Innovation Intelligence

Commoditization. Digitalization. Acceleration.
Major Pressure on Innovation Drivers.

Albert Meige, PhD • Jacques Schmitt, PhD

ABSANS PUBLISHING
Innovation Intelligence
Albert Meige and Jacques P.M. Schmitt

Copyright © 2015 by Albert Meige and Jacques P.M. Schmitt
All Rights Reserved

Copyeditor: Louann Pope
Cover Design: Naeem Jee
Interior Design: Albert Meige, based on the Legrand Orange Book
All rights reserved. This book was self-published by the authors Albert Meige and Jacques P.M. Schmitt under ABSANS PUBLISHING. No part of this work may be reproduced or transmitted in any form or by any means, electronic or mechanical, including photocopying, recording, or by any information storage or retrieval system, without the prior written permission of the copyright owner.
PUBLISHED BY ABSANS PUBLISHING
ISBN 978-1-326-12582-0

First printing, April 2015

INNOVATION-INTELLIGENCE.COM

to Maya and Iseline... and Ane
– Albert

to Aline
– Jacques

Contents

Preface by Jean-François Minster ix

Preface by Marc Giget xii

Acknowledgments xix

About the authors xxii

0 Introduction 1

0.1	Adapting innovation to a new world	1
0.2	Why did we write this book?	2
0.3	Innovation Intelligence: story of a book title	4
0.4	Organization of the book	5

1 The Internet of Skills & Knowledge 9

1.1	Toward the third Industrial Revolution	11
1.2	Mega-trends in employment and work organization	14
1.3	Toward the Internet of skills and knowledge?	17

2 The Parrot AR.Drone Case 21

2.1	Introduction	22
2.2	Parrot: a successful SME that had to diversify	23
2.3	The atypical, self-taught, visionary entrepreneur	25
2.4	The young genius	28
2.5	The technology outburst of helicopter drones	30
2.6	The Commando team	31

2.7	The Launch	33
2.8	Epilogue	35
2.9	Conclusion	36

3 Knowledge, the fuel of innovation 39

3.1	Knowledge and innovation: a tight interdependency	40
3.2	Knowledge-source mapping	43
3.3	Innovation cycle and risk management	56
3.4	Innovation waves	60
3.5	Conclusion	69

4 Commoditization in a digital world 71

4.1	Knowledge flood and change acceleration	72
4.2	Permanent fight against commoditization	108
4.3	Disruptive digital tsunami	121
4.4	Conclusion	137

5 Expert and expertise 139

5.1	Definition of expert and scope of this work	140
5.2	Becoming an expert requires a strange mindset	143
5.3	Experts in the enterprise	151
5.4	Expert role shifting with rapidly changing trends	169
5.5	Conclusion	181

6 Toward Innovation Intelligence 183

6.1	Introduction	184
6.2	TOTAL: organization vs. agility	188
6.3	Rise of the Chief Innovation Officer (lever #1)	197
6.4	Innovation labs (lever #2)	210
6.5	Innovation intelligence (lever #3)	220
6.6	Conclusion	233

7 Tools for Innovation Intelligence 235

7.1	Intelligence channels	236
7.2	Tools for speeding up the innovation process	246
7.3	Digital tools for innovation intelligence?	255

7.4	Conclusion	270
8	Conclusion and Perspectives	273
	Bibliography	277
	Table of figures	285
	Index	293

Preface by
Jean-François Minster

Innovation is a key element of present day economic activities. It is essential to addressing the major challenges of humankind, particularly the economic development and well-being of the vast majority of the world's growing population. It is also necessary for companies to face the fast evolution of our complex world and the resulting competition. Our societies are being affected by major game-changers: the digital wave, the proliferation of massive communication capability worldwide, the continuous introduction of new business models and new uses, and the application to industry of many advanced technologies (biotechnologies, new material sciences, nanotechnologies, and so forth).

Without any doubt, innovation is not primarily technology-driven; as new business models or new uses are fast to implement and frequently cause quite profound evolutions. Yet technology is one essential element of innovation. In this book, Albert Meige and Jacques P.M. Schmitt analyze technology innovation, its processes, and tools which are being used successfully in companies; this is what they call "innovation intelligence."

The strategic dimension of innovation deals with major trends, such as technology (the digital world), people (the worldwide market of skills), and practices (the management of innovation). Existing elements of innovation are not disappearing: industrial production will always be needed across the value chain (for example, a digital world needs a microelectronics industry), advanced skills must rely on production and functional teams, and even the open-innovation approach must protect differentiation. Yet companies are continuously evolving to face a convergence of drivers.

Managerial commitment and managerial approaches are an essential element of innovation. In my view, the key factor is management's capacity to take the risk and to accept the idea and the benefits of a potential failure. Another essential element of innovation is comprised of approaches that allow new ideas to emerge and be nurtured. Such approaches require a means for innovators to exchange views, notably about new knowledge or technologies, and the capacity of management to accept new ideas in a positive way even if the ideas disrupt the current business. The implementation of such exchanges should be thought of in a very dynamic way, because the tools themselves can benefit from ongoing innovation. Open-innovation approaches are found to be efficient, particularly as a means to develop fast, complex systems that can create and reach the market in a short time.

Companies aim to differentiate themselves, even when they are essentially producing commodities. They always hope to cause disruption, which could give them an advantage over their competition. The disruption is rarely due to technology alone: reaching the market, creating or satisfying customer needs or societal needs, benefitting from the appropriate infrastructure that our modern economies rely heavily upon, and making sure that regulations adapt themselves to the new world, are all factors of importance.

Whatever the processes and managerial commitment, innovation is dependent on people. These people have the capacity to elaborate new ideas, to convince others that there is something to consider, or to take the risk of introducing disruption. Some of these people are experts, as described in detail in this book. They are a precious asset to any company and should be managed with great care. They must

Innovation Intelligence

be put in an environment that can benefit from the value they add. Many innovation intelligence tools exist to achieve this: open calls for ideas, internal frame programs allowing unanticipated developments, innovation laboratories, and prizes that recognize innovators. There is no magic solution for success. Companies have to strive to continuously adapt to facilitate, manage, and promote innovation and the innovators.

However, the most difficult part of the innovation process always seems to be the transition from an experimental phase to an actual, significant, successful new business case. While it may look fast, based on the extraordinary success of digital businesses, for industrial companies that produce goods, or even commodities, needed by our societies it is risky, capital-intensive, and slow. Yet companies have to do it; we have to build the future.

Jean-François Minster
Senior Vice President Scientific Development, TOTAL SA
Paris, France
February 25, 2015

Preface by Marc Giget

Integrate the best state of knowledge in the world

To innovate is to integrate the best state of knowledge into creative products and services with the aim of improving life in society and for individuals. These three components: the knowledge, the creation, and the improvement of life constitute the fundamental elements of all innovation processes. They can each, depending on the players and the periods, act as the initiating factor for an innovation. Albert Meige and Jacques P.M. Schmitt walk us through various approaches and sensibilities with regard to innovation processes:

- technological push and innovations originating primarily from knowledge,
- validation of the vision of the creator, designer, entrepreneur, and
- human-centric innovations originating from expectations, dreams, and wishes of individuals such as consumers.

Of these three approaches, we resolutely share that the opinion of Steve Jobs: "You've got to start with the customer experience and work back toward the technology – not the other way around. You can't start with the technology and try to figure out where you're going to try to sell it." Because this vision places the individual rather than the technologies at the center of innovation, it is much more demanding in terms of knowledge than a simple search for applications of a technology or a concept. It demands that the innovative company seek the most relevant knowledge and technologies, whatever they are and wherever they come from, because the company can combine them in the best way possible in order to improve real life.

This universal vision of sciences, technologies, and knowledge as the raw materials of user-friendly innovations is at the heart of the success of Apple, which is the leading company in the world in terms of value even though its R&D expenditure is extremely low compared to other electronics companies – less than 4% of revenues over the past ten years compared to 10-20% for its competitors.

An iPhone is an extremely simple and easy-to-use product for the consumer, but at the same time it is extremely complex internally, with the complexity resulting from combining the best technologies from around the world (Germany, Korea, Japan, China, the United States, and dozens of other countries). In a way, the iPhone is a kind of "best of" of the skills in the world of mobile technologies. In fact, Apple doesn't score above thirtieth place in the list of mobile-phone patent holders; Apple's main competitor, Samsung, is twenty places higher in the list. Another fundamental aspect of Apple's strategy of renewing its products rapidly, with clockwork regularity: iPhone 3, 3S, 4, 4S, 5, 5S, 6. This short innovation cycle means refreshing all of the constituent technologies at an annual, if not semiannual, rate!

This just goes to show how much the world has changed compared to thirty years ago when large companies, closed to anything "not invented here," ruled and designed most of the technologies involved in their products whose development took several years if not dozens of years. This open and rapid approach to the design of new, extremely complex products has shaken up the world of innovation. It is into the heart of this revolution that Albert Meige and Jacques P.M. Schmitt, with their great advantage of having lived close to leading companies that they were precursors in the research and design of tools for open innovation, lead us.

Already 300 years ago

The question of continuous progression in knowledge and its segmentation into multiple and ever more compartmentalized disciplines had already preoccupied the great thinkers of the Renaissance and the philosophers of the Age of Enlightenment. Gottfried Leibniz, a great thinker and polymath genius, "the philosophers' philosopher" but also a mathematical genius and great innovator, is considered the last scientist capable of understanding all the scientific works in a library. He was well aware that, in spite of his genius, he was living off his job as a librarian.

The perspective of knowledge that would, from that time onward become ever more fragmented, each person, even the most intelligent, only mastering an increasingly limited part of knowledge, made him think the worst. That is to say, he anticipated erroneous decisions would be made based on partial knowledge. He warned his contemporaries and looked for solutions, first asking scientists for conciseness and going so far as to suggest that each author be limited to writing no more than two books, and to oblige the author to send only his real and original contribution, under penalty of not being read.

Understanding that the evolution toward increasing complexity was unavoidable, he devoted his research to ways of dealing with complexity by using simple tools. In the field of mathematics, he achieved this in masterly fashion by creating in 1679 the binary number system, which uses only two symbols, 1 and 0. This very simple language replaced all previous complicated numbering. It allowed for the most complex of calculations and paved the way to the digital revolution, which was to be adopted three centuries later upon invention of the technology required to exploit it, the transistor.

Without wishing to directly compare our two authors to Leibniz, their quest – an absolutely necessary one – for simple tools to enable understanding of the complexity, the diversity, and the renewal of knowledge has made them his direct spiritual heirs.

A vital challenge for companies today

As shown in surveys carried out each year to describe the strategic stakes of innovation that is performed in the world's leading companies, access to new knowledge and technologies never ceases to progress. Today, it is a major brake on innovation, despite everything seeming to be available on the Internet. Why is abundant knowledge, paradoxically, limiting innovation?

The GE Global Innovation Barometer is a survey-based innovation report published by General Electric annually and recognized worldwide. The 2014 edition, based on more than 3,000 interviews with innovation managers in 26 countries, identifies knowledge growth as both vital and very badly mastered by major companies.

In fact, the measure of progress in technology sciences and knowledge shows the breathtaking scale of the problem. At the rate of more than a million new researchers and engineers in R&D each year, their population will have grown from 10 million to 20 million by 2020. The trends of rapid growth in publications, which will soon reach 5 million per year, and patents, which have already exceeded 2 million per year, are not expected to reverse any time soon.

How, amid this mass of information, can a company correctly identify those inputs of knowledge and technologies necessary for its innovation process and, at the same time, protect itself from their rapid obsolescence. The problem is even more complicated due to the existence of major interactions between different technologies and the fact that horizontal, or adjacent, innovation strategies have considerably enlarged the competitive landscape.

Thus, Michelin, which dominated the world of road maps for more than a century, took a long time to identify Google as a real competitor; Google, though coming from an entirely different world, overthrew Michelin's leadership.

In the same way, at the start of 2015 SNCF, the French national railway company, surprised its audience when presenting its strategic goals. The surprise was that it cited Google as its main competitor,

Innovation Intelligence   xvii

followed by BlaBlaCar, a start-up in carpooling that is becoming the leader in Europe with more than 10 million members and 2 million people users every month. Then the SNCF presented its digital strategy for the future – particularly ambitious because digital was very far removed from its core skills just five years ago.

Even in their sectors of excellence, leading companies no longer feel safe from the rapid technological evolution or from technologies they master but which are then replaced by exogenous technologies they cannot control and which may prove more efficient. If the problem of an overwhelming volume of knowledge is already very difficult to for large companies to deal with, how will medium-sized companies and start-ups deal with it?

A salutary and visionary work

In this book, Albert Meige and Jacques P.M. Schmitt first show us the magnitude of the problem by explaining the fragmentation of knowledge, its exponential growth, and the speed of its renewal. They justify the irreversible evolution toward open innovation, tied to the necessary synthesis between this splintering of knowledge and the growing complexity of products.

They then question the nature and the role of experts, who are vital interfaces – even, and above all, in a digital world – between the vast amount of raw, unprocessed knowledge and the companies that want to identify and use it. They also categorize the tools and approaches used by companies to deal with the new environment in which new forms of knowledge management are available, by analyzing notably:

- the emergence of the function of Chief Innovation Officer, which in no way calls into question that of the Chief Technology Officer,
- the development of innovation labs, and
- the generalization of user-centric innovation approaches, notably design thinking.

Finally, the most important and creative part of the book addresses the future by proposing tools for innovation intelligence that could meet the expectations of this new world.

In this book, the authors examine the relationships between skills and both internal and external experts, between preformatted and ad hoc information services, among exploration, investigation, and experimentation, and between the use of automatic systems and human intervention.

This study has the double advantage of being supported by both the unique experience of Presans, which has played a major role in the emergence of crowdsourcing of skills, and by the interviews conducted with innovation managers from major companies and start-ups; this advantage guarantees the inclusion of proposed solutions into the concerns and real-world experiences of companies today. The case study on Parrot, the champion start-up in the emerging sector of drones, shows how the new generation of entrepreneurs is perfectly comfortable with outsourcing skills to support its vision.

The ambition of this book is to lead to innovation intelligence tools that enable companies to create value through faster and more relevant innovation, by giving them real-time access to the latest state of sciences and technologies.

I therefore thank Albert Meige and Jacques P.M. Schmitt for this salutary work in which there is no doubt that Research & Development Managers, Technical Managers and Innovation Managers in companies will all find the material to help them meet the challenge of making the best use of this enormous flow of knowledge.

Marc Giget
President of the European Institute for Creative Strategies & Innovation
and the Club de Paris des Directeurs de l'Innovation
Member of the French Academy of Technologies
Paris, France
March 3, 2015

Acknowledgments

The authors would like to thank everyone who contributed to this book and without whom it would never have been possible.

First, we would like to thank Marc Giget, the innovation master who served as a source of inspiration, and Jean-François Minster who kindly gave to us some of his precious time. We are also grateful for the excellent prefaces they wrote.

This book was written based on material that we collected through dedicated interviews and discussions with more than forty people who deal with innovation (Chief Innovation Officers, among others) and research and development (Chief Technology Officers, among others), as well as founders and CEOs of companies that provide third-party digital tools. Many concrete examples included in this book were compiled thanks to them. These people agreed to answer our questions, in some cases spending more than three hours explaining how their world was changing and how they were trying to adapt. In particular we would like to thank the following[i]: Isabelle André (Le Monde Numérique), Christophe Aufrère (Faurecia), Yann Barbaux (Airbus), Jean Botti (Airbus Group), Troy Breiland (HCL Hewlett Packard), Sylvie Breton (Lesieur), Nathalie Brunelle (Total), Nicolas Bry (Orange), François Callou (Parrot), Yves Caseau (AXA), Albert David (Université Paris-Dauphine), Olivier Delabroy (Air Liquide), Eric Duceau (Airbus), Alain Dufossé (Pernod-Ricard), Didier Dumont (SKF), Philippe Du-

---

[i] In alphabetical order.

vivier (Parrot), Axel Flaig (Airbus), Marc Giget (European Institute for Creative Strategies and Innovation), Frédéric Guillou (GRTgaz), Christine Halliot (Total), Sihem Jouini (HEC), Franck Landrieve (SKF), Catherine Langlais (Saint-Gobain), Sam Levy (Marlin & Associates), Pascal Magnier (Expernova), Matthieu Marquenet (Smart Me Up), Chritophe Midler (École Polytechnique), Jean-François Minster (Total), Grégory Olocco (Air Liquide), Jean-Philippe Paré (Danone), Jean Parizot (Total), Guillaume Pinto (Parrot), Hervé Plessix (Danone), Stéphane Quere (GDFsuez), Didier Roux (Saint-Gobain), Raphael Schoentgen (GDFsuez), Dan Serfaty (Viadeo), Henri Seydoux (Parot), Jean-Christophe Simon (SEB), Virginie Simon (MyScienceWork), Vincent Sinchole (InVivo), Nicolas Tenzer (IDEFIE), Trond Undheim (Yegii), Andy Zinga (NineSigma), and Pascal Zunino (Novadem).

Thank you also to Philippe Letellier, an expert on the digital wave who wrote a small portion of Chapter 4. Special thanks to the young Eliott Joseph, who helped us at the beginning of the project to perform preliminary literature research regarding experts and expertise.

Special thanks also to our beta-readers, who have suffered with us: Hervé and Truls.

We are also very grateful to the rest of the Presans team, who have all contributed in one way or another: Darko, Damien, Fabien, Guillaume, Hervé, Jacques K., Marc, Sarah, Truls, and Vassilis.

Finally, thank you to Louann Pope, who did an amazing job on the copy editing.

Thank you to the authors of a few comments that we received on

Innovation Intelligence

LinkedIn [ii]. Thank you to the crowd of designers [iii] and voters [iv] who helped us design the cover of the book.

Jacques would like to thank Aline and apologize for a temporary shortcoming with regard to gardening.

Albert would also like to give a special thank you to his family members who have supported him during this journey: Tusen Takk, Maya, Iseline, and Ane.

[ii] Mark Piekny, Bob Chalfan, Warren Huang, Lee Sellenraad, Rodrigo Ferro Ruiz, Delyth Samuel, and Florian Roques.

[iii] IgnacioIdeas, ekkia, RedOne22, DejaVu, Omini, Randy Robert, Mala Baranove, Dandia, Sopwani, kata83, Martis Lupus, Solidnorthds, 9greenstudio, Forza Design, Dakir, GraphixArt, Progressive15, GladlyART, Kirestring, Resentinel, Adjayceency, Art Concept, Imperius, and MJWdesigns.

[iv] Adam Wojnicki, Alain Mathieu, Ale the Great, Arthur Goujon, A. Bergeron, Bianca Roatis, Virginie Carteron, Cedric Rauschen, Chantal Meige, Damien Lemaire, Didier Roux, Dominique Meige, G. Durand, Eric Petit, F. Plais, Fabien Coulon, Graham Wallis, Gregory Olocco, Henri Seydoux, Hervé Arribart, Isabelle de Melo, Jaime Ulloa, Kelly, Laura Faulconer, Marc Grunnagel, Marlene Lieberman, Gabrielle Vaissière, Mikael Berrebi, Olivier Delabroy, Olivier Lucas, Philippe Mourant, Samuel Huber, Sébastien Santos, Stéphane Quere, Thierry Pardessus, Yann Barbaux, Agnes Marotte, S. Carzon, Christophe Laux, Chuan-Dong Wen, Daniel M., J.C. Simon, Jean Parizot, Kathleen Konecek, Markus Durstewitz, Nico P., Nicolas Decayeux, Sophie Mariotti, Thibaut, and thirty one anonymous voters.

About the authors

Albert Meige has been active in the field of entrepreneurship, innovation, and new business development since he was a teenager. He is the founder and CEO of Presans, a company organizing worldwide expertise and making it available to others. Before founding Presans, he was a researcher in plasma physics at the École Polytechnique, the Australian National University, and the Université Paul Sabatier. At the age of sixteen, he founded and served as President of an entertainment agency selling magic shows, starring himself and other magi-

Albert Meige

cians, in Europe and Australia. Albert Meige holds an MBA from HEC Paris business school, a PhD in Physics from Australian National University, and a telecommunications engineering degree. He was awarded the École Polytechnique Innovation Prize in 2008, and he coauthored the book *A Guide to Open Innovation and Crowdsourcing*, which was foreworded by Henri Chesbrough. He is also a conference speaker on the subjects of open innovation, innovation intelligence, expertise, and entrepreneurship, giving talks at various engineering schools and universities (including École Polytechnique and École Centrale), companies (including TOTAL and Schneider Electric), and public events (including Mardis de l'Innovation). He has authored fourteen peer-reviewed scientific articles and two patents. He solves the Rubik's Cube in less than fifty seconds and enjoys urban underground exploration. linkedin.com/in/meige

Jacques P.M. Schmitt

Jacques P.M. Schmitt is a Fellow at Presans, and he teaches Innovation Management and Industrial Property in Engineering and Business Schools. His career has had three stages. The first stage was spent in academia and research: he studied physics (and theater) at École Normale Supérieure, and then he did research at Le Centre National de la Recherche Scientifique (CNRS) and taught Physics at École Polytechnique. The second stage of his career was spent in industry: after spending a sabbatical at Xerox PARC, he joined a start-up firm (Solems), then a large Swiss corporation. He began by driving a new business (flat-panel display manufacturing equipment) and later became CTO of the Unaxis group, where he managed innovation strategy and patent portfolio. He developed hands-on experience in shifting a corporate culture from close innovation to open innovation before the term was even coined. In the third stage of his career, he became a Fellow and partner at Presans. His broad interest in technology has gradually extended to innovation and change management. Jacques Schmitt has authored approximately sixty scientific papers and thirty patents. linkedin.com/in/jacquesschmitt

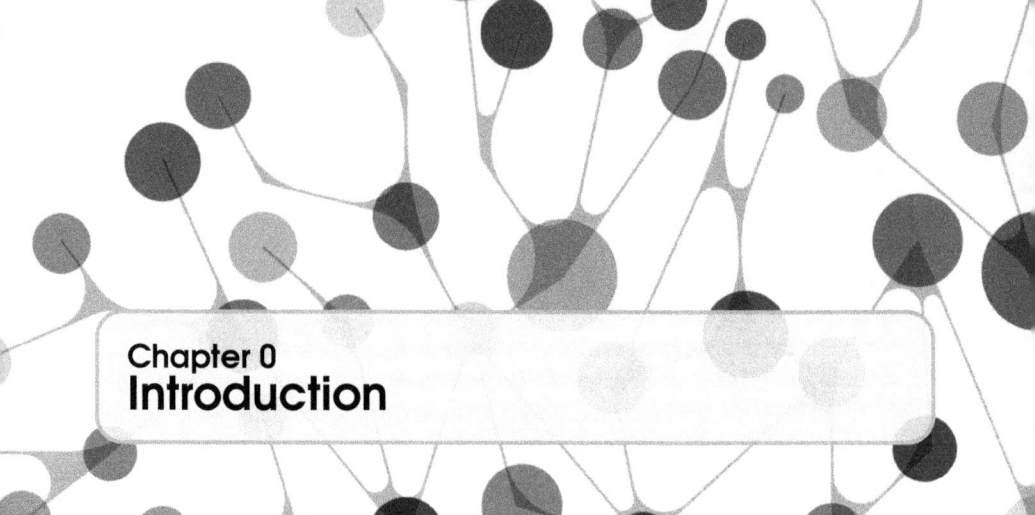

Chapter 0
Introduction

The oldest and strongest emotion of mankind is
fear, and the oldest and strongest kind of fear is
fear of the unknown.

H. P. LOVECRAFT

0.1 Adapting innovation to a new world

To innovate, companies must combine multiple and disparate areas of knowledge outside of their core businesses, and they must do it faster and faster. Accessing knowledge and skills has never been so easy and so difficult at the same time. It is easy, because new tools facilitate the task. It is difficult, because it requires finding the needle in the haystack. The problem is that the haystack is growing and the needle must be found more and more quickly.

Ten years ago, Facebook didn't exist. Ten years before that, the Internet didn't exist. Following in the footsteps of the Industrial Revolution, the transition to new manufacturing processes during the late-eighteenth and early-nineteenth centuries, and the second Industrial Revolution, also called the Technological Revolution, of the late-nineteenth and early-twentieth centuries, we are on the verge of a third

Industrial Revolution: the optimization of resources by using digital technologies. Work in the year 2030 won't look the same as it does today. Work, helped by digital tools, will probably be more flexible, fluid, freelance, and collaborative.

There are many questions. How will knowledge be accessed? How will top-level experts be engaged? How will these rapid changes affect the way companies manage innovation? What is the future organization of innovation in large corporations?

In this book, we provide an up-to-date overview of recent, disruptive trends forcing companies to implement new practices to improve the performance of innovation. We analyze the ongoing role of redistribution for nearly all participants in the hot innovation race. It is essentially a matter of positioning with respect to an immaterial but essential resource: knowledge. Researchers, experts, innovation drivers, and company decision makers are all affected. We seek to understand the underlying forces that drive this major turmoil. These forces generate turbulence, but even in that blurry context trends for maintaining competitiveness can be delineated. One of them centers on *innovation intelligence*.

0.2 Why did we write this book?

Founded in 2008 by Albert Meige, Presans sees itself as the next-generation provider of open-innovation services. With a network of over three million experts worldwide, Presans injects new perspectives into business, fueling breakthrough innovations. Presans helps the worlds leading companies to access worldwide intelligence and knowledge, by identifying, qualifying, and engaging for them the best experts across a broad range of industries and disciplines. Our clients need the best experts to help them build and foresee the future, a future in which strategic decisions are made in a complex system environment and technological problems are solved at the frontier of science.

Collaborating with Chief Technology Officers and Chief Innovation Officers in a wide range of industries worldwide, at Presans we have worked as both observers and active participants. We observe the new ways companies develop to deal with innovation and analyze how new tools could potentially improve the innovation performance of their users.

In late 2013, because we had accumulated a fair amount of knowledge from the field, I felt compelled to write a thirty-page white paper focusing on the evolution of the role of the Chief Innovation Officer and of experts in relation to innovation. I hired a young consultant, Eliott Joseph, to help me with gathering additional information and writing the white paper. The white paper was never published. Why? Because I realized that it would be difficult to achieve our vision if I myself was not deeply involved in the writing. I also knew that the material would be more interesting if I involved my collaborator and friend Jacques Schmitt who has over forty years of experience in innovation management. As a result of our collaboration, the simple white paper became a book of over 300 pages. The scope of the book is also much broader than the white papers scope would have been: it shifted from a simple focus on experts and expertise to a broader look at innovation practices at large, including organization, process, tools, and so forth. The content is a much more anchored in reality and in the current concerns of companies with regard to innovation.

For this book, we have conducted approximately forty interviews with key people who deal with innovation and research and development in large international groups and with the founders and CEOs of companies that provide new digital tools (the interviewees are mentioned in the acknowledgments). We are deeply grateful to everyone who spared time from their busy schedules to discuss openly with us the challenges they are facing. Indeed, we are living in disconcerting times: the philosopher Hartmut Rosa calls it a "shrinking of the present"[1] because the future is hardly predictable and experience from the past is hardly relevant.

The consolidation and analysis of these interviews, and of course of other literature, has given us a solid understanding of the current challenges of companies, what they are implementing to overcome

4 Chapter 0. Introduction

these challenges, and where this ongoing reorganization might go in the coming years. However, the content of this book is not exhaustive or conclusive, but should rather be considered a dynamic observation of experience from the field.

Although we have endeavored to write the book as a whole, in a consistent manner, it was a two-person job with (most of the time) a shared vision. Given our background and respective experience, the division of writing was natural: Jacques, the Thinker, focused on history and its analysis, while Albert, the Doer, focused on the current situation, recent trends, digital barbarians and expectations for the future.

0.3 Innovation Intelligence: story of a book title

> One of the main activities of the Breakthrough Innovation Group is to do Intelligence to feed innovation. Bad Intelligence yields bad innovation.
> **Alain Dufossé, Head of the Pernod-Ricard Breakthrough Innovation Group (BIG)**

The title of this book, *Innovation Intelligence*, was chosen near the end of the project. We think that the title contains the essence of our message. Intelligence in this sense has its origins in military jargon. Military *intelligence* is a set of activities consisting of gathering data from various sources, analyzing the data to transform it into information, and using that information to guide or support strategic decision making or operational actions.

One of the key messages of this book is that the innovation function occupies an increasingly high position in companies and that it oversees functions such as marketing, business development, and research and development: innovation is not only technology but also business. In addition, in most industrial sectors (and eventually likely all sectors), innovation is less and less concerned with knowledge creation and more

Innovation Intelligence 5

and more concerned with the smart integration of the appropriate bricks of skill, knowledge, and technology. This selection and integration of bricks of knowledge raises the question of sourcing and qualifying the bricks in a multidisciplinary manner. Even in the most structured companies, activities of technology watching, market analysis and megatrend analysis are not coordinated. They are not done by the same teams. The teams are not in the same locations. The teams don't share knowledge. And, most importantly, the teams do not necessarily serve innovation. This lack of coordination is a serious issue. Chief Innovation Officers, at companies where they exist, are the most mature on this topic: they are currently trying to find ways to coordinate, at the highest level, the various actions of intelligence to feed innovation. This is what we call innovation intelligence.

0.4 Organization of the book

In the first chapter, we position the change in innovation practice in a broader framework than that of innovation alone. We find it interesting to see three trends converging to increase the efficiency of innovation: (i) the third Industrial Revolution, spurred by digital technologies, (ii) employment returning to a marketplace of skills, and (iii) companies inventing and implementing various practices and tools.

In the second chapter, we present a concrete innovation case, the Parrot AR.Drone, providing a detailed description and analysis of this recent and extremely interesting example of rapid innovation. In order to diversify, Parrot, the French leader in Bluetooth hands-free car kits, successfully managed to catch the innovation wave of drones even though drones represent a market and a technological domain initially very far outside its core business. We tell the story on how Parrot's team assembled the bricks of external knowledge in a short time, and we pinpoint the key steps.

In the third chapter, we examine knowledge as the fuel of innovation. At a strategic level, knowledge is used to fill the innovation pipe with new concepts and to make sound strategic decisions and

6 Chapter 0. Introduction

investments. At an operational level, knowledge is used to develop and screen new concepts. Ambitious disruptive innovation requires intelligent acquisition of new knowledge.

In the fourth chapter, we provide an overview of the recent landscape changes that large companies in various industries must face. The changes are forcing companies to wipe the slate clean with regard to their innovation habits. We focus on both knowledge growth and fragmentation. We emphasize the drastic acceleration of the innovation cycle and product commoditization, zooming in on the main agents of this change, the *digital barbarians*, newcomers of the digital wave who are rapidly attacking traditional companies.

In the fifth chapter, we describe the new face and the new role of experts, the vehicle of knowledge. To be able to maintain an ever-increasing pace of innovation, companies must implement new and more open innovation tools and processes. In this context, the modern expert stands at the apex of a human network of knowledge workers, and he or she must branch out from technical knowledge to embrace all of the parameters of market creation and value creation. The modern expert's focus is not on generating knowledge. Instead, the expert seeks knowledge and then combines it to generate business propositions. We call this modern expert a meta-expert.

In the sixth chapter, we review recent drastic changes in the way companies deal with innovation to adapt to the landscape change. The Chief Innovation Officer, a gradually emerging figure, oversees functions such as strategy, marketing, business development, and research and development. At the same time, *innovation labs*, small, agile structures tasked with predicting the future and potentially even killing the current business, have appeared. Intelligence dedicated to innovation is becoming increasingly important and complex.

In the seventh chapter, we propose new tools to help companies achieve better performance in terms of innovation intelligence: open-innovation intermediaries, expert network and micro-consulting platforms, knowledge data-mining software, professional social media, and so forth. Yet certain bricks are still missing.

Innovation Intelligence

In the eighth chapter, we conclude the book with some highlights from chapters one through seven.

Chapter 1
The Internet of Skills & Knowledge

Exploring the unknown requires tolerating uncertainty.

BRIAN GREENE

In Short... This short chapter elaborates on works by Jeremy Rifkin and also Stefan Heck and Matt Rogers. They see our world entering a third Industrial Revolution. The first Industrial Revolution, which took place during the late-eighteenth and early-nineteenth centuries and was associated with steam and steel, boosted industrial productivity. The second Industrial Revolution, also called the Technological Revolution, took place during the late-nineteenth and early-twentieth centuries and was associated with urbanization and corporate creation, mainly with regard to corporate banking and research and development (R&D). We are entering a new period, during which the focus will be on sound management of resources. Although Rifkin focuses mainly on energy, we agree with the prediction of Heck and Rogers that nearly all resources will be globally managed as they become increasingly scarce. The third Industrial Revolution will exploit the power of Internet to change many wasteful aspects of our lives. For example, Uber may be the first sign of an attempt to temper the waste of energy and space associated with individual ownership and use of cars. Another resource which may be managed differently during and after the third Industrial Revolution is the work force. During the first Industrial Revolution, the work force was on hire, but during the second Industrial Revolution permanent employment became the rule. Companies were retaining, by contract, their skilled employees who were driving internal innovation. We think this approach may change again during the third Industrial Revolution. Trends are indicating that we may be returning to an open market of skills. All scenarios describing professional life in 2030 include a considerable increase in workforce flexibility, in particular for those workers who have the most valuable skills. Digital technology will play a strong role in matching demand and offers for technology experts and market insiders. Digital technology will help entrepreneurs to find and enroll, on demand, the skills required for assembling the knowledge bricks of a daring innovation project. In parallel, skilled experts will use their channels to be known by teams they think would benefit from their input.

While this book focuses on how companies deal with innovation, and in particular, how companies access external knowledge and engage external talent to make innovation more efficient, we would like to set the stage in a broader perspective: the economist Jeremy Rifkin sees the third Industrial Revolution as one of energy, while Heck and Rogers see it as one of resources in general (energy, transport, housing, and so forth). Would the third Industrial Revolution apply to the resource of knowledge and skills? Rifkin speaks about the *Internet of Energy*; we have decided to speak about the *Internet of Skills and Knowledge*. In this chapter we aim a provocative flashlight toward the future, focusing on both the third Industrial Revolution and mega-trends in employment. Such a predictive exercise is always a bit like science fiction, but the rationale is more important than the description. We wonder if modern companies will return to a marketplace of skills and knowledge, powered by digital technologies and, if they do, how this shift will affect the world of innovation management.

1.1 Toward the third Industrial Revolution: optimizing resources

The economist Adam Smith identified three key factors for economic growth: labor, capital, and resources. While the first and second Industrial Revolutions were mostly concerned with optimizing labor productivity and capital allocation, the third Industrial Revolution is expected to focus on optimizing resources. Resources are understood in a broad sense to include land, raw materials, energy, workspace, knowledge, human resources, and so forth.

1.1.1 First Industrial Revolution: optimizing labor

The first Industrial Revolution spanned from the late eighteenth century to the early nineteenth century and was characterized by dramatic improvements in the methods of producing material goods. The steam engine, invented by Jerónimo de Ayanz y Beaumont, commercialized by Thomas Newcomen and much improved by James Watt, replaced more traditional power sources – human power, horses, windmills, and watermills – to run machinery. The textile, paper, and metal industries were deeply

James Watt

revolutionized: large factories replaced the midsize traditional manufacturers. Capital needs to build these firms were also at the origin of the capitalism. Although productivity in the United Kingdom, the United States, and continental Europe increased by a factor of ten and higher wages pulled many people out of poverty and famine, work

12   Chapter 1. The Internet of Skills & Knowledge

conditions did not really improve.

1.1.2 Second Industrial Revolution: urbanization, capital, and corporate R&D

By the end of the nineteenth century, the first Industrial Revolution had transformed Europe and the United States: productivity had experienced a tenfold increase, but urbanization was becoming a serious issue. The second Industrial Revolution, with its wave of inventions for building modern cities and transportation networks, allowed cities to become much larger and denser. For example, the population of New York City grew from 800,000 in 1860 to 7.5 million in 1925, a tenfold increase in just sixty-five years. The second Industrial Revolution, like the first, focused on materials, for example steel rather than wood for buildings. It also focused on electricity, which was used for lighting and for powering appliances, air conditioning, elevators, assembly lines, and so forth. In addition, the second Industrial Revolution also focused on the combustion engine for use in transport.

Finally, the second Industrial Revolution introduced radical changes in the way firms were organized and managed: the first national and multinational corporations and corporate banks (to finance all of these capital-intensive infrastructures) appeared during this time. Corporate research and development became critical for the first time.

1.1.3 Third Industrial Revolution

The Internet of energy

Economic and social theorist Jeremy Rifkin, in his best-selling book *The Third Industrial Revolution: How Lateral Power Is Transforming Energy, the Economy, and the World*,[2] describes a whirl of change with energy converging with the Internet and creating new businesses and employment. Rifkin has proposed five pillars of the third Industrial Revolution:

- renewable energy as a greener and more sustainable energy source;

Innovation Intelligence   13

- buildings as micro-power plants, leveraging local renewable energy;
- energy storage technologies in all buildings to adjust local supply of and demand for energy;
- the Internet as a technology for managing global supply of and demand for energy, via a global grid; and
- fuel-cell vehicles for transporting energy to various points of the continental grid.

Although Rifkin's theory is controversial, he thinks that once these five pillars are brought together, synergies will be generated and we will be on the verge of a new economic paradigm. The bottom line, according to Rifkin, is that the Third Industrial Revolution will be about the Internet of Energy. Leading IT companies worldwide are already building the required infrastructure: IBM and its *Smarter Planet* initiative is one of the most famous examples.

The Internet of resources

In their book *Resource Revolution*,[3] Stefan Heck and Matt Rogers go even further than Rifkin: they say that the third Industrial Revolution will focus on optimizing not only energy resources but any kind of resources used by individuals and companies.

Let's consider the example of cars. When you think about it, cars are extremely inefficient vehicles for moving people around. They are inefficient in terms of energy consumption: with a typical weight of over 1.2 tons, each car transports an average of 1.6 people, with only a very small amount of the consumed energy moving the passengers. Cars are also inefficient in terms of capital: although cars represent a significant investment for their owners, the cars are parked most of the time. To address these inefficiencies of cars, a number of companies are currently reinventing the way in which people can be moved around. Zipcar allows you to rent a car where you are, when you need it, by the hour or day, on demand via a simple smartphone app. Uber connects passengers with drivers of cars.

An incredible number of new services are trying to address such

14   Chapter 1. The Internet of Skills & Knowledge

inefficiencies in various domains. The iTunes Store changed the way people buy music. Amazon.com changed the way people buy books and many other products. eBay changed the way people sell and buy stuff to each other. Spotify, an online music-streaming service, changed the way people listen to music. Airbnb changed the way people rent accommodations when traveling. This list could go on and on.

Uber: they change the way you take a cab

Founded in 2009 by Garrett Camp, Travis Kalanick, and Oscar Salazar, the highly controversial car-hire app Uber has reached a valuation of over EUR 13 billion as of 2014, four years after the app was deployed for the first time in San Francisco – it is said to be the second richest start-up in history. The concept behind Uber is to connect passengers with drivers of cars. Uber is an efficient tool that addresses one of the above-mentioned car inefficiencies: the passenger pays for the car only when using it, there is no need for most passengers to own a car. In addition, a driver provides a low-cost, high-end service to the passengers, making Uber an excellent substitute for traditional cabs.

The bottom line is the following: look at all the resources used by individuals and companies, spot the inefficiencies, and rethink the system as a whole by leveraging information technology.

Because there are significant inefficiencies in accessing knowledge and engaging talent, it is legitimate to wonder how digital technologies will affect the way in which companies access knowledge and engage workers who have the required skills.

1.2 Mega-trends in employment and work organization

In parallel to the third Industrial Revolution, the world of work and employment is changing rapidly.

Innovation Intelligence   15

1.2.1 Birth of the enterprise: from a marketplace of skills to employment

Blanche Segrestin and Armand Hatchuel give a very clear history of employment and of the notion of an enterprise in their book *Refonder l'Entreprise*.[4]

A traditional factory, such as a textile factory, before the first Industrial Revolution, differed from today's factories in two important ways. First, people rented out their skills to the factory – the worker was a supplier. The notion of a work contract did not exist, but rather there was a real marketplace of skills driven by demand (by factories) and supply (by workers). Second, the factory relied on inventions and innovations made by others – the factory did not invest in its future. Inventions were made by individuals, and firms could buy these inventions.

With the first Industrial Revolution and the steam engine, things changed. Firms could no longer rely only on discoveries made by external parties. Instead, they had to take control over their own futures. Firms realized that the activity of invention can and must be collective and controlled. For example, the British engineering and manufacturing firm Boulton & Watt, which played a major role in the first Industrial Revolution, fully rethought the entire work organization, leveraging an important knowledge-creation activity.

The enterprise, in its modern sense, is relatively new, having appeared in the late-nineteenth century; before that time there were companies, factories, workers, and bosses, but no trace of an enterprise. The modern concept of an enterprise radically changed the classical notions of work, capital, and power. According to Segrestin and Hatchuel, the modern concept of an enterprise appeared in response to the need to collectively organize inventive activities using a scientific approach and to harness innovation. Since that time, technological advances have been organized, managed, and brought to market by enterprises.

The modern enterprise was born to manage complexity and build its future. With the invention of the enterprise, the marketplace of skills was replaced by the work contract.

16   Chapter 1. The Internet of Skills & Knowledge

1.2.2 Modern trend: return to a marketplace of skills?

Despite the triumph of the concept of modern enterprise, a number of recent reports[5,6,7] and books[8] have shown that there may be a megatrend pushing employment toward a return to a marketplace of skills. As of 2014, mobile has overtaken desktop as a method for accessing the Internet. Private life and professional life are becoming more and more difficult to distinguish: mobile devices allow you to perform your professional tasks while remaining in contact with your private sphere anywhere, anytime.

In the report *The Future of Work: Jobs and Skills in 2030*,[5] the authors have looked at both stable trends (societal, technological, economic, ecological and political) and potential disruptions (reverse migration, changing values of employees, zero-hour contract, anytime and anywhere capability, artificial intelligence, and so forth) to forecast a four scenarios related to jobs and skills in 2030 based on solid, factual evidence. It is interesting to note that these scenarios include a number of common features:

Fluidity: Employers will need to develop capabilities to leverage more fluid employment and to manage and develop skills across a global network. Employers have already started doing this: for example, in France eight out of ten employment contracts were made on a temporary basis. What will happen when this trend is pushed to its limit? How can this trend be pushed?

Diversity: Employers will face an increasing diversity, based on both culture and generation, in the workforce. How will employers deal with that? How will they help people to work together?

Flexibility: Information and communications technology (ICT), including the smartphone, has already created a revolution in the organization of work, in terms of time, duration, and place. The smartphone allows a continuous link with work, increasing flexibility in the organization of the work in terms of both time and space. In addition, the workspace itself is being reconfigured: working at remote worksites and working in shared offices are becoming increasingly common.

Innovation Intelligence   17

Adaptability: Companies are looking for employees who have a spectrum of skills and who can adapt. How can they find the needle in the haystack?

1.3 Toward the Internet of skills and knowledge?

For younger generations, work has already changed. The famous Generation Y, the Slashers, don't trust companies. They don't rely on companies to train them. They change jobs every twelve to eighteen months to gain new experiences, to add lines to their résumé or CV. In fact, rather than a résumé or CV, they have a LinkedIn profile. Talented professionals market themselves. Young professionals are no longer telecom engineers or project managers. Instead, they are developer/designer/DJ or consultant/magician (and I am not speaking about myself!). This "/" is the reason they are called Slashers.

1.3.1 Digital tools

Professional social networks provide new tools for headhunting companies to use in finding talented professionals, especially those who are not necessarily actively looking for jobs. Professional social networks provide new tools to young professionals for building their careers based on what other people have done before them. Powerful tools are currently being shaped to facilitate the matching of needs and talents. We can imagine what could happen if the Slashers? trend were pushed to its limit. We can imagine that talented professionals wouldn't stay for even one year in a given company, but rather would offer their expertise for a short-duration project or for a consultancy to address a spot problem. Professional social networks don't yet offer the infrastructure to easily enable such arrangements. Other platforms do, however. Expert-network platforms such as Maven or Clarity facilitate the matching of people who have a specific set of skills with people and companies that have a given need. You need somebody to help you write your first business plan? You'll find someone to do that. You need a carpenter? You'll find one. You need a plasma physicist who is

18 Chapter 1. The Internet of Skills & Knowledge

specialized in particle-in-cell modeling? You'll find such a person. We anticipate that there will be a convergence between professional social networks and these expert-network platforms to enable both employment and micro-consulting. These digital tools, together with other trends such as the zero-hour contract (an employment contract in which the employer has the discretion to vary the employee's working hours, usually anywhere from full-time to zero hours), will make work more fluid, more flexible, and less secure. We predict that companies will return to such a marketplace of skills, at least in part. Unfortunately, such a result would further stretch the gap between educated people and less-educated people. We can imagine in a future not so far away the rise of the Uber of Skills.

In parallel to these tools that focus on talents, other tools are focusing on the mining of knowledge. Google does already a good job at this, but data searching dedicated to the conception of innovative projects can be improved even further. Big Data is one of the buzzwords. New data and knowledge are being generated at an increasingly rapid pace. For example, two to three million scientific and technical publications are published each year. Over half a million patent applications are made each year. Most of this new knowledge is available in unstructured documents. Current search engines are very good at finding the most popular documents given a set of keywords, but they are not yet very good at interpreting the query made by the user, searching by concept, or finding rare documents buried in the depths of the Internet. However, many companies are working on filling these gaps. Machines will soon outperform humans at such tasks. A few years ago, computers began beating humans at chess. Today, machines even beat humans at game shows like *Jeopardy!* In *Jeopardy!* players must determine the question that matches a given answer. The program Watson, developed by IBM, was able to interpret spoken, natural language, search on the web for the most likely questions, and win the game against the best players. Other companies are specialized in applying Big Data to scientific papers or patents. These tools are currently limited by their capacity to interpret what the user really wants, but, once again it is

Innovation Intelligence

just a question of time until search engines also help users to ask the right questions. We can imagine the eBay of knowledge.

1.3.2 Impact on innovation?

It took about a century for the steam engine to radically change both industry and economy. It will take far less time for digital technologies to change our entire world. Digital technologies have already changed the way we listen music, the way we watch films, the way we buy and sell stuff. Now they are changing the way we use cars, the way we move around, the way we pay for products, and the way we use energy. Digital technologies will reshuffle the cards in all industrial sectors and disrupt all the value chains.

In parallel, and amplified by digital technologies, employment trends seem to indicate that we are returning to a marketplace of skills. This marketplace will be a global one in which a switch can be made in the blink of an eye. How will that landscape affect innovation? In this fast-paced world, companies will need to change the way in which they deal with innovation. There is no magic recipe for facing these changes – it will be a trial-and-error trajectory in which the most attentive and agile will gain while others will lose.

Chapter 2
The Parrot AR.Drone Case

You don't have to be a genius or a visionary or even a college graduate to be successful. You just need a framework and a dream.

MICHAEL DELL

In Short... This is a case description based on interviews of the actors. The story is the birth of the Parrot AR.Drone, which was created by a company that makes peripheral interfaces for mobile phones. The CEO, Henri Seydoux, drove the project himself. The project was daring, because much of the required knowledge was absent in Parrot. Henri needed to grow and diversify the company. Disruptive innovation would be needed. The company's lab was pushing an electric toy car – Henri decided that it should fly. The necessity of finding outside knowledge was recognized and dealt with by the combination of a systematic approach and opportunistic moves. Pascal Zunino, a student who had built a quadricopter drone in his garage and won an innovation contest organized by ONERA (The French Aerospace Lab), was found in Grenoble, France. He was not yet finished with school when he struck a deal with Parrot to

22 Chapter 2. The Parrot AR.Drone Case

assist in designing the flying object. He joined Parrot's Commando team, which included experts in electronic drives and stabilization sensors, on a part-time basis. A PhD student was hired to determine how to stabilize flights; an original solution was developed based on image analysis. Three years later, after many challenges, the quadricopter was ready. The product was launched at the International Consumer Electronics Show (CES) in Las Vegas, Nevada in 2010. A memorable demonstration was conducted in the conference hall and received significant media coverage. The product was a great success. Parrot is now working on the product's fourth generation. Henri Seydoux was sure that his market would be gamers who could use the drone and its camera to obtain a 3-D view of any scene in a game. However, its customers turned out to be people who wanted to film themselves from an aerial perspective. As a result, Parrot has focused subsequent generations of the product on the challenges experienced by photographers.

2.1 Introduction

"It must fly!" This was it! Our Wi-Fi remote-control car must fly! That was exactly when Henri Seydoux got the idea that would become one of his most difficult but most exciting challenges as an entrepreneur.[i]

It was January 2007 along the Canal Saint-Martin in Paris. It was early in the morning, very early. In fact, it was before dawn. It was very quiet. There were hardly any sounds, because it had snowed during the night. The streetlights gave the street a surreal atmosphere. There was nobody in the street. Well, almost nobody. Henri Seydoux,

---

[i]Although the story of the Parrot AR.Drone told in this chapter was slightly dramatized, it is based on the true story. All the characters are real. The story was constructed based on secondary research and on a series of interviews of the key participants: Henri Seydoux (cofounder and CEO of Parrot), Guillaume Pinto (Chief Technology Officer of Parrot), François Callou (AR.Drone Project Leader), and Pascal Zunino (cofounder and CEO of Novadem and consultant for Parrot). Discussions with Parrot employees who were not involved in the project, such as Matthieu Marquenet and Philippe Duvivier, also helped to shed light on certain aspects of the story.

Innovation Intelligence 23

the co-founder and CEO of the French company Parrot was walking slowly toward the headquarters of the company he had founded almost thirteen years earlier, as he did every morning. Henri was slightly upset this morning, because he was remembering telling the team in charge of the video remote-control car that "it's not fun enough!" They had been working on this project, meant to diversify Parrot's business, for three years already. They had gone through numerous challenges, numerous prototypes, and even test batches. The product was ready for production... but it was not fun enough. Henri decided to cancel the project. This was it, the end of the story.

Without realizing it, Henri was also upset because he was not the first person to walk in the fresh snow. As he was trying to walk exactly in the footsteps of the stranger who had taken away the snow's virginity, he saw the stranger's tracks end suddenly. It was as if the stranger had disappeared into the air. "This guy can probably fly," he thought, raising his head, his rectangular, plastic glasses fogged. "He must fly."

It must fly!

Just like that Henri got the idea that would give new life to the project. He knew that this was the solution. He also knew that the challenge he had given to his team three years earlier was a piece of cake compared to this new challenge he was about to give the team. He knew that large chunks of knowledge and technologies would need to be sourced from outside of the company.

This was so exciting!

2.2 Parrot: a successful SME that had to diversify

"Henri, we need to sell Parrot!" In those words Olivier Protard started the conversation. Olivier Protard, a partner at Sofinnova Partners, a venture-capital firm based in Paris, had called Henri Seydoux a few days earlier to make plans to meet at one of the quiet lounges of Café de la Paix on a Wednesday afternoon in September 2003.

Parrot was the company, based in Paris, that Henri Seydoux and Jean-Pierre Talvard had founded in 1994. As of 2003 Parrot's core

24 Chapter 2. The Parrot AR.Drone Case

business was the development and commercialization of high-tech products for using mobile phones inside cars. Specifically, Parrot offered the largest range of hands-free car kits. Over the years Parrot had developed a globally recognized capability in technologies related to voice recognition and signal processing for embedded and mobile applications for telephony in a car environment: chipsets, algorithms, Bluetooth, and software applications. By 2014, Parrot would grow to employ 850 people and generate revenues of EUR 235 million, with the vast majority of those sales abroad. Parrot is seen as an exception in an industry landscape dominated mainly by companies based in California, China, and Japan.

When Henri entered Café de la Paix that afternoon in 2003, he had already guessed what Olivier Protard wanted to discuss with him. Henri had cofounded Parrot almost ten years earlier, and the company had grown rapidly to about seventy employees and was generating good profit. This profitability had not always been the case: Parrot had undergone several crises. For Sofinnova Partners, which had invested in Parrot seven years earlier, it was time to sell its shares, and Sofinnova wanted Henri to sell the company. For Henri, selling was out of question; he still had projects planned for the company. He promised Olivier that he would find another investor to buy Sofinnova's shares.

This was just two years after the collapse of the Internet bubble and just two years after September 11th. Henri knew that finding an investor to buy Sofinnova's shares (with the cash going to Sofinnova rather than to Parrot) would be difficult, but that was what he wanted, and that was what he would do. It took him more than a year to close a deal with new investors that would not only buy out Sofinnova but also inject cash into Parrot.

By late 2004, Sofinnova was out, new investment funds were in, and Parrot had just received EUR 6 million in cash from the new investors. Parrot was still profitable. Henri was ready for new projects – it was time to think about the future and diversification. Since Parrot's historical activity was centered on Bluetooth peripherals for mobile phones, Henri started investigating what else the company could do

Innovation Intelligence   25

related to mobile phones. Music, photo, and video were appealing. Parrot would launch projects in all three of these domains.

With regard to music, Parrot bet on the fact that the mobile phone would become the device on which consumers also listened to music. They were wrong, as the opposite happened – mobile phone capabilities were added to music players such as the iPod. With regard to photos, Parrot launched a digital photo frame. It was a flop.

The video opportunity took a bit longer to develop. The idea was to enter the video-game toy business. The code name for Parrot's project was BTT (Bluetooth Toys). The first project was a Bluetooth (BT) remote-control car.

Two years later, in 2006, the verdict fell: the BT remote-control car worked, it was ready to be commercialized... but it was really not fun at all. Henri had tried to pitch his video-game toy project to various companies, including Nintendo, Sony, and Nokia. The idea was to pair a remote-control car with a video game. Henri was convinced that this combination would be the future of video games. Unfortunately, nobody wanted to buy it. Parrot had already spent a lot of money on the project and progressed quite far – everything was ready for industri-

Henri Seydoux.

alization: prototypes, test batches, industrial molds, and so forth. In terms of "good" innovation management, the project should have been cancelled much earlier, because there was simply no market for the product. Other than the project team and Henri, there was no strong support for it from within the company. The project, this time, would be killed.

2.3 The atypical, self-taught, visionary entrepreneur

At least, in a normal company, the project would have been killed. But Parrot was not a normal company. And Henri Seydoux was not a normal CEO. A bit like Steve Jobs, Henri is an atypical, self-taught, visionary entrepreneur.

Atypical. Henri is atypical for various reasons. First, he is self-taught, which is fairly exceptional considering the level of responsibility that he has reached (we will return to this aspect later). Second, he is also a glamourous CEO who does not hesitate to mix various spheres. For example, when he married the former model Farida Khelfa at the almost mythical Palace Theatre in 2012, he invited all of Parrot's employees, as well as a number of famous people, including Arielle Dombasle and Bernard-Henri Lévy, Elle Macpherson, Jean Paul Gaultier, Carla Bruni-Sarkozy and her husband, the former President of France Nicolas Sarkozy... and the Rolling Stones lead singer Mick Jagger! He invited all of his employees and a world famous rock star. Henri is also an atypical boss. He does not hesitate to take a nap at the desk of his nice see-through office, right in the middle of the open space where Parrot's young engineers sit at their workstations.

Self-taught. Henri was born in 1960. He is now recognized as a successful entrepreneur. The company that he cofounded in 1994, Parrot, is one of the world's leading companies in the field of wireless peripherals for mobile phones. Yet it was not obvious from the start that this talented, atypical, self-taught man would play such an important role in the high-tech sector. Not very interested in studies, calling himself a dunce, he began his career as a journalist from 1978 to 1980. During this period he met Roland Moreno, the inventor of the smart card, who convinced him to get into computer science. Henri defines himself as a rat de bibliothèque (a bookworm), because everything he knows he learned on his own. The self-taught aspect of Henri is very important: searching for missing pieces of knowledge is hard-coded into his DNA. It is part of his culture. It has become part of Parrot's culture. Passionate by philosophy, Henri himself is a sort of modern Enlightenment philosopher. He knows how to search for knowledge in the global encyclopedia. Passionate about open-source software, he knows how to rapidly assemble the best technologies to be the first to market with superior, innovative products.

Visionary. Henri is also visionary and intuitive. Although according to the best practices in terms of innovation management the remote-control car project should have been killed and the AR.Drone should never have been a project for Parrot in the first place, Henri had the intuition that the project should be pushed forward. The car project should not have gone as far as it did, because there was obviously no market for it. As for the drone project, it required leveraging technologies and market knowledge that were both very far from Parrot's core business and core competencies. The project was simply too risky. But Henri trusted his gut enough to launch the project and to continue it, against the rest of the company's resistance. He wanted Parrot to be the first to master indoor flights of drones. In addition, he wanted to use Wi-Fi as the remote channel, in order to place the drone within the phone ecosystem.

Entrepreneur. Finally, Henri is also a successful entrepreneur who has not always been successful. In the early 1980s, Henri realized that he did being an employee did not suit him very well and that he would be better off creating his own companies. During this period he started several companies: one in operating systems, another in 3-D imaging, and a third one – mainly as an investor – in luxury. The first two companies were not very successful. Then, in 1994, he cofounded Parrot. Henri's entrepreneurial spirit was transmitted to him mainly by his family members, for whom successful ventures were not rare. His father was copresident of the Pathé cinema and his brother is CEO of Gaumont Film Company. His great-grandfather Marcel Schlumberger founded Schlumberger Limited in 1926 (it currently employs 120,000 people worldwide. Like most entrepreneurs, Henri is extremely pugnacious and does not hesitate to get his hands dirty in business. For example, at some point during the drone project the team realized that it would be much better to be able to manage two video streams – one for controlling ground speed and one for the user. Unfortunately, having two video streams was not compatible with Parrot's P5 microprocessor. Henri decided that Parrot's next-generation processor (P6) should be able to manage two video streams. Another

28   Chapter 2. The Parrot AR.Drone Case

example of Henri's operational involvement can be found in the story
of how he tracked down the young geniuses he needed to help him to
complete the AR.Drone and take it to market.

2.4 The young genius

Pascal Zunino (right) and his team

OK, done! thought Pascal
Zunino. He saved the Pow-
erPoint file, closed his brand-
new MacBook Air, turned his
head, and looked at the landscape
through the window of the first
Grenoble-Paris Train à Grande
Vitesse (TGV) train of the day. It
was still very dark outside. He
could imagine himself floating in
the fields. He started thinking
about how he had gotten there. About how in a few hours he would
meet the CEO of a company that he hoped would become well known
by the general public for its drones.

Seven years earlier, when he had been only eighteen years old,
Pascal had succeeded in making a drone fly. This wasn't just any drone.
It was a drone that he had designed and built in his garage. The project
had not been easy, in particular because the required microelectrome-
chanical systems (MEMS) sensors were not yet available. But Pascal
was a real entrepreneur. He had been passionate about robotics (embedded electronics) and aeronautics (propellers) from a very early age,
and he was extremely resourceful: he managed to obtain piezoelectric
sensors for free through a friend of a friend in Switzerland.

This early success had been just the beginning; five years later
Pascal was still tinkering on amazing things in his garage. He was
now an engineering student at the Grenoble Institute of Technology
(INPG). His professors were so impressed, by both his passion and
what he could achieve with almost nothing, that they advised him

to enter the prestigious ONERA/DGA university innovation contest. Pascal assembled and managed a team of eight other smart engineering students. A few months later, they won the competition with their CPX4 drone, a 350-gram drone for use in urban scoping missions. Winning the prize was exciting and gave Pascal and his collaborators a lot of press coverage. Pascal knew that it was an important event, but he did not expect it to be so important that it would change his life to such an extent.

A few months had passed since the contest. Pascal had completed his engineering degree, but he was still working on his drone, and he was even thinking of starting his own company. On a cold Friday evening in the winter in Grenoble, Pascal was sitting at his kitchen table having eaten a quick dinner. He was mechanically playing with a breadcrumb when his old Nokia 3310 mobile phone started vibrating and spinning on the table. The phone number displayed on the screen was unfamiliar to him. Who could it be?

"Oh, hi, this is Henri Seydoux speaking."

Not knowing who that was, Pascal didn't say anything.

"I am the CEO of Parrot.

– Hmm?"

Pascal had never heard of Parrot and he was getting ready, one more time, to say that he was not interested in changing his phone plan or buying life insurance.

Henri explained Parrot's business to Pascal (at that time Parrot was much less known by the general public than it is today).

"We do wireless devices for the automobile... "

Pascal listened for a few minutes without saying a word. He could not understand where the conversation was leading. He was starting to think that this guy, Henri Seydoux, may have wanted to speak with someone else who had the same name as Pascal. Pascal was getting lost in his thoughts. Why is this guy telling me all this? He was not really listening anymore.

"We are thinking about making a drone!" Henri finally said.

This was a few days after Henri had become convinced that Parrot should make the car fly. Since that day, this CEO of a company employing two hundred people had spent all of his time exploring the Internet for information on drones. Henri is a man of passions: when he gets hooked on a topic, he wants to know everything about it. It did not matter if the company was in the middle of closing its annual accounts. Even the financial director could not get his attention. He was somewhere else. He was dreaming of the future. He was dreaming of Parrot drones. During that scouting he stumbled on a press release about Pascal Zunino and his team winning the ONERA/DGA contest for their CPX4 drone. He was stunned. I have to meet this guy! he thought. He had to meet him, because what he had achieved by himself with hardly any materials was incredible.

As soon as Henri said, "We are thinking about making a drone!" Pascal started paying attention. This was his passion.

"Could you please come over to Paris to tell us about what you are doing?" Henri asked.

That was how Pascal had ended up on the Grenoble-Paris train so early in the morning. He was heading to the Canal Saint-Martin in Paris. Pascal was so excited to show what he had been working on over the past few years, to people who immediately understood his passion, that he told them everything without thinking about secrets, confidentiality, intellectual property, and so forth. Parrot's Commando team had so many questions. He explained in detail all of his technological choices.

That was the beginning of a collaboration that would last for three years. The collaboration would save Parrot precious time – probably several years. And it would enable Pascal to start his own company, already having a first client: Parrot, from which he had learned a lot.

2.5 The technology outburst of helicopter drones

Henry Seydoux's project and Pascal Zunino's hobbyist passion were part of a new breed of technology that was blossoming at the time. While large drone technology was exclusively focused on military applications, the miniature automated flying objects were being made pos-

Innovation Intelligence 31

sible by the development of many new components related to consumer applications. High-performance lithium batteries, telecommunications network-connection components, miniature cameras, and position sensors were developed and made available at reasonable cost thanks to the markets for laptop computers and mobile phones. High-performance electric motors had been made available by the development of advanced ceramic magnets and other power electronics at the turn of this century.

2.6 The Commando team

François Callou was working at Sagem DS, on autopilot and feeling like he needed a change. That was when he came across a job posting at Parrot in automation. The position was somewhat obscure and did not really fit into Parrot's core business. During the series of job interviews, he came to understand that there was something brewing. A small team, which he would later lead, was onto something big, something secret. He understood that he would have to make the car fly. What a challenge that would be. François started working at Parrot in August 2007 and he was put in charge of automation.

Going to market with a toy drone would be challenging. In fact, it would require the creation of a new market segment. On one side was the model building segment, comprised of expensive (up to several thousand euros) remote-control helicopters made and used only by specialists. On the other side were inexpensive (less than one hundred or even fifty euros) remote-control toys with a trend towards small indoor flying objects such as PicooZ (also sold under the brand name of Air Hogs Havoc Heli in North America). At the same time, another trend emerging – action video, led by companies such as GoPro. Would 2004 be the beginning of the convergence for making videos in improbable conditions? Parrot would bet on creating a new segment: mass-market drones.

The challenges of the project were numerous and Henri knew that he would not be able to do everything by himself. Many of the required pieces of knowledge were not available in-house: aeronautics (propellers and engines), mechanics (resistance and lightness), cameras (optics, sensors, and image processing), and control algorithms.

What would be outsourced? Who could help? How would Parrot find the missing bits of knowledge? What value would Parrot add? To bring in the required knowledge and skills, every type of arrangement would be allowed: hiring, consulting, codevelopment, and so forth.

In early 2007 Parrot assembled the new team, the Commando team, that would be in charge of making the car fly. Claire Jonchery was hired to solve the problem of drift control by video, a key point to being able to display the drone's absolute position (she was able to write her PhD dissertation on this topic as well). François Callou, who is now the project manager for the Bebop Drone, was originally hired to manage automation for the first AR.Drone. And Pascal Zunino joined the Commando team as an external consultant. Pascal and his newly formed company, Novadem, helped Parrot to develop various key aspects of Parrot's drone: propeller design, control system and stabilization algorithms, ultrasound telemeter, benchmarks (for example, for sensor choices), noise reduction, and testing procedures. While Parrot focused mainly on video, Pascal focused on flight. The relationship worked very well. Pascal would spend three days each month at Parrot, in Paris, another five days each month working remotely for Parrot, and the rest of his time on his own drone projects. The arrangement was ideal for both parties.

The Commando team was like a small startup within Parrot. The main rules were secrecy and efficiency. A number of products were already available on the market, but none of them was good enough for the general public. Henri wanted to sell a drone that would be plug-and-play for the consumer.

Because Parrot wanted to reach the prototype phase quickly, traditional V-model development methods were out of the question. (The V-model is one of many ways to formalize the sequential steps in the development of an innovative project). Instead, the Commando team moved forward using more agile methods: quick prototyping, boot-

Innovation Intelligence 33

strapping, and so forth. Their philosophy was the following: let's quickly get something in the air, put our electronics on it, and see what happens. They did exactly that. In fact, for one of the first prototypes, the team used the mechanical structure of an existing toy, the X-UFO manufactured by Silverlit.

The team's first objective was to measure the latitude, the angles of the drone, accurately. This required building a small inertial measurement unit (IMU), a subsystem generally used for aeronautical applications and therefore expensive. An IMU has two main components: an accelerometer and a gyroscope. Fortuitously, at roughly the same time these components were becoming more inexpensive, the prices having been pulled down by the markets for digital cameras and smartphones.

The team's second objective was to measure altitude and drift. The device for measuring the drone's altitude would also be sourced in the mass market. An ultrasound telemeter, used in the automotive industry to measure the distance between the back of a vehicle and an obstacle, would suit. For measuring drift, the speed of the drone relative to ground, a video camera would do the job.

2.7 The Launch

The morning of the launch, the whole Commando team was excited. Although it was January, almost exactly three years after the "it must fly" epiphany, the temperature was much warmer on this day and there was no snow outside. The launch took place in Las Vegas, Nevada, almost 9000 kilometers away from Parrot's headquarters. Why was the team so excited? Because the drone was functional and they were there, in Las Vegas, to officially launch the AR.Drone at the 2010 Consumer Electronics Show (CES).

It was impossible to miss this strange flying object with its four propellers, as it flew above the people milling about and walking along the corridors of the show. The pilot stood a few meters away, using his iPhone to control the drone via Wi-Fi. It was absolutely amazing.

Henri Seydoux at Le Bourget

Henri Seydoux was thrilled.

He was thrilled because in mid-2009, just a few months prior to the CES but three years after he had come up with the idea to make the car fly, he had still been telling his team, "It must be stable!" Results were encouraging but not yet successful. "It must be stable!" was Henri's new directive. "I want anybody to be able to control this drone. Stability must be drastically improved. Either you stabilize it by the end of the year so we can demo the drone at the 2010 CES, or we stop the project." It sounded impossible to achieve in such a short time, but somewhat like Steve Jobs with his "reality distortion field"[9] Henri Seydoux knew how to mobilize a team.

And there they were: the AR.Drone was the star of the 2010 CES. It was the first Wi-Fi augmented reality quadricopter drone. The drone was loaded with sensors and video cameras. It had debuted just in time to surf the wave of the famous, miniature, remote-control helicopter PicooZ. In fact, Parrot was not just catching the wave but was extending it: the various embedded sensors (gyroscope, accelerometer, and ultrasound sensor) enabled a perfect flight: stable and ultrasimple to maneuver. The video camera placed underneath the drone enabled both

Innovation Intelligence   35

measurement of ground speed and stationary flights. The video camera placed at the front of the drone streamed video directly to the pilot's iPhone screen, enabling the pilot to control the drone by simply moving the iPhone.

The AR.Drone would hit the market just a few months later, with a global launch beginning in August 2010, starting in Hong Kong and France before spreading to the rest of the world. This initial product was a major success: 120,000 AR.Drones would be sold by the end of the year. That was just the beginning. The team immediately began working on the next-generation drone, the AR.Drone 2.0, which would be launched in 2012. Then, in late 2014, the third-generation drone, the Bebop Drone, was launched. While Parrot basically had the market to itself in those early years, competition is now catching up, with the main competitor being DJI. Parrot has again begun to diversify, for example, by looking into professional applications for the drones. As part of this effort, Parrot recently acquired the Swiss company senseFly.

2.8 Epilogue

Although Parrot's drone project should have been killed on various occasions based on "good" innovation-management practices, it survived. Ten years after Parrot started its initiative to diversify, seven years after the beginning of the drone project, four years after the launch of the AR.Drone, Parrot has realized two additional generations of the drone and has acquired other drone companies for expanding the drone's professional applications. Of Parrot's revenues today, 50% are generated by drone sales.

Parrot successfully achieved diversification with short time to market. This achievement was made possible by Parrot assembling the necessary puzzle pieces, most of them coming from outside the company. The success has much to do with Henri Seydoux's background: not being an engineer, he has the attitude in his DNA to search outside for information and to ask the right questions rather than trying to solve problems by himself.

36   Chapter 2. The Parrot AR.Drone Case

Despite the success of the AR.Drone, Parrot's entire process, specifically with regard to plugging in external bricks of knowledge or talent, introduced risk. For example, there was intellectual property risk: the propeller design is protected as a piece of art and it belongs to the designer, the young genius Pascal Zunino. This is not a problem as long as Pascal's company, Novadem, and Parrot are not pursuing the same market segment, but what if Novadem changes its strategy? To this question, Henri Seydoux replies that patents are irrelevant, that what really matters is having an original positioning, early time to market, and a superior product.

2.9 Conclusion

The story of Parrot's AR.Drone is interesting for various reasons.

First, the product was a true innovation, in terms of both its technological innovation and its market positioning[ii]. It was a technological innovation, because it was the intelligent integration of new, specially-developed technologies (propeller designs, stabilization algorithms, and so forth) and other technologies available on the mass market (including MEMS). It was innovative in terms of marketing positioning, because it debuted almost perfectly in time to catch the convergence of two waves: the wave of mass-market flying objects and toys such as PicooZ and the wave of action-video cameras such as GoPro. Parrot's successful global launch of the product globally, starting in Hong Kong, is still fairly rare for French small and medium-sized enterprises, which makes the achievement even more impressive.

Second, the story is interesting because Parrot was not, at first sight, the company best suited to provide the product. For Parrot the project was particularly risky, because most of the required technologies and skills were not available in-house. The Commando team, led directly by Henri, had to fight the rest of the company, which was skeptical of

---

[ii] Actually, the only mistake Henri Seydoux made was to initially position the AR.Drone as a video game. That application never caught on. Instead, people started using the drone for other applications: flying and filmmaking.

Innovation Intelligence | 37

the project. While other projects were killed, the AR.Drone project was kept alive, against all standard innovation-management practices.

Third, the story is interesting because its risk was mitigated by careful engagement, leveraging, and management of external sources of knowledge and skills.

The story of Parrot's AR.Drone, like the story of Apple's iPod, raises a number of questions. Parrot's CEO, Henri Seydoux, had the right intuition to guess quite accurately what the market would want soon. (By the way, the market does not want anything and does not demand anything. The market does not know what it wants.) He had the right intuition to source and engage the required technological bricks and talent. This is what we call *innovation intelligence*. Henri carefully managed the integration of all of these external bricks. And he did it based on intuition and gut feeling. Is there a way to systematize and organize innovation intelligence on a larger scale – at the scale of large industrial groups such as corporations?

Chapter 3
Knowledge, the fuel of innovation

Our behavior is driven by a fundamental core belief; the desire and the ability of an organization to continuously learn from any source, and to rapidly convert this learning into action, is it's ultimate competitive advantage.

JACK WELCH

In Short. . . Creativity and knowledge are the yin and yang of innovation. No creative idea is any good without a solid base of knowledge. No quest for knowledge is meaningful without the goal of generating an innovative idea. Performance of the innovation cycle accepts risk but not waste. A good innovation process first addresses the most risky aspect of a project. Often risk is created by a lack of knowledge. Technical inventions penetrate industries as waves of innovations. For strategic positioning, knowledge must be acquired early in the wave. For market entry, piping in external knowledge is faster than learning on one's own.

40   Chapter 3. Knowledge, the fuel of innovation

Inventions and discoveries are essentially novel combinations of existing pieces of knowledge. The winners at the innovation game are always best-in-class at gathering and acquiring knowledge and combining it to serve their customers' needs. In this section we map the multiple sources of knowledge for companies' innovation processes, analyze the dynamic aspect of the process, and derive the following themes:

- Knowledge is the most important component of innovation.
- Innovation is renewed as new knowledge emerges.
- Important discoveries in an industry can cause waves of innovation converging to generic product features.
- Good timing in knowledge acquisition is a key for performance.

3.1 Knowledge and innovation: a tight interdependency

Any innovator knows from experience that knowledge is as important to him or her as mortar is to a mason. Knowledge is required at every step of the innovation process. Knowledge is the key resource in the generation of an innovative concept. We speak here about all types of knowledge, not only technical knowledge but also knowledge of markets, user ergonomics, business trends, geopolitics, and so forth. When an idea is found worth pursuing, further knowledge is needed during the engineering phase to implement the concept. In parallel, another layer of knowledge is required, this one to back one of the most critical phases of innovation – the process of shaping a business model and defining a marketing strategy for the new product. Finally, even more knowledge is required for the product's lateral diffusion phase, the possible extension of the innovation to other applications. Such extension can generate value for the company by either licensing in industries in which the company does not operate or by creating new business development opportunities in its current industry.

This close connection between knowledge and inventive design is well perceived and analyzed within the framework of concept-

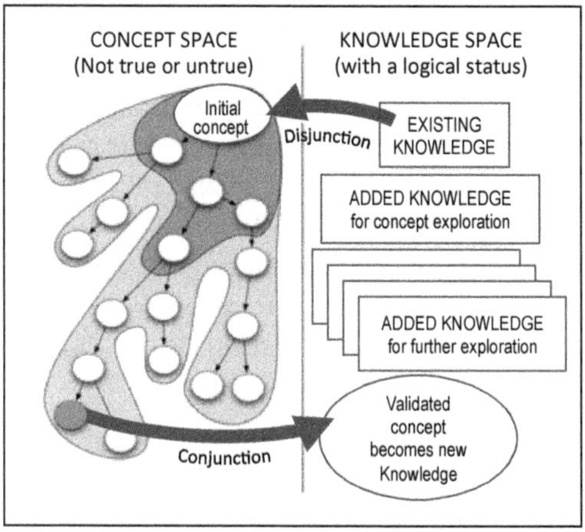

Innovation Intelligence

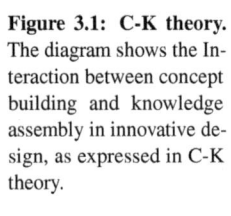

Figure 3.1: C-K theory. The diagram shows the Interaction between concept building and knowledge assembly in innovative design, as expressed in C-K theory.

knowledge theory (C-K theory).[10,11]

While C-K theory is an analytical tool for describing the process of designing innovative concepts, it is also an operational guide for the creative design process itself. One of the benefits of C-K theory is that it facilitates understanding of the mechanisms that operate at the instant of creation, the mechanisms that cause the iconic inventive lightbulb to ignite.

The steps in developing the famous Swatch were analyzed by C-K black-belt analysts (see the inset). The Swatch concept was first proposed by employees who were studying plastic manufacturing, a field alien to the company, ETA, a master of fine mechanics. The Swatch concept had to go through several design loops, from shaping the preliminary concept to incorporating new pieces of knowledge into the design.

As described in C-K theory, innovative design must incorporate novel pieces of knowledge as a way to extend an existing concept into new, innovative concepts. The more innovative the concept, the further the design team must explore, seeking and incorporating new knowledge. At some point, the required addition of knowledge is no

42 Chapter 3. Knowledge, the fuel of innovation

longer straightforward for the design team, as its members may not themselves have such knowledge. This is the critical moment that will make the difference between a successful team and an unsuccessful team. The successful design team remains tenacious in acquiring additional knowledge that may help in building a coherent concept. Such knowledge can be acquired by many possible means, by luck or serendipity,[i] by self learning, or by introducing external expertise into the design circle. In other words, the most fertile moment in an inventive process is the moment when a design team has the opportunity to introduce into its thinking pattern "alien" knowledge.

The story of Swatch as seen by C-K theoreticians

The creation phase of the famous Swatch is analyzed in the book titled *Innovation Factory*.[13] C-K theory is used to illustrate how knowledge is used to put forward a concept and how the transformation of an emerging and immature concept into a practical product capable of value creation requires further knowledge. It the case of the Swatch, the initiating knowledge was:

- Polymer injection molding for small and precise parts
- Polymer-to-polymer ultrasonic welding
- Design for the improved reliability of watches by the use of fewer parts

This knowledge formed the basis for the initial, vague concept for a low-cost watch, but far more knowledge had to be incorporated into the thinking process, in particular by marketing personnel. Only then was the initial concept made precise and complete:

---

[i]See, for example, "The serendipity equations" by A. Dias de Figueiredo and J. Campos, Proc. Of the 4th Int. Conf. on case based reasoning, (2001).[12] We discuss this concept further in chapter 5.

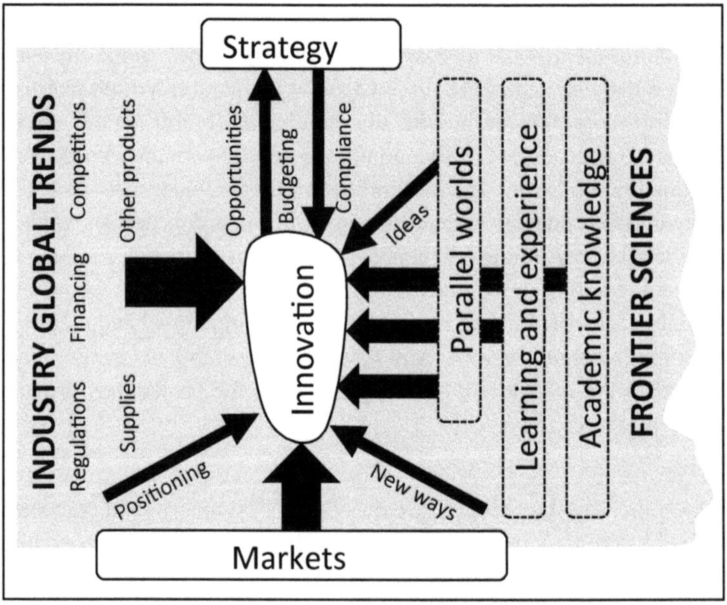

Figure 3.3: Origins of knowledge. The diagram shows the origins of knowledge relevant to appropriate decision making during an innovation project.

- A watch that becomes a fashion accessory
- A classic watch that ticks but at the same time looks futuristic
- Rapid renewal of the watch's visual design

3.2 Knowledge-source mapping

3.2.1 Internal knowledge flow

Relevant knowledge comes first from within the company contemplating the new endeavor. Although it may be considered obvious, we take this opportunity to stress the importance of the internal knowledge transfer shown as the upper vertical arrows in figure 3.3. Above all,

44   Chapter 3. Knowledge, the fuel of innovation

the innovation drive must be consistent with the company's strategy. This requirement is not as easy to satisfy as you may think. In real life, company strategies are often vague, wishful, and written mainly as tool for communicating with shareholders. Moreover, innovative ideas are conceived by creative minds whose ideas are the results of a combination of dreams and possibilities; it is rare when such ideas fit nicely into the company's stated strategy. Such new concepts should be considered opportunities by those who shape the company's strategy, but the adaptation to take advantage of those opportunities requires a reliable flow of information between the company's headquarters and its innovation warriors. Any flaw or delay in this exchange may jeopardize the innovation, in particular when the project has grown sufficiently large to be visible.

Another key knowledge stream within a company relates to the potential product's market (the lower vertical arrow). A successful company has a strong knowledge base with regard to its existing markets. This source of information is of paramount importance in both shaping and guiding any innovation project. That internal knowledge may be insufficient, as when the potential of the new concept is expected to lie outside the company's usual customer base or outside its existing business model. A common threat to reliable flow of such internal knowledge is poor communication between the sales and marketing and research and development departments.

Both vertical flows of knowledge within the company are important. In the remainder of this book, however, we will focus primarily on access to lateral knowledge, or knowledge from outside the company. However, you should keep in mind that the digestion and integration of knowledge from the various areas within the company is a priority and thus should not be omitted when considering a long-distance knowledge quest. As we all appreciate the strategic importance of innovation in today's modern economy, this point is more important than ever.

Innovation Intelligence   45

3.2.2 Trends and environment for innovation deployment horizon

We have positioned on the left side of figure 3.3 all knowledge related to the industrial and social environment in which a potential innovation project should be considered. This knowledge is typically acquired by a company when defining its strategy. However, when an innovative concept is proposed, it is very important to revisit the environment for the proposed project. By *environment*, we mean the broad, slowly changing landscape in which the innovation will exist. This environment includes the following:

- Socioeconomic factors and fashion trends
- Availability and cost of raw materials
- Standards, regulations, and export taxes
- Emergence of competing solutions
- Megatrends such as urbanization, climate change, and so on

Trends may be easy to discern in the foggy contour of the future, but what is difficult to grasp with a reasonable level of accuracy is the time scale for the establishment of a new equilibrium and the turbulence that may accompany the transition. Deeper and wider knowledge is required to assess the most probable environment that a new product will encounter.

Let's consider an example: a company is planning to create an innovative version of an electric car. Please feel free to imagine your own version of this innovation – there is still room today for creativity because the electric-car market is not yet mature. For now, however, let's consider a foldable car[ii]. Such innovation shall project in a business environment. Let us focus on only two important elements of the environment.

First: urban life. Urban life will change rapidly during the coming decades. The increasing population in cities that will grow larger and larger will need to cope with more traffic congestion and atmospheric

---

[ii]We found two published projects regarding an electric foldable car: the Michelin Design Challenge "Soleil Concept Car"[14] and the Hiriko Car already in pre-series.[15]

46   Chapter 3. Knowledge, the fuel of innovation

pollution. This will result in more severe regulations and constraints. Will cities become wild, permanent traffic jams? Or perhaps cab-only zones or high-toll zones? The answer will probably vary based on the average wealth of the specific city's population. Positioning a new product in its future market and shaping its design accordingly requires valuable expertise on the socioeconomic trends of the individual cities around the world.

Second: batteries. A key element for this electric foldable car is lithium-battery reliability. It will have a significant effect on the car's business model. So far, lithium batteries have a reliability horizon which is significantly below both car-industry standards and consumer expectations. Today, many companies that sell electric cars are leasing the battery in order to lower the risk perceived by consumers. A key question is how fast the electrochemistry industry will progress along the experience curve for high-powered lithium batteries. Theoretical analysis of reliability growth in general was initiated in the 1960s[16] somewhat in parallel with the famous theory relating production cost and cumulative volume via a learning curve,[17] Predicting the reliability improvement for the modern lithium battery is a challenge requiring a combination of knowledge in progress modeling, production engineering, and electrochemistry. It is a difficult task, but an experienced expert in the field can narrow the window of uncertainty.

Deep and thorough analysis of the environment is highly recommended when any innovation project is expected to grow to require a significant budget. A deficiency in this area may lead to poor positioning of the product and therefore disappointing business results. For example, when Roussel Uclaf, a French pharmaceutical company, developed RU-486, a version of the morning-after pill, it underestimated the power of the antiabortion organizations in the United States. Although the product was effective, it was not successful in the United States,[18] the largest potential market. The obstacle posed by the antiabortion organizations was not well estimated when predicting the environment for the product, and that led to disappointment for Roussel Uclaf's shareholders.

Innovation Intelligence 47

Conversely, when the Swiss watchmakers realized that the trends for wristwatches were being increasingly driven more by fashion than by the need for keeping time, they shaped the future Swatch accordingly. Environment-related knowledge is bread and butter for a company; indeed shaping its strategy requires that a company have a permanent in-house intelligence activity. However, in many cases, specific complementary knowledge is needed for each innovation project, particularly when the project aims further into the future or targets market segments that are new to the company. With regard to this environment-related knowledge, companies are often blinded by self-confidence.

3.2.3 General knowledge

The right-hand side of figure 3.3 shows the rest of the required knowledge base. These areas are broader than knowledge of a technical nature; for example, personal experience in included here. This complex tissue of knowledge has such diverse and unpredictable origins that it is rarely available entirely from within a company. In the extreme case of a very large corporation, the knowledge may be present but difficult to locate unless it belongs to a well-identified group of people. This ensemble that we call *general knowledge* is broad, complex, and difficult to map. In an attempt to delineate a pattern, we have chosen to organize it into simple, generic subgroups.

Frontier sciences

Further away from the daily activity of most companies, we have located the new knowledge generated by basic research or emerging application fields. We call these the *frontier sciences*. At the beginning nobody knows how soon this new knowledge will be relevant to industrial innovation. However, this new knowledge certainly has an intrinsic potential for creating novel combinations that will affect the industry eventually. Important discoveries penetrate industry as waves with associated delays. The typical delay and duration varies widely; electricity came as huge wave but slowly, stretching on for half a century. Conversely, it took only a few years for giant magnetoresistance to

48   Chapter 3. Knowledge, the fuel of innovation

progress from Nobel-Prize-winning papers[iii] to the marketing of hard disk thin-film heads[iv]. Frontier knowledge penetrates even faster when it is immaterial knowledge such as algorithms or new applications of an existing infrastructure, for example the onset of cloud computing.[19] Currently, the entire economy is being shaken by a wave that is both large and rather fast-moving, the digital wave (we will revisit the digital wave in chapter 4).

Note that this frontier activity can be segmented into two types:

Scientific research and discoveries. This *scientific research* activity is conducted in basic research labs and is primarily intended to contribute to human knowledge. Currently this activity is conducted mainly in universities and public research organizations, although in the past groups inside private companies such as Bell Telephone's Bell Labs and the IBM Zurich Research Laboratory in Rüschlikon, Switzerland made contributions that led to several Nobel Prizes. It is not impossible for major scientific discoveries of the future to emerge from a private research center, but it is rather unlikely. Public research has become powerful, and private research is too busy struggling with the complexity of applied research.

Start-up activity. There is an increasingly active sector focused on applied research via *start-up activity*. Such activity battles at the frontier of knowledge, but its goals are concrete rather than the general objective of contributing to human knowledge. Examples include the following: creating a process that would improve oil recovery from an oil pit, developing image-interpretation software that can look through turbulent media, creating an algorithm that would detect an epidemic at an early stage, creating a miniature electric motor, proposing a new, secure way to perform financial transactions via the Internet. In each of these cases a clear application has been identified and that application is the motivation for the research. This type of critical activity is undertaken in both the public and the private sectors. Public research

---

[iii]The papers by Albert Fert and Peter Grünberg were both independently published in 1989.

[iv]IBM launched the first hard disk with a giant magnetoresistance head in 1996.

Innovation Intelligence

centers are urged to engage in such activities. If a project's initial results are promising, the project is often spun off from the public organization into either a start-up firm or an established company. Industrial laboratories also conduct this type of research.

This applied frontier-science activity is often confidential or at least not publicized because of its business potential. As a result, teams involved in such projects are not linked to an open network for knowledge exchange. Even so, they need to exchange knowledge with others in order to maintain their expertise. For them, the exchange is done via the networks associated with the knowledge bricks they are assembling in their project. As we will see later, exploring frontier knowledge in what we will call the *start-up nebulae* is quite difficult, because this knowledge is fragmented, rarely disclosed fully, and often strongly tainted by communication-driven optimism.

Despite its challenges, observation and analysis of new knowledge at the frontier of science is a must-do task for large companies. Such new knowledge will, with a high probability, trigger a later wave of innovations for which the key players must be prepared.

Alan Turing and the genetic algorithm

The genetic algorithm was conceived in the 1950s by Alan Turing. It mimics the Darwinian evolution process by generating random variations of a program sequence, selecting them by testing, and then proceeding from the best resulting breed to another set of mutations. The concept is calculation-intensive. For decades the concept was applied and refined by a small circle of academic specialists in genetic sciences and algorithm theory. It was only at the dawn of the twenty-first century that the engineering modeling community developed an interest in genetic algorithms. Several applications, such as antenna design optimization[20] or gas turbine design,[21] have demonstrated the potential of genetic algorithms, specifically because they fit naturally with parallel computing.

50　　　　　Chapter 3. Knowledge, the fuel of innovation

There are still many jewels of knowledge resting in secluded niches of academia!

The natural fate of frontier knowledge is to rapidly pass to the most advanced laboratories and academic teams in the relevant field, as indicated by the box labeled academic knowledge and shown to the left of the one labeled frontier sciences in figure 3.3. They then reprocess and test the new discovery and evaluate all fruitful applications and potentials extensions of the concept. A critical task usually done at this stage is the reformulation of the new knowledge into wording more accessible to a larger number of people and disseminating it via review papers and conference keynote speeches.

As the new knowledge matures, it is taught first at the postgraduate level then later at the graduate level or in specialized engineering schools. Extension of the knowledge base can be slow. For example, more than a century after their discoveries, complex theories such as quantum mechanics or relativity theory are still confined to graduate-level education. The extension can also happen quickly, as it did in the cases of solid-state energy band structure in physics and Polymerase Chain Reaction (PCR) in genetics.

Academic knowledge, at least to mature knowledge, is relatively accessible. Textbooks are published and special-focus summer schools are proposed. The difficulty with this type of knowledge is not in its access but rather in its breadth. Academic knowledge is so broad, so diverse, and dispersed across so many disciplines that nobody can examine it all. Innovation players may miss the opportunity to apply a valuable piece of knowledge from academia, simply because they are not aware that it exists. This potential failure highlights the importance of assembling innovation teams that are comprised of people who have diverse origins. Such diversity, with its wider coverage of academic knowledge, increases the probably that the team will identify a relevant piece of knowledge. Moreover, teams that include a diversity of experi-

Innovation Intelligence   51

ence are more inclined to admit that their knowledge is still limited[v] and, surprisingly, to invest more in actively searching for additional knowledge around the world.

Learning and experience

Example of the fire piston

Rudolf Diesel has always ac-knowledged that his invention of the sparkless internal com-bustion engine was directly in-spired by a demonstration he witnessed while a student at the University of Munich. He saw his professor of thermody-namics ignite a fire by using a primitive fire piston. The traditional method of some tribes in Oceania for starting a fire is to violently compress air inside a wooden tube with a tight piston, a fire piston. Years later, when Diesel was trying to simplify the design of the internal combustion engine, he remembered this piece of ancestral knowledge.

Example of the velcro example

George de Mestral was in-trigued by seeds, commonly called burrs, attached to his dog's fur. Burrs, the envelopes of fruits, are dispersed by an-imals (this is called epizoo-

---

[v] Johann Wolfgang von Goethe said the following: "We know accurately only when we know little; with knowledge doubt increases" (Sprüche in Prosa, 1819).

chory) enabling reproduction
at great distances. In his microscope, de Mestral saw tiny hooks
at the end of these burrs. Such hooks were already shown in the
drawings in various botany books. The difference was that for de
Mestral – an engineer who specialized in weaving technology –
the knowledge came by serendipity. As soon as he saw the burrs'
tiny hook, the logic was straightforward. This "discovery" was
the first step in the invention of the product now known as Velcro.

Learning and experience, the accumulated knowledge carried by
an individual, is the box shown to the left of academic knowledge
in figure 3.3. It is the sum of an individual's education, which also
belongs in the area of academic knowledge, and experience. As such,
it is a complex collection peculiar to each individual. When trying to
understand and explain the mysterious mechanisms that made them
follow a path that nobody ever followed before them, many inventors
refer to some long-ago, fortuitous event that left a mark on his or her
mind.

A person who has been exposed to a wide variety of circumstances,
including travel, and various cultures, will have a larger collection of
knowledge waiting in his or her "attic" for a fortuitous occasion when
it will be reactivated as a creative process calls for it. Furthermore,
a team of people who have accumulated various educations and life
experiences will have access to a larger base of knowledge and will
therefore be more likely to generate innovative concepts.

Parallel worlds

Parallel worlds, shown in figure 3.3 as a box between learning and
experience and the company's in-house knowledge, contain industrial
knowledge far from the standard knowledge base of the company's
own industry. The piece of knowledge may be unexpected and not
present in the existing knowledge base of the company's industry but
applicable to the company's situation. For example, a metal packaging
company trying to conceive a fraud-resistant container for medicine

Innovation Intelligence

will have a good chance of being inspired by exploring knowledge in the banknote and credit card printing industry. This is a magical instant when a concept is taken from a given industry and combined with the traditional elements of another industry to create value. It is called creative addition. Fruitful knowledge often comes from areas that are not necessarily connected to the original industry. We call these seemingly disconnected silos of knowledge *parallel worlds*. Next, we will provide two rich examples of sourcing of knowledge from parallel worlds.

Cross-Industry Propagation. Finding a good idea, a better material, a better process, or simply a new perspective from a different industry is a fertile route for innovation. Examples abound. We have provided two brief examples in the inset, but we could have included additional examples, such as Fischer Sports GmbH limiting the vibration in skis by using an old technique for limiting the resonance in violins or Henry Ford drawing inspiration for his automobile assembly line from the belt system used for meat processing by large slaughterhouses in Chicago, Illinois.

Example of the Schindler rope

The Schindler Group is a leader in elevator manufacturing. In the 1990s, the company assigned a student to perform an exploratory survey for a better material than steel for lift cables. The student explored many fields and found that aramid ropes, developed decades earlier for rock climbing, performed far better than steel cables in terms of strength, flexibility, and longevity. The corresponding detailed knowledge was gradually acquired and reworked by

54   Chapter 3. Knowledge, the fuel of innovation

Schindler. After a long qualification phase, aramid-rope-based elevators are now manufactured and marketed by the Schindler Group.

Example of video game players and BMW

BMW was searching for new human machine interfaces (HMIs) for adapting cars to modern numerical services such as GPS and hands-free telephone. The BMW project team members used their networks of contacts in Silicon Valley to explore and connect with the video-game community. Thanks to various collaborations with joystick designers, BMW developed its iDrive, a simple and intuitive switching system which drivers can use while keeping their eyes on the road.

Biomimetics. Another rich parallel world is Mother Nature. In countless cases creative thinking has been derived from the incredible performances of bacteria, plants, and animals through the ages of natural selection. In the insets, we have given two recent examples, but there are many other familiar examples, such as honeycomb structures used in many applications, bullet train noses being inspired by kingfisher birds, and robot actuators being influenced by elephant trunks.

Innovation Intelligence   55

Example of the Nanopass needle

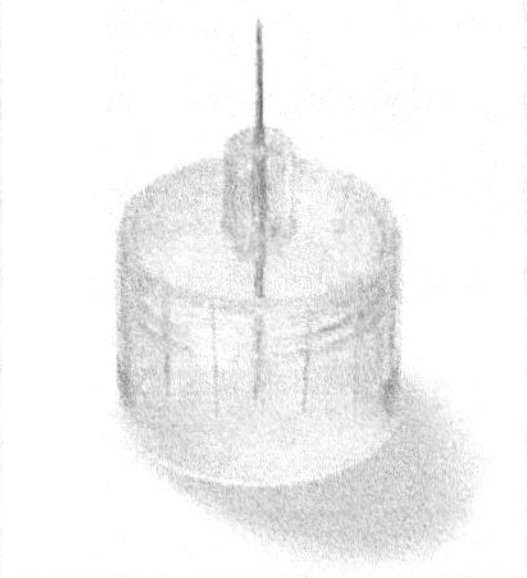

Researchers in Japan decided to
study a type of mosquito that stings
people without hurting them (at least,
at the biting phase). They were seeking a novel design for an injection
needle that would cause less pain for
patients. As a result of this research,
they designed the Nanopass 33, a
sharp, thin, conical needle which was
released in 2005. Millions of these
needles have been sold.

Example of the Geckskin

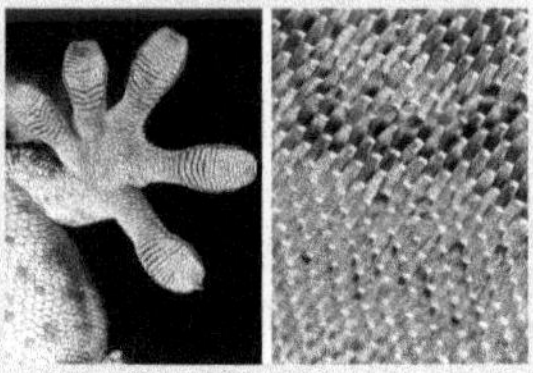

Humans are fascinated by the geckoes' capability of walking on a ceil-
ing. Geckoes can do this because
of the temporary adhesion of their
feet, this adhesion being termed van
der Waals force. For decades nan-
otechnologists have tried to mimic
the hairlike structure of the skin on the sole of a gecko's foot.
Recently, a group led by Professor Al Crosby[22] at the University
of Massachusetts, Amherst designed a textile-like pad, Geck-
skin, which indeed has a remarkable adhesion without wetting the
contact surface. The invention is now pushing its way through
applications.

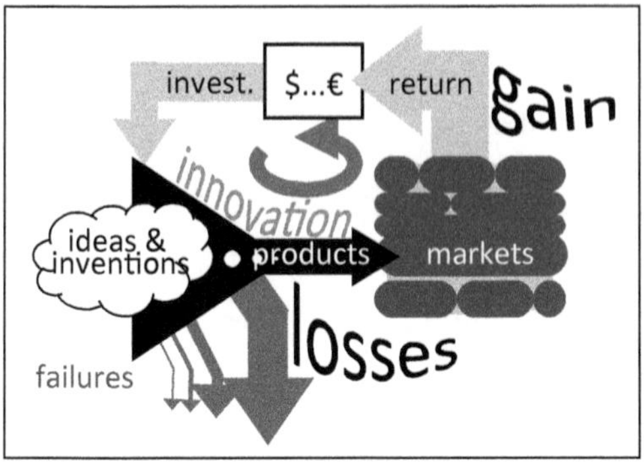

56 Chapter 3. Knowledge, the fuel of innovation

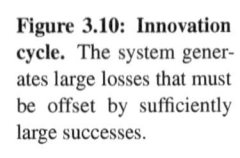

Figure 3.10: Innovation cycle. The system generates large losses that must be offset by sufficiently large successes.

3.3 Innovation cycle and risk management

3.3.1 Innovation as a risky venture

Innovation is the process of pushing a new concept toward its implementation in the society with the objective of creating value. At least in the early phase of its process, innovation is always an endeavor with a low probability of success. Innovation is risky, because it explores paths that have not yet been visited or mapped and in which the presence and location of treacherous obstacles have not been recorded. Uncertainty is the key, unavoidable aspect of innovation.

The economics of innovation can only be regarded as a statistical average of the performance of the innovation cycle represented in figure 3.10. At the core of the process, the innovation cycle itself can be represented by the famous funnel into which many ideas are introduced. As an innovative project progresses along its individual path, a better understanding of the ideas is formed, and, unavoidably, a large fraction of the ideas are determined to be non-viable so are dropped. The abandoned ideas may be seen as failures and the resources that were used to foster them as losses, but hopefully all is not wasted. From failure can come valuable learning, a benefit that accounting may not take into consideration.

Innovation Intelligence 57

A fraction of the projects continue along their innovation courses and become products that enter the market and generate the premium revenue associated with an innovative item. A portion of the financial gain can be reinvested in new, innovative projects, perpetuating the innovation cycle. If gains exceed losses, the innovation cycle continues. Due to its large losses and the low probability of successes (as noted, at least in the early stages of each project), innovation is like gambling. This metaphor raises the following key question:

Is there a winning system for the gambling game called innovation? The answer is both yes and no. There is no simple system, no miracle algorithm, for eliminating risk from the innovation cycle. Eliminating risk would mean avoiding newness, and that would destroy the very substance of innovation. However, there are a couple basic rules that separate the winners and the losers at the innovation game:

- Maximize gains by collecting the maximum value that can be created by successful innovations. Recommended ways of achieving this include patents, an optimized business model, solid market projections, international distribution, speed to market, and spin off or licensing in situations when the innovation does not fit in the company's strategy.
- Minimize losses. This does not mean that only riskless or low-risk projects should be pursued but rather that the risk associated with each project should be carefully and objectively managed. The concept is summarized precisely in a well-known motto found in many management books: "fail fast, fail cheap, fail often." Although, like many authors, we do not like the impression of ease that may be suggested by this motto. Managing innovation risk does not mean simply dreaming up ideas – it is difficult, intensive work that requires focusing on the sources of uncertainty that quench the project's viability, finding the smartest and fastest way to shed light on such key factors, and accepting the heartbreaking decision to cancel a project early when its probability of success is low.

3.3.2 The stage-gating approach to risk management

The process leading to killing a "good idea" with a hidden flaw deserves attention as it is based on knowledge and requires expertise to be done efficiently. A creative idea is born in an environment of uncertainty. A fool will attempt the daring exercise of assigning a budget to the venture and then will rush straight into the fog and blow through the entire project budget. Instead, it is highly recommended that you do some planning, even though the very concept of planning may be surprising in such an environment of uncertainty. Our recommended approach is to first list all of the unanswered questions that are critical to the viability of the initial idea. Then, make a list of *killer questions*, and reorder the question in a hierarchy with the most risky at the top of the list. The creation of this list is where innovative genius is revealed, by combining experience, business sense, and operational knowledge. Finally, address each of the questions in sequence[vi]. Such a rational, step-by-step approach to the planning phase of innovation is a type of stage gating.[23]

By addressing the most risky aspect of an idea first, the average spending per project is minimized, as shown in figure 3.11. Indeed, if a project is cancelled after its first killer question, the most risky, receives a bad answer, then only a relatively small portion of the budget has been spent and the rest of the budget and resources can be reassigned to other, more promising projects. This is a key improvement in the efficiency of the innovation cycle. Killing non-viable projects quickly is rarely a natural approach, however, as a project manager tends to champion his or her idea and is often reluctant to consider in priority the idea's potential weaknesses.

Now let's focus on knowledge in relation to innovation process planning. For an innovation project team, any question that is raised in an environment of insufficient knowledge bears significant risk. The

---

[vi] If a question can be modeled as a multistep Markovian gambling model, the priority index will be the probability of failure associated with the question divided by the budget necessary to answer the question.

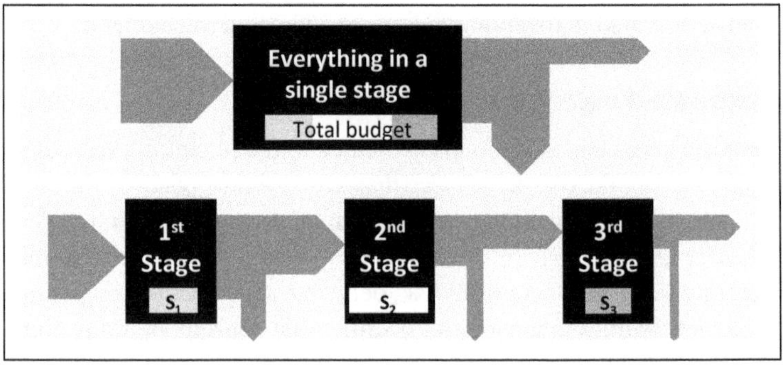

Innovation Intelligence

Everything in a single stage

Total budget

1st Stage S_1

2nd Stage S_2

3rd Stage S_3

Figure 3.11: Stage gating. Schematic of an innovation process in a single stage (the top of the figure) or divided into three stages, each with a specified failure risk and budget. The gray arrows indicate movement through the process in the case of success (movement from left to right) or failure (movement down to the recycling bin).

lack of knowledge may result in a flawed concept or suboptimal project planning and strategic orientation. As a result, in the earliest stages of the innovation process a team should consciously go against its natural tendency, and address any priority areas for which it has insufficient knowledge.

Indeed, at these early stages project teams are often victims of type of streetlight effect.[24] They are tempted to tackle first the aspects of the problem for which the team already has sufficient skills and knowledge and postpone the more unknown aspects.

Calling on an expert in the desired specialty is probably the fastest and safest approach. This injection of specialized, outside expertise into the project should take place as early as possible, ideally while the project is still in its early evaluation phase. Based on the expert's input and the project team's analysis, the team will be able to construct a detailed plan for how, where, and when the team will integrate in-house and activate the required new knowledge.

In this chapter we have recommended a sequential approach to the innovation process, question after question, stage after stage. In some cases the innovation process must be accelerated; key considerations

60 Chapter 3. Knowledge, the fuel of innovation

for an accelerated innovation process are addressed in chapter 6.

3.3.3 Unexpected obstacle

Even when care and attention is dedicated to the planning phase of a project, there still exists the chance that a treacherous obstacle, missed in the list of killer questions, is hidden in the fog of uncertainty. The issue may be discovered in a late stage and pose a severe threat to the project by suddenly increasing risk, delay the schedule, or increasing the budget. Failing to identify some difficulties during an innovation project is normal – it is a natural consequence of the basic uncertainty associated with innovation. However, an unexpected obstacle is more likely to appear in situations in which the driving team has insufficient knowledge. Regardless, when such an unexpected problem pops up, it creates stress and induces an immediate feeling of urgency in the entire team. The project is already in progress, it has a significant daily fixed cost, and, as a result, the unexpected obstacle must be addressed rapidly.

On such occasions, companies rarely hesitate to call upon external expertise. The expert is then seen as a proverbial firefighter. There are several technical sectors (software development, Internet security, corrosion consulting, acoustic engineering, and so forth) in which experts regularly act as firefighters, but any area in which the team has insufficient knowledge can cause an unexpected obstacle to arise during an innovation project.

3.4 Innovation waves associated with invention and discovery

Looking at innovation from a historical perspective reveals that the long series of innovative products generated by the industrial world have come in a progression of waves, with each wave originating from an invention or a discovery. The following are a few examples of inventions and discoveries that have changed drastically the world in

Innovation Intelligence 61

which we live today:

- Liquid-crystal display (LCD) technology (including electro-optics), first a scientific discovery then the basis for products such as flat-panel LCD displays and LCD projectors
- Signal compression, first as mathematical algorithms then the basis for products such as music files (MP3), image files (JPEG), high-definition TV (HDTV)
- The Internet first as a means of global communication then the basis for products and services such as data mining, networking, online businesses

After its birth, an invention or discovery is known initially only within a small community. Gradually, applications are found. Eventually the spread of knowledge gains momentum, triggering many development initiatives. After a lag time which can vary widely depending on the technology, the invention or discovery deeply affects the industry sectors in which it can provide direct benefit. At that point, many innovation projects are taking place in a competitive atmosphere. The invention or discovery reaches its maximum penetration rate when the related patent filings peak. Penetration then continues, at a slower rate, as the invention or discovery spreads to adjacent industrial fields for which the benefit is more indirect.

Figure 3.12 displays the rate at which the U.S. Patent and Trademark Office (USPTO) has granted patents each year since its creation in 1836. Note the sharp growth in the past thirty years and notice that World War I and World War II each had less effect on the patent rate than did the Great Depression or the drastic policy change in U.S. jurisprudence in 1982.[25] In the figure we have also noted the approximate innovation wave peaks associated with several key inventions and discoveries. One of the champions of these was electricity, which experienced decades of lag time because its application had to wait for shops and homes to connect to the grid, which was a slow but impressive tsunami. Today's digital wave seems to promise a similar reshaping of the economic landscape.

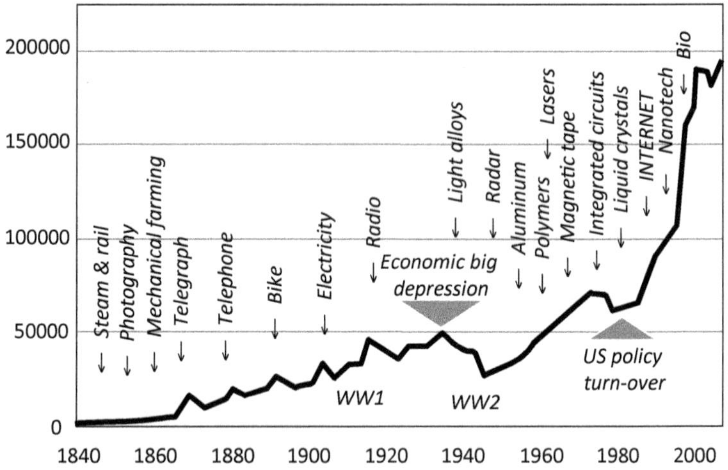

62   Chapter 3. Knowledge, the fuel of innovation

Figure 3.12: U.S. patent rate. This chart shows the rate at which the U.S. Patent and Trademark Office has granted patents each year since its creation. Significant key events contributing to waves of innovation are indicated.

In contrast to slow but massive waves, we have also experienced a rapid mini-wave associated with *giant magnetoresistance*. An explanation of the physical effect of giant magnetoresistance was first published in 1988. Its key application, thin-film heads for hard disks, was marketed by IBM in 1997 – this period from 1988 to 1997 was probably one of the shortest lag times ever. Giant magnetoresistance is also now applied to some MEMS.

3.4.1 Time sequence for innovation waves and their applications

As an example, let's consider GPS, a tool for geographical positioning and that was initially created by the military. The annual rate of GPS-related innovation can be represented by GPS-related patents granted by the USPTO. As shown in figure 3.13, the GPS-related innovation wave appears as an S-shaped curve with an acceleration peak in the late 1990s.

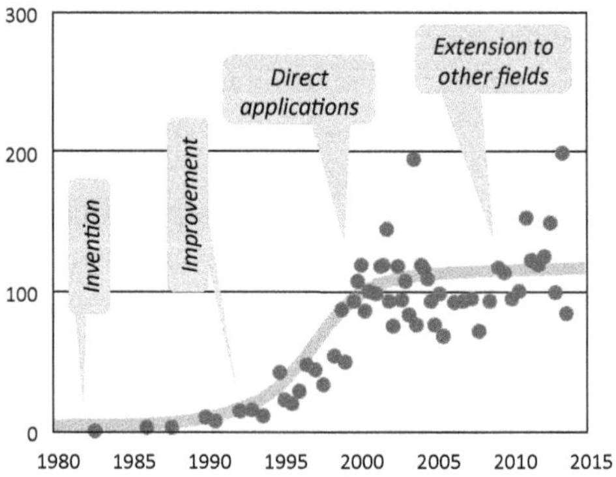

Innovation Intelligence

Figure 3.13: GPS patent rate. This chart shows the evolution over time of the rate at which the U.S. Patent and Trademark Office has granted patents for inventions related to GPS. The thick S-curve in grey shows the typical shape of an innovation penetration wave, with a starting point at the time of initial discovery followed by a lag period, then rapid penetration, and then a slower consolidation and lateral diffusion.

The early phase following the invention of GPS was the lag time. The industry was contemplating GPS, a new push technology, with prudence. Eventually, its successful introduction into plane, ship, and finally automobile navigation systems propelled GPS into an innovation wave that has also included tracking of other mobile systems such as buses and containers. In the past decade, GPS has even been extended to less straightforward applications such as mobile phones, photograph tagging, and outdoor gaming.

The typical S-curve shape shown in figure 3.13 applies to all innovation waves. Its length may range from one decade to several decades depending on the implementation difficulty. The first, steeper slope corresponds to the rapid penetration for straightforward applications of the invention or discovery. The second slope shows the more gradual diffusion to less obvious or adjacent technical domains.

Innovation waves are the bread and butter of industrial innovation. Leading companies know how to quickly recognize and incorporate such inventions and discoveries into their product lines. Even companies that are less eager to change will need to do so: no compromise is possible. Winning companies are not necessarily those who jump on the bandwagon first but rather are those that incorporate the invention or discovery at the right time to create the most value. If you would like an example of this, we recommend that you research the effect on commonplace products, such as kitchenware and office appliances, of polymers becoming readily available.

The digital wave, now taking place, is inducing a performance jump for both speed and distance related to data-based transactions. Telecommunications companies were affected years ago, and everybody remembers the famous Internet bubble of the 1990s that burst in 2001. Now the digital wave is spreading to adjacent industries, changing the rules of the game, creating opportunities for new entrants, and posing severe threats for industry sectors that fail to anticipate its effects.

How Kodak missed the turn...

In the mid-1970s, Steven Sasson, a young electrical engineer, was hired by Eastman Kodak, at that time the world leader in silver-based photography. He was a member of a team that was incorporating electronic commands into film cameras. He was asked to evaluate a new CCD chip from Fairchild Imaging (containing ten thousand pixels!) and took the concept so far that he actually invented the first portable digital camera. The prototype was a proof of concept but was very clumsy compared to a film camera. Steven's prototype camera weighed four kilograms and took 23 seconds to transfer the ten thousand black and white pixels. At that time, in part due to Steven's invention, a small entity within Eastman Kodak was at the forefront of the future digital photography wave. Unfortunately, on that day, Steven's invention made everybody in the room at Eastman Kodak smile but then was rapidly forgotten. For his own pride, Steven patented the digital camera – that patent is a testimony of the sad ending to Eastman Kodak's potential early entry into digital photography. Instead of pursuing digital photograph, the company launched a clone of Polaroid's instant camera, which led to a historical case of patent infringement.

Eastman Kodak was a chemical company, and all strategic decisions were made based on its deep knowledge of photochemistry. Despite all the efforts of this junior electrical engineer, nobody in the company had appreciated the rapid, significant innovation wave that was heading for the semiconductor industry. In an article in Electronics Magazine in 1965 Gordon Moore had expressed his "law" that the number of transistors in a chip will double approximately every two years, and by 1975 there was enough data to support Moore's speculations.

In the aftermath of the Polaroid v. Eastman Kodak patent-infringement lawsuit, Eastman Kodak did make a strong move toward digital photography. In 1986, the company hurried to catch the innovation wave and managed to design the best digital imager of that time (1.4 megapixels). Again, however, due to the company's poor understanding of electronics, it focused on the professional market. Eastman Kodak had failed to recognize what consumer-electronics experts already knew – that the mass market was the key driver of technology. Semiconductor experts knew it, but chemists did not.

3.4.2 Knowledge distribution during an innovation wave

When an invention or discovery is born, only very few experts, researchers specialized in the specific topic, can understand it and foresee its full potential and limits. If the concept is indeed fruitful, other laboratories will try to reproduce the results and will distribute the knowledge further within a small international community of experts.

66   Chapter 3. Knowledge, the fuel of innovation

Time	Phase	Knowledge status	Knowledge location
0	Discovery	Partial, incomplete, and confidential	Laboratories and internal seminars
2 – 5 years	Scientific	Basic patent filed and principles understood	Academic labs and conferences
5 – 10 years	Pre-industrial	Patent applications filed, R&D results published, and basic applications identified	Institutes, some private laboratories, research consortiums, and journals
10 – 20 years	Application	Development by pioneer companies and publication of basic tutorial books	Postgraduate education and specialized summer schools
15 – 30 years	Maturity	Application performance known, technology accepted by the market, potential further improvements may cause a resurgence of the innovation wave	Engineering schools, textbooks, and consultants

Table 3.1: Knowledge distribution during an innovation wave

This process of knowledge distribution is summarized in table 3.1. In the early phases, the knowledge associated with the invention or discovery is not widespread, and it is generally missing within the companies whose business models may be affected. However, even during these early phases, companies do require sufficient knowledge to evaluate the potential of an invention or discovery. One way or another, they must gain access to this knowledge in order to outline their R&D plans. Because innovation often requires the incorporation of a new ingredient from outside the company, this early learning process is of paramount importance.

The acquisition of even deeper knowledge is necessary when the innovation wave finally strikes the industry. At that point, far more knowledge sources are typically available, but the knowledge-acquisition effort may still be challenging and costly. In addition, the number of options for knowledge acquisition may lead to difficult decisions: finding the least risky trajectory is especially challenging in the heat of a competitive atmosphere. Seeking assistance from external players

Innovation Intelligence 67

who are already experts in the knowledge area is often a wise approach.

3.4.3 Timing and process of knowledge acquisition during an innovation wave

Early strategic phase: knowledge acquisition to mitigate risks

At the onset of a potentially fruitful innovation project, many companies need access to a portion of the relevant new knowledge while performing their minimum duty, roadmapping. This includes strategically evaluating the potential impact of the new invention or discovery on the company's current business and then defining if, how, and when the company should introduce the new concept into its innovation pipeline. By definition, the invention or discovery is new, so the relevant knowledge is confined to a narrow circle of a few pioneering laboratories. The relevant knowledge is absent from most companies.

However, there may be one exception: a start-up firm that has just been spun off from a laboratory that played a key role in the invention or discovery. Indeed, such a start-up would have an advantage over its competitors due to its capability to more easily and rapidly put the new knowledge to use.

Aside from this hypothetical spun-off start-up firm, the rest of the industry would face a knowledge deficit. Several approaches are currently used for rapidly acquiring knowledge during the early phases of an innovation wave:

- Engage a consultant who is expert in the new field. Make sure that he or she is qualified in terms of both technical knowledge and headquarters confidence and is not working with any of your competitors. Secure a solid confidentiality contract with the consultant and foster the relationship between the consultant and your company's executives. You may want to use a stepwise approach such as the Presans process described on www.presans.com.
- Assign one or more internal engineers to learn about the new invention or discovery. Such an approach requires allocation

68 Chapter 3. Knowledge, the fuel of innovation

time and budget to activities such as reading scientific papers, visiting laboratories, and attending international conferences on the topic. All knowledge-acquisition processes bear some risk. For example, a consultant may be too driven by his or her own enthusiasm to spot treacherous obstacles. In addition, a consultant may not be reliable in terms of confidentiality even after signing a confidentiality agreement.

The consulting option is faster than the self-learning option. The cost of self learning is far from negligible. A company that chooses the self-learning option will have to make an often painful trade-off between spending more time learning, which will delay a decision, or making an early decision based on only a partial understanding.

Note that for the strategic early phase we have excluded the option of hiring an expert as an employee. At such an early stage, because the company does not yet know if it will incorporate the new concept, it would be too risky to hire an employee and integrate him or her into the company.

Technology entry: knowledge acquisition for fast time to market

When a company knows enough about a new invention or discovery has decided to pursue it, the company needs to acquire operational knowledge in the new field in order to make its time to market as brief as possible. As already stated, self learning is possible but slow and costly. The required operational knowledge is not widespread but rather is still confined to research laboratories. Hiring experts as employees is the fastest option. In fact, large conferences on particularly hot topics have an unofficial function as hiring offices. In the United States, a large company that wants to hire experts in a new field frequently rents a suite in the hotel at which the conference is taking place and offers refreshments and on-the-spot interviews to interested candidates. For example, at the onset of the blue LED innovation wave, several companies that attended key meetings of the Materials Research Society (MRS) followed this approach to hiring the best specialists in compound-semiconductor crystal growth. A few years later, when the

Innovation Intelligence   69

first steps of LED technology had been done, the same companies attended the American Physical Society (APS) conferences, looking for experts on Maxwell-equation 3-D modeling in order to address the next steps.

Also during this phase, a company may need assistance in determining which knowledge is the most suited to its purpose and therefore which research area should be the highest priority. The recommended approaches for acquiring this guidance are the same ones recommended for the early strategic phase.

We should remind you that, even if an invention or discovery is certain to affect a company's business, there is an excellent alternative to acquiring the full knowledge by hiring experts: the company can partner with a company that has already the proper knowledge. The two companies can agree to share the knowledge, and perhaps even future effort, to develop new products.

This approach, *open Innovation*, is probably the most efficient and flexible. However, it requires that both companies have some high-level skills in terms of collaboration and setting up contracts. When relying on open innovation, a company is not exempt from the need to integrate a solid understanding of the invention or discovery, at least at a strategic level. Indeed, it is impossible to conceive and conduct a successful collaboration with a partner company without having someone in-house who understands the value generated by the new concept and has a positive feeling about the required innovation-related efforts.

3.5 Conclusion

In this chapter, we have seen that knowledge and innovation are interdependent. A company cannot outperform its competitors by attempting to innovate without acquiring external knowledge. The knowledge map is complex because knowledge exists everywhere; companies must learn how to navigate on that map. Innovation is a risky venture in which knowledge is the key ingredient for risk mitigation. By looking at history, we found that knowledge and innovation are interdependent, forming innovation waves that wash over industries and give birth to new products. Proper timing for the acquisition of knowledge is one of the main drivers of successful innovation. In the next chapter, we will look at a series of megatrends and consider how the changing environment may affect companies' innovation processes.

Chapter 4
Commoditization of Knowledge & Technologies in a Digital World

The universe (which others call the Library) is composed of an indefinite and perhaps infinite numbers of hexagonal galleries, with vast air shafts between, surrounded by very low railings. From any of the hexagons one can see, interminably, the upper and lower floors.

JORGE LUIS BORGES,[26] 1944

In Short. . . Knowledge is being generated at an increasingly rapid pace, a flood pouring out from multiple sources. This faster and faster tempo is also affecting innovation and innovative practices. In the map of knowledge sources, breadth and fragmentation are apparent. A new breed of players, start-up firms, can be seen as innovation activists, and these new players are leading the innovation game, particularly in the digital arena. Knowledge is becoming a commodity. It is now more effective to seek knowledge that has already been acquired by someone else than to create it. This has led naturally to the paradigm shift called open innovation. A faster rate of innovation and associated market response poses the risk of product commoditization. In response to this threat, companies are making their products increasingly complex, converging toward a total-service offering. Finally, the major task of innovative companies today is to search deeply in the wide collection of technology bricks and to combine them to best serve their customers' needs. The beauty is in the assembly. The digital innovation wave is extremely disruptive for most of the traditional economy. Digital innovations are much cheaper and run much faster. Furthermore, they have affected the relationships between most businesses and their customers. Traditional industry is unprepared and severely short on managers with digital skills. For traditional companies digital technology could be an opportunity, but it could also be a severe threat. Waiting is not recommended!

4.1 Knowledge flood and change acceleration

Examining the past century, we can see that the rates of both knowledge creation and innovation have accelerated.

It is sometimes difficult for people of our time to appreciate the quantity of knowledge that humankind has accumulated throughout history. A mental exercise that may help consists of scanning the inventory of knowledge that forms the basis for modern items such as the mobile phone, the hybrid car, weather forecasting, breast cancer treatment, and so forth. Let us begin with the oral wisdom of our ancestors, and then consider the knowledge of ancient Greek philosophers as Archimedes and Pythagoras, and finally proceed, layer by layer, through knowledge created from the Industrial Revolution up to the present day. By following this progression, we can assemble a huge pyramid of intricate and additive pieces of knowledge.

The difficulty lies in transforming this intellectual vertigo into quantitative data. Let's explore some illustrative facts and driving factors.

To follow the time variations of knowledge creation, let's use a simple proxy relevant to both knowledge and innovation: the number

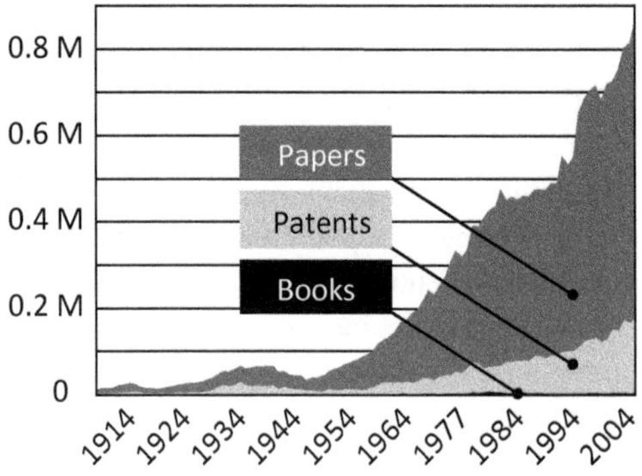

Innovation Intelligence   73

Figure 4.1: Scientific publication rate. The chart shows the historical publication rate of scientific documents, papers, patents, and books listed in Chemical Abstracts Service.

of peer-reviewed scientific publications as recorded by the American Chemical Society's Chemical Abstracts Service (CAS)[i] . The CAS databases cover most hard sciences with the exception of medicine and applied engineering. Although CAS does not cover all knowledge, what it does cover represents a significant portion of the knowledge that is used as a basic ingredient for innovation.

Note that all the publications counted in our proxy are assumed to contain some new knowledge, as guaranteed by a review from a referee, an examiner, or a journal editor. As a result, the proxy should serve as a meaningful indicator despite some redundancy. The data shown in figure 4.1 covers the century from 1904 to 2004. The publication rate took small dip during World War II, but the growth in the second part of the twentieth century has been spectacular. A small pause, which we will discuss in the following section of this chapter, is also apparent from the shape of the curve during the 1980s. Note that the chart stops short after the year 2000. By that time the number of paper publications was no longer a good proxy due to the turbulence associated with the Internet gradually displacing printing as a media for knowledge transfer.

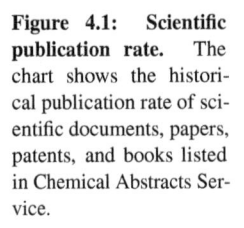

---

[i]Chemical Abstracts Service ended its paper publications in 2010. It is now exclusively a digital service.

74   Chapter 4. Commoditization in a digital world

Despite the difficulty of reliably tracking publication rate since the advent of the Internet, there is not the slightest doubt that the pace of knowledge creation is faster than ever, despite persistent doubts about the newness and quality of material published on the Internet.

Although we have used scientific publications as a proxy for global knowledge dynamics in general, we must keep in mind that knowledge has a much broader base than solely scientific and engineering. Knowledge of business models, market trends, socioeconomic trends, public moods, pop culture, public regulations, and politics are all important. One of the key difficulties in shaping an innovative strategy or conceiving a new product is to collect, filter, link, and concentrate all of the relevant information from the chaotic web of available knowledge. The necessity of extending knowledge by seeking a way beyond the technology frontier was emphasized by nearly all of the innovation managers we interviewed. As we will see later, in chapter 6, they are still searching for the optimal processes and organization to coordinate the collection and the analysis of disparate knowledge for feeding and managing innovation.

4.1.1   Globalization of knowledge creation

For the first time in 2012, Chinese residents accounted for the largest number of patents filed throughout the world.
WIPO[a], 2013 World Intellectual Property Indicators, December 2013

---
[a]WIPO is the World Intellectual Property Organization.

The same Chemical Abstracts Service data were analyzed with regard to the geographical origins of the authors. The resulting geographic distribution of each year's publications is shown in figure 4.2.

It appears that the growth deficit observed in figure 4.2 during the 1980s was due to the collapse of the USSR and the associated countries

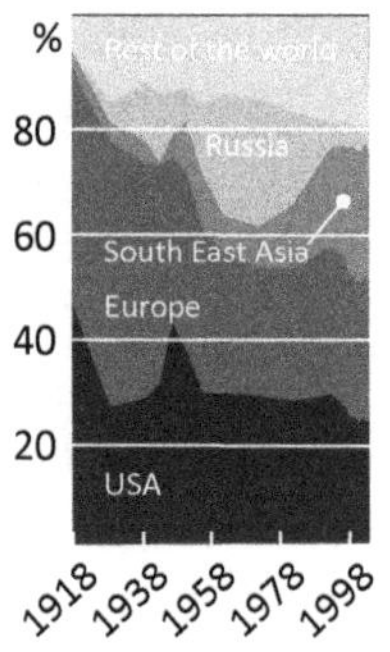

Innovation Intelligence

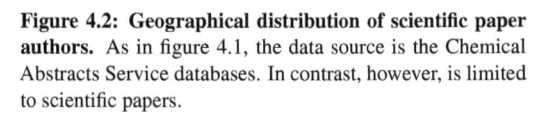

%
80
60
40
20

Rest of the world
Russia
South East Asia
Europe
USA

1918 1938 1958 1978 1998

Figure 4.2: Geographical distribution of scientific paper authors. As in figure 4.1, the data source is the Chemical Abstracts Service databases. In contrast, however, is limited to scientific papers.

pulling out of the knowledge-creation race, presumably temporarily. The most significant long-term trend is the globalization of knowledge creation. At the beginning of the twentieth century, Europe and the United States were dominant, generating more than 90% of scientific publications; by the turn of the twenty-first century, Asia and the rest of the world accounted for about 50% of scientific publications. The most recent data show that emerging countries, such as China, India, and Brazil, now account for a growing share of knowledge creation.

In these so-called emerging countries, there an increasing number of engineers and researchers producing knowledge. Never in history have so many people worked in research laboratories. Is the rate of knowledge creation increasing simply because there are more educated people to contribute to the effort? It is certainly one of the drivers, but many thinkers are pointing at even more basic roots for acceleration of knowledge creation.

4.1.2 Exponential knowledge growth

> Knowledge begets knowledge as money bears interest.
> **Sir Arthur Conan Doyle, The Parasite, 1885[27]**

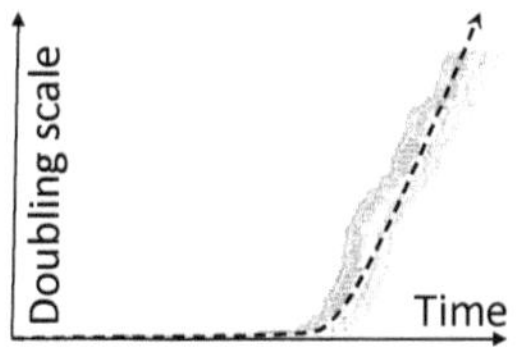

Figure 4.3: Doubling rate for accumulated knowledge. Buckminster Fuller's data, shown here in gray, displays his estimate for the doubling rate for accumulated knowledge. The time scale begins with Johannes Gutenberg, who lived from approximately 1398 to 1468, and ends in the 1970s. Doubling scale is the inverse of the time required to see the volume of accumulated knowledge double. As emphasized by the black dashed arrow, the doubling rate increased dramatically during the twentieth century.

The above quote from the father of Sherlock Holmes provides a simple, basic explanation for accelerated knowledge growth. Indeed, new knowledge is built on an existing base of knowledge. If one assumes some proportionality between initial and resulting knowledge created during a given period, this is enough to lead to exponential growth. Derek J. de Solla Price,[28] the father of *scientometrics* proposed optimized ways of measuring the production of scientific knowledge, and his conclusions leaned toward exponential growth. Other authors elaborated on his work; one refinement was the introduction of an additional parameter, the quality of the new knowledge..[29]

Measuring the growth of knowledge is difficult, particular over a long period of time. The definitions of quality and newness have changed over the years. In the first millennium, manuscripts were a means of propagating knowledge by reproduction rather than of publishing new contributions. Recent electronic publications are also difficult measure in a sufficiently rigorous and consistent manner.

The measurement challenge has not stopped some daring authors, however. Many authors claim that knowledge creation is accelerating at a rate even faster than an exponential one. Mere exponential growth would imply that accumulated knowledge doubles at a consistent pace. One of the first people to analyze the growth of knowledge was Buck-

Innovation Intelligence

minster Fuller[ii]. He estimated the historical variation in the doubling time of knowledge.[30] Fuller used printed materials as a proxy for knowledge; as shown in figure 4.3, he found that although knowledge had doubled approximately every century up until the eighteenth century, then sometime during the nineteenth century its growth rate accelerated dramatically.

Fuller's analysis demonstrated a recent acceleration in knowledge growth since the nineteenth century. Sir Arthur Conan Doyle's simple explanation does not provide a reason for knowledge "interest" to be generated at a faster-than-exponential rate. This acceleration, specific to the era since the Industrial Revolution, may have multiple root causes. We have already mentioned the increasing number of people working of knowledge creation, a result of population growth combined with an increasing proportion of educated people. The faster communication system, which speeds up feedback loops among thinkers and thus limits losses of time and efficiency associated with redundancy, is another cause. Some authors are exploring additional causes. According to Gerald S. Hawkins, progress generally proceeds via *mindsteps*, dramatic and irreversible changes to paradigms or world views.[31] Indeed, humankind has achieved spectacular advances in the way it thinks as a collective body, introducing new mindsteps such as speech, writing, printing, symbolic calculus, computers, data mining. Hawkins has further explained that key mindsteps are appearing at an accelerated rate and humankind is indeed learning, discovering, and inventing faster now, as such mindsteps are incorporated into its collective mind.

[ii] Buckminster Fuller (1895-1983) was a famous thinker and architect. He designed the bucky ball, a geodesic structure that was later discovered to be similar to fullerene molecules.

Acceleration of change

> I assert that continued growth is essential to the rational and empirical character of scientific knowledge.
> **Karl Popper**[32]

Knowledge is expanding at an accelerating rate. Because knowledge and innovation go hand in hand, the rate of innovation is also accelerating. New products and new technologies are reaching the market today at an impressive rate, faster than ever before. The same is true for product life cycles, which are becoming shorter and shorter[iii]. As we will see in chapter 6, industries that are accustomed to designing product platforms that can support several product generations are struggling to cope with the rapid rate of innovation. As product developers and manufacturers progress along the famous experience curve,[33] they incorporate faster, learner methods, which decrease production cost but also the time required for the product-design phase. Everything happens faster, even the market's response. Ray Kurzweil, a director of engineering at Google, gathered information on the market-penetration time for major technological breakthroughs. As shown in figure 4.4, the market-penetration time has decreased by a factor of five from the earliest days of Bell Telephone to the recent days since the Internet entered our lives.

The digital revolution is also spurring traditionally slow response to speed up, particularly in the areas of customer relationships and business model migration.

Everything happens faster and faster. Imagine knowledge as a large pot of boiling water, surging, occasionally erupting, with increasingly frequent burst of innovation jumping out of it. Theorists of social change have studied and refined this metaphor. In their analyses,

---

[iii]For example, the life cycle of a typical computer game is measured in months. However, the airplane engine is an exception, with a life cycle of three to four decades.

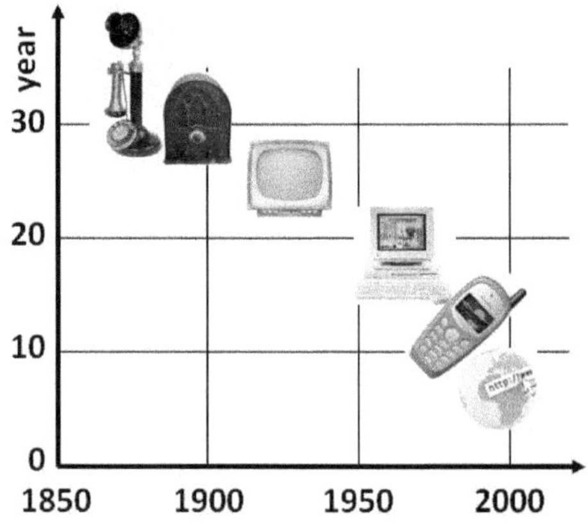

Innovation Intelligence 79

Figure 4.4: Market penetration time. The chart shows the market-penetration time for six major inventions: telephone, radio, television, personal computer, mobile phone, and Internet broadband connection. Data, taken from Ray Kurzweil,[34] provides a reasonable estimate of the delay between market introduction and penetration to 25% of the consumer market in the United States.

knowledge and innovation are often treated as a homogeneous whole. However, some theorists have attempted to incorporate categories such as energy and information in reworking and extending the visionary predictions of Gordon Moore[iv].

Hartmut Rosa, a German philosopher, in his book *Social Acceleration*,[1] performed a critical analysis of this accelerated change. He distinguishes three parallel fields: technology, social life, and personal life. The pace of change is accelerating in all three areas, contradicting the expectation that progress provides humans with leisure time. He also notes what he calls a shrinking of the present, an increased difficulty in predicting the future by simple extrapolation of past and present. Rosa sees today's motto, "faster, faster, faster!" as opening to a rather grim future.

[iv]Gordon Moore, father of the famous Moore's law, is mentioned in an inset in chapter 5.

Flash flood of data

> Knowledge doubling every 12 months, soon to be every 12 hours!
> **David Russell Schilling**[35]

We often read flabbergasting announcements on an incredible growth rate of what is mistaken as knowledge. These announcements come from the Big Data battlefield, and we will take this opportunity to cool down from the excitement of those announcements and return to some clear definitions. Knowledge does not double in less than a day; those who make statements that it is doing so are mistaking knowledge for data, which may indeed be doubling that rapidly. Data should not be confused with information, which is a coherent and meaningful set of data, or with knowledge, which is an innovator's favorite raw material. Milan Zeleny[36] described the four successive steps in elaboration of material for human learning:

- Data, or know-nothing,
- Information, or know-what,
- Knowledge, or know-how, and
- Wisdom, or know-why.

The same hierarchy is shown graphically in figure 4.5. Knowledge is the key ingredient in innovation. Wisdom is an even higher level of knowledge, at which global structures emerge from a cloud of details. Wisdom is very powerful, especially for strategic guidance, but R&D teams operating at the frontier of knowledge rarely have access to wisdom. Indeed, wisdom takes time to emerge after a turbulent wave of fresh knowledge.

Data is a conglomerate of many things, such as street-camera recordings, telephone and text-messaging traffic, online chats, and signals sent from various sensors. Knowledge has a higher level of elaboration: it is a ready-to-use, coherent set of information. In this book we focus mainly on knowledge level. Experts are knowledge mediators and

Innovation Intelligence

WISDOM

KNOWLEDGE

INFORMATION

DATA

Figure 4.5: WKID pyramid. A representation of the famous WKID pyramid, this is an attempt to emphasize by use of an image the large difference in value and usefulness of the four elements constituting the knowledge chain.

expertise is the art of leveraging a given knowledge base. Transformation of information into knowledge is a task generally performed by researchers and analysts. Experts typically have a research background but also know how to deal with and apply both information and knowledge. Data is accumulating at an incredible rate; however, only a small fraction of it can be transformed into information, and even less into knowledge. Knowledge is indeed growing but at a more reasonable rate than are data or even information. We would be inclined to accept for today an estimate of, say, ten years for the doubling rate of knowledge, with an error margin strongly dependent on the exact definition of knowledge.

Growing, growing... to where?

Theories on social change are usually meant to enable prediction of the future. Such predictions vary widely, however. John M. Smart[37] goes so far as to state that the acceleration we are witnessing is of an explosive nature and that, as predicted by mathematics, it will reach infinity in a finite time, finally entering a singularity similar to that of black holes. Ray Kurzweil, one of Google's flamboyant managers, also predicts that we will soon enter such a singularity and that it will result in a sudden expansion of our universe.

Other thinkers predict a peak and subsequent decline in this impressive acceleration. For example, Theodore Modis[38] speculates that too-fast changes will stall a result of human cognitive jamming. Jonathan

Chapter 4. Commoditization in a digital world

Huebner[39] claims that the growth rate of knowledge is already declining if one accounts only for really significant innovations and normalizes progress to economic measures such as the total budget for education.

Regardless, we will not contribute to the many speculations on the outcome of the observed acceleration. We will remain humble in the midst of a knowledge flood that was triggered by our own society. We will avoid the risk associated with predicting the behavior of a machine of which we ourselves are part. It will be sufficient to face the facts, keep up with short-term trends, and attempt to infer how the facts and trends will change our lives.

A physicist joke...

> **SPEED LIMIT 3 10^8 m/s**
>
> Let's end this glance into the future with a physicist joke. In the 1970s one of us attended a seminar by Guy Laval on the subject of electromagnetic wave propagation. He exhibited a semilogarithmic graph of the rate of growth of the stack of Physical Review[a] issues on a library shelf. The few experimental points were aligned, indicating exponential growth. He then extrapolated the line into the future and stated that, one day, the stack of journals would grow at a rate faster than the speed of light. With a smile, he added that the seminar's attendees should not worry – this result did not contradict Albert Einstein's theory of relativity because, indeed, that stack of journals would no longer carry information.
>
> ---
> [a]*Physical Review* and its young satellite, *Physical Review Letters* are journals published by the American Physical Society.

4.1.3 Knowledge distribution and fragmentation
Knowledge-base stretching
Knowledge has continued to increase in quantity but, at the same time, it stretch to cover a wider range of subjects. Indeed, if we

Innovation Intelligence

visualize knowledge as many piles of books, the piles labeled "algebra," zoology," and "astronomy" are still growing today, but new piles have been created. "Genetics," "informatics," and "microelectronics" are piles that have existed for only a few decades but during that time they have grown rapidly. From the traditional sciences, related disciplines have emerged: life sciences gave birth to ecology, arithmetic produced cryptology, and medicine produced bioengineering. The net result is that knowledge has grown both vertically and horizontally. Most of these new fields have bases of fundamental knowledge in common with their originating field but have grown to such a degree of sophistication that they have become disciplines of their own, with their own experts.

Moreover, a new discipline develops different practices for different applications. For example, the field of radioisotope physics and chemistry is specialized for nuclear fuel recycling, archeological dating, and medical applications. As a result of this lateral growth, knowledge is now distributed across a more numerous and complex set of sectors and disciplines.

Organizational diversity and knowledge fragmentation

During the past century, nearly all countries have built up and grown their public research organizations, whether those organizations are public, semi-public, or even private (for example, foundations and consortium institutes). Most new research organizations, other than universities, are focused on specific application fields. In these cases, the objective is not, as it used to be for academic laboratories, solely the creation of knowledge. Some of these specific applications, as well as examples of the organizations that are conduct the research, are the following:

- Sensitive topics related to nuclear energy, space, and the military: in the United States, the Atomic Energy Commission (AEC) and the National Aeronautics and Space Administration (NASA); in Japan, the Japan Atomic Energy Agency (JAEA); in France, the Atomic Energy and Alternative Energies Commission (CEA); in Europe, the European Space Agency (ESA); and other similar organizations.

- Public causes, such as health, meteorology, timekeeping, and various national standards: in the United States, the National Institutes of Health (NIH) and the National Institute of Standards and Technology (NIST); in the United Kingdom, the Atomic Energy Research Establishment (AERE), the Met Office, and the National Standards Body (NSB); in France, the Pasteur Institute; in Germany, the Robert Koch Institute (RKI); in Japan, the National Institute of Health Sciences (NIHS), the Japan Meteorological Agency (JMA), and the Japanese Standards Association (JSA); and other similar organizations.

- Large-scale initiatives requiring joint investment, such as high-energy physics, fusion, and telescopes: the European Organization for Nuclear Research (CERN), International Thermonuclear Experimental Reactor (ITER), the Square Kilometre Array (SKA), and other similar initiatives.

- Promotion of local resources: in the United States, Harbor Branch Oceanographic Institute (HBOI) at Florida Atlantic University (FAU), the U.S. Forest Service's Forestry Sciences Laboratory in Olympia, Washington, and the Colorado School of Mines (CSM); in Iceland, the National Energy Authority (NEA); in Japan, the National Research Institute of Aquaculture (NRIA); in France, the French Research Institute for Exploitation of the Sea (IFREMER); in Scotland, the Institute of Petroleum Engineering (IPE); and other similar organizations.

- Support for local industries: in Germany, the Fraunhofer Society; in France, CEA-LETI; in Switzerland, the Swiss Center for Electronics and Microtechnology (CSEM) and the Swiss Association for Horological Research (ASRH); in Japan, the National Institute of Advanced Industrial Science (AIST); in Canada, the National Optics Institute (INO); in South Korea, KAIST (Korea); in Taiwan, the Industrial Technology Research Institute (ITRI); and other similar organizations.

- Promotion of a new field: in the United States, the MIT Media

Innovation Intelligence

Lab, the Laser Biomedical Research Center (LBRI), and the National Human Genome Research Institute (NHGRI); in Germany, the Fraunhofer Institute for Intelligent Analysis and Information Systems (IAIS) and the Max Planck Institute; in France, the French Institute for Research in Computer Science and Automation (INRIA); and many institutes focusing on nanotechnology and MEMS devices.

- Topics of interest to industry associations: in the United States, SEMATECH and the Institute of Scrap Recycling Industries (ISRI); in the United Kingdom, British Textile Technology Group (BTTG) and the Institute of Food Research (IFR); in France, the Centre Technique du Papier (CTP); in Germany, the Welding and Joining Institute (ISF); and other similar organizations.

This list is intended to illustrate the diversity of semi-public research organizations today. Not only are the topics dispersed, but the organizations are numerous and often intricate. It should also be noted that these research operations driven by applications or industries are less coordinate with one another and communicate less with one another than do universities who perform basic research. They are not ruled by the famous "publish or perish" rat race.

Proliferation of start-up firms

Not listed in the previous section, but extremely active at the frontier of applied science, are start-up companies. Their origins are diverse, but the following scenarios are most common:

- Spin-off from a public research organization. Prior to the effective creation of a start-up company, the team is often incubated in source public research organization. Today, entrepreneurship is strongly supported by most governmental agencies.
- Direct or indirect spin-off from an existing company. When a project is determined to be outside a company's strategy but the project has strong potential, its champions are sometimes allowed to pursue the project on their own by forming a start-up firm. In such case, the existing company typically retains a stake

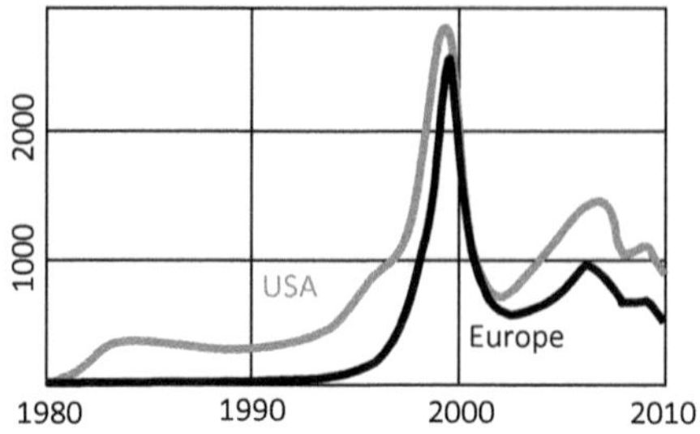

Chapter 4. Commoditization in a digital world

Figure 4.7: Start-up firm creation rate. The chart shows the rate of start-up firm creation in Europe and the United States, as estimated from first venture-capital investment deal. The peak around the year 2000 corresponds to the famous Internet bubble. Europe was late to the start-up trend but has been catching up during the past two decades. Data is from Dow Jones VentureSource.[40] The data is only indicative, because not all start-ups are funded by venture capital (some are funded privately, by existing companies, by angel investors, by incubators, and from other sources).

in the spun-off start-up firm in order to reap a benefit from the potential success that it initiated. Sometimes the spin-off is less peaceful; key engineers may resign and become independent entrepreneurs.

- Students or groups of students, often who have not yet finished their education, often start business around an idea, frequently but not necessarily based on the Internet. Examples include Pascal Zunino, described in the Parrot case, and Leetchi.com, described below.
- Former start-up firm that failed but is later reborn in a different form with an improved business model, thanks to lessons learned from the experience.

It is difficult to keep track of the action in this vibrant and ever-changing landscape of start-up firms. They appear, change names, and then die or are acquired quite rapidly. In the early phase, they have little visibility and may focus on only one or two referring customers. They have great potential for creativity, and by submitting their ideas to the market at a very early stage they provide valuable knowledge.

Innovation Intelligence   87

More than 80% of the innovation managers we interviewed empha-sized their high degree of interest in the fertile world of start-ups, but at the same time they all stated that it was difficult and time-consuming to search and find interesting picks in this informal, complex, and ever-changing landscape (we will discuss this further in chapter 7).

A start-up is a young, small company that has virtually no revenue and is investing in developing an innovative product or service. The risk pattern for start-up firms is similar to that for all innovation projects: the probability of success is relatively low, but success creates value of ten or more times the initial investment. It is difficult to count innovation-driven start-ups. They are sometimes lumped together with the entrepreneur's other ventures, such as opening a restaurant. In figure 4.7 we have counted only the start-ups supported by venture-capital firms, but the trend associated with these start-ups is likely indicative of the trend for start-ups financed by other means. As shown in the figure, today about 1,000 start-ups are launched in the United States each year, slightly fewer than in Europe. A start-up launch, as shown in this figure, is proxied by the company receiving its first round of venture-capital funding. This figure also shows the Internet bubble in the year 2000, during which the rate of start-up creation was more than three times higher than it is today. The hype that generated the Internet bubble was based on the digital innovation wave. This same theme, along with medical science, populates the majority of today's start-ups. As we will see later in this book, venture capital is still fond of digital innovation. This digital topic is still popular for start-ups and approved by venture-capital firms in part due to the shortcomings of large, established companies with regard to the digital revolution; the large, established companies have left so much room that start-ups stand a good chance of finding a market slot and creating value. This observation is less valid in the mainstream business-to-consumer (B2C) arena, because Google, Facebook and others are in the competition, but it will remain true for years in niches and in the business-to-business (B2B) arena.

88   Chapter 4. Commoditization in a digital world

Also demonstrated in figure 4.7 is the fact that Europe almost did not exist on the venture-capital scene before 1995, but it is now gradually catching up. Europe's start-up creation trend began in northwestern Europe, perhaps because the Protestant culture is more keen on entrepreneurship. Scandinavia, in particular, is booming today, and we have highlighted one example (see the inset below). Israel is also a popular place for start-up creation today. In Asia, the start-up culture is at an early stage of its development; however, clear signs of activity are coming from South Korea, Taiwan, mainland China, and India. According to experts, conditions are favorable for Brazil and Russia to soon join in this new form of innovation.

The example of Coworks

Coworks, one start-up out of many in Scandinavia, was founded in Stockholm, Sweden in 2010. A very small operation, it has developed a freelancing job website focused on the creative professionals (designers, writers, translators, online market analysts, web developers, etc.). Cofounders Mattias Guilotte and Henrik Dillman want to create a social network. They are not trying to offer you a choice from hundreds or even thousands of freelancers; instead, they want to focus on your social networks to find freelancers who your friends and other connections know and may be willing to recommend. Basically, they want to digitalize word of mouth. An interesting event in this start-up's development is that Matthias Guilotte (pictured) has now migrated to San Francisco, California to foster the company.[41]

Innovation Intelligence

The example of Leetchi.com

Leetchi.com, founded in 2008 by Celine Lazorthes while she was still a student, is gaining momentum. The website is a digital tool for social communities to use for collecting funds. Applications range from a group of friends or colleagues contributing to a gift to fundraising for a group trip or even crowdfunding for a charitable organization. The service is now spreading across Europe with success.

As mentioned above, it is difficult to count the start-ups in operation. We propose the following approach to making a rough, low-end estimate: assume approximately 2,000 start-up creations per year worldwide (based on figure 4.7 plus an estimate for the rest of the world) and an average five-year life for a start-up company (some of these firms die, some are acquired, and some become profitable and endure). By multiplying 2,000 start-ups by the average five-year life, we arrive at a low-end estimate of 10,000 active start-ups around the globe. Incorporating a rough guess of 10 skilled employees, on average, in each start-up, we estimate an army of 100,000 skilled persons employed by start-ups; the true number is probably significantly larger, perhaps twice that many. Compared to the estimated five million[42] researchers in the world (academia and industry), this remains a relatively small number. But this 2-4% minority is growing and is composed of creative activists who are battling hard at the frontier where knowledge intersects with business. Their relative effect on the future economy far exceeds this small ratio.

Most start-ups, like our examples in the inset above, focus on the digital economy, but a decent proportion of them are in more traditional businesses, from MEMS to beauty cream. And it's important to note that the knowledge created by start-ups is not only technical. As emphasized by Henri Chesbrough,[43] start-ups are willing to consider

Chapter 4. Commoditization in a digital world

any business model, because they are tied to none (in contrast to established companies). The knowledge created by start-ups, then, is not only technical but also related to the market's response to alternative business models.

An estimated 100,000-200,000 creative persons, enthusiastic and fully involved in their projects at start-up firms; this is not insignificant, particularly given that they are innovation activists. Unfortunately, start-up firms' knowledge is the most dispersed knowledge. Exploring the start-up nebulae is a difficult challenge: start-ups belong to the most fragmented fraction of frontier knowledge (see chapter 7).

4.1.4 Direct impact of knowledge growth on innovation practices

> The great driver of scientific and technological innovation [in the last 600 years has been] the increase in our ability to reach out and exchange ideas with other people, and to borrow other people's hunches and turn them into something new.
> **Steven Johnson**[44]

There a straightforward way to interpret the current new situation, in which knowledge is everywhere and is produced by multiple competing sources: knowledge is becoming a commodity. The capacity to produce it the ability to store it in large volume are no longer differentiators of company performance.

The old way: innovation in an environment of knowledge scarcity

The float-zone

Around the time of World War II, Bell Labs was pushing the idea of using solid-state devices as alternatives to vacuum tubes in electronic systems. However, key knowledge had to be acquired prior to the development of a transistor. Most importantly, new concepts and processes would be needed to allow the growth of quality semiconductor crystals. A major foundational-knowledge effort was conducted at Bell Labs by people such as Jack Scaff, Russell Ohl, and Henry Theuerer[a]. They developed the float-zone crystal-growth technique[b]. John Bardeen[c] noted in his 1956 Nobel lecture that "of great importance for our research program was the development during and since the war of methods of purification and control of the electrical properties of germanium and silicon."

[a]In 1939 Ohl engaged Scaff and Theuerer, two of Bell Lab's metallurgists to purify silicon.[45]

[b]The Czochralski process for the growth of ingots of single-crystal silicon, inspired by a metallurgy technique, was developed at Bell Labs by Gordon K. Teal and Ernest Buehler.[46]

[c]The 1956 Nobel Price was granted to William Shockley, John Bardeen, and Walter Houser Brattain, all from Bell Labs, for their discovery of the bipolar transistor; the first functional device was made in 1947 from a germanium crystal.

For major innovation projects conducted half a century ago, companies created most of the adjacent required knowledge in-house. As shown in the example above, when Bell Labs, around World War II, was working on developing what would become the transistor, the researchers had to create on their own most of the underlying and adjacent knowledge, particularly that related to the purification, growth,

92 Chapter 4. Commoditization in a digital world

and doping of crystalline silicon.

In the first part of the twentieth century, most major inventions originated from large corporate research centers. Competition, if any, was between these large laboratories: Siemens versus Westinghouse Electric, Dunlop Rubber versus Michelin and Firestone Tire and Rubber, or Pilkington versus Saint-Gobain and Pittsburgh Plate Glass (PPG). While they were developing the polymer industries, large players like DuPont, Imperial Chemical (ICI), and Bayer had very little to expect from the open world, because the most significant publications of applied technology were patent applications. There was little to learn that these big research centers could learn from other parties: they were ahead, public research was trailing behind, and no small or medium-sized business or start-up firm was trying to enter the game. The general policy during the course of a research project was secrecy.

The epitome of all large innovations projects driven in a confidential framework in which all necessary knowledge was developed in-house was the famous Manhattan Project[v]. It was a military project with its own rationale for secrecy, but during that era, strategically important industrial research projects were also enclosed in metaphorical double-stranded barbed-wire fences.

After industry had demonstrated the great potential for applications of polymers, dedicated public research centers were created. For example, in 1946 the Polymer Research Institute was founded in Brooklyn, New York and in the same year, the *Journal of Polymer Science* published its first issue. In Europe it was only in 1958 that English researchers began holding conferences on a regular basis. It was only in the 1970s, when many academics were wearing Nylon shirts, that the field of polymer science began organizing in Europe. In the postwar era, most large industrial innovation projects, such as radial tires, jetliners, nuclear reactors, antibiotics, and halogen lamps, were still conducted in private research centers.

---

[v]The Manhattan Project, the design and construction of the atomic bomb, was driven by the U.S. Department of Defense during World War II.

Innovation Intelligence

Except for a few pioneers (see the inset below), it is only in the mid-1970s that the practice of seeking knowledge bricks outside of the company was increasingly used in innovation projects. One of the leading players in this process was the automobile industry, which was experiencing gradual fragmentation of its value chain.

Early example of the new way to do industrial R&D

In the early 1950s, large players such as RCA and General Electric were feverishly struggling to develop a commercial color-television vacuum tube. As part of the development process, they had to learn a lot about vacuum electronics, precision mechanics, image coding, and the chemistry of phosphorus. In this race between large corporate research centers, an interesting and anomalous event occurred: a man developed a color-television vacuum tube in his university garage[a]. This man, Ernest O. Lawrence, was a special person, a professor at the University of California, Berkeley (often called simply Berkeley). He had been won the Nobel Prize in 1939 for inventing the cyclotron; he was a man of large research projects. Having just returned from the Manhattan Project, he was developing what he called Chromatron as a side hobby. Lawrence could do this because he had access to a very large knowledge base from various sources including Berkeley, Oak Ridge National Laboratory, and Los Alamos National Laboratory (the site of the Manhattan Project). He succeeded in turning his TV tube into a large project, first with the support of Paramount Pictures, then starting his own company, and finally selling the license to a newcomer, Sony Corporation. This story is an early example of the new way to do industrial research and development; naturally, it took place

94 Chapter 4. Commoditization in a digital world

near San Francisco, California. However, Chromatron was developed while knowledge was still scarce but by a man who had an excellent personal network of connections to knowledge.

---

[a]Let us recall how iconic the garage's symbolic myth is in California. Hewlett-Packard (HP) and Apple were both born in garages. In fact, Lawrence's Chromatron was not the first garage development: Hewlett and Packard started in their Palo Alto, California garage in 1935!

Innovation in an environment flooded with knowledge

> We have always been shameless about stealing great ideas.
> **Steve Jobs in an interview for the 1996 Public Broadcasting Service series "Triumph of the Nerds"**

The story of Ernest Lawrence and his Chromatron was rather unique in the environment of the 1950s. Such a story would be common today, probably with younger actors. The general level of knowledge is much higher today than it was in the past, and knowledge is disseminated by a wide diversity of sources, including public research teams, institutes, small university laboratories, start-up firms, and consultants. The shift to seek knowledge from external sources rather than creating it in-house happened gradually. Companies retain control of their core knowledge, but they build innovation projects by complementing their internal strengths with specific elements from external sources, combining them to create new products. They search the world, identifying opportunities, integrating the new knowledge, and combining it with their core knowledge to shape a new product or service. Table 4.1 lists some examples of companies who have followed this process.

Today, due to the fantastic growth of knowledge, it is impossible for even a large company to own experience and expertise in every field. If a company contemplates a project involving an emerging technology, it is safe to expect that there exist external sources superior to the

Innovation Intelligence

Company	Time period	Core competency	External knowledge	Process or tool	Products
Apple	1980s – present	Design and user interface	IT devices and databases	Contracts and royalties	Electronic appliances
Parrot	2000s – 2010s	Remote control and phone apps	Flight stability and propeller design	Hiring employees and engaging consultants	Drones
Cisco Systems	1990s – present	Network integration	Telecommunication components and data transfer	Purchase and integration of companies	One-stop-shop for telecommunications
IBM	1990s	Production and market access	Sensor-device design and magnetic film stacks	Licensing and technology transfer	Thin-film heads for hard disks
Telefónica	Present	Global network and market contact	Applications and cloud computing	Wayra,[47] the company's start-up accelerator	Telecommunications applications

Table 4.1: A few examples of companies that use external knowledge in their innovation projects

96   Chapter 4. Commoditization in a digital world

company's in-house sources of knowledge about the new technology. This is probably true for nearly all fields, except for the company's own core knowledge, which, we may reasonably assume, is carefully maintained.

The lesson is to seek non-core knowledge and identify the various knowledge centers that have mastered it. Knowing the best-in-class sources of such knowledge, the company's next step is to decide how to acquire the knowledge. Self learning remains an option, and at least the best places to learn from have been identified. Targeted hiring is also an option, and here again the potential sources of employees have been identified. The fastest approach, however, remains partnering in some fashion with the external knowledge source; there are many potential structures, with the ideal outcome that both parties benefit from the interaction. In any case, the best-in-class source of knowledge should remain on the company's radar screen as both a source of inspiration and a benchmark of success.

4.1.5 Open innovation

In this section, we focus on one of the consequences of the trends we have discussed thus far: a paradigm shift in the innovation process. The term open innovation was coined for the new approach by Henri Chesbrough.[43] We will provide a brief descript of the transition from closed innovation to open innovation; the transition was a result of a convergence of trends affecting the world of innovation at the turn of the twentieth century.

Closed innovation: the old way

"In the 1880s, 'General' Henry du Pont proudly told an applicant for an engineering position that 'we build our own machinery, draw our own plans, make our own patterns and have never employed anyone to design or construct our mills and machinery, dams or races, roads or anything else.'"[49] Close innovation consists of applying that same principle to R&D. Within the paradigm of closed innovation, the innovation process is confined within the company. In other words, most

Innovation Intelligence 97

knowledge and intellectual property is developed internally until the new product is launched. The company's research center is like a bank of proprietary knowledge enclosed by a tight security fence. Such an approach was common historically; opening connections to the outside was not considered worth the potential risk of industrial secrets leaking, and besides, there was not much knowledge available outside the company.

The Bell Labs

Bell Labs[48] is the archetype of large, central corporate laboratories. Founded in Murray Hill, New Jersey in the early 1940s, it grew to employ a staff of 5,000 people before it was further extended to other locations in the United States. The very long hallways were intended to spark spontaneous encounters between scientists, ideally resulting in knowledge sharing. Rows of laboratories were each driven by a lead scientist. The white lab coats worn in this photograph from the mid-1970s were staged – the actual atmosphere was far more informal, blue jeans more common than neckties and good science the sole rule. Bell Labs did not survive the breakup of Bell Telephone's monopoly: in the 1980s, it was divided across several companies, and its efforts were scaled back.

At the beginning of the twentieth century, universities and governments had little involvement in applied research for non-military applications. Large corporations each created their own R&D department to manage the cycles of product development. The research world was simple: universities pushed out the frontier of basic knowledge, and their output was the subsequent publications and teachings; industries developed applications and the required subsidiary knowledge, and their output was products.

98 Chapter 4. Commoditization in a digital world

The period between the end of World War II and the mid-1970s was the golden age of corporate R&D. Many private-company R&D departments were at the leading edge of scientific research. In addition, this large volume of in-house knowledge was perceived as a solid barrier to entry by potential new competitors; indeed, large investments had to be made to learn enough to be capable of entering and competing.

Closed innovation implies deep vertical integration (from raw material to after-sale services), because the company can count only on itself. During this gold age of corporate R&D, not-invented-here (NIH) syndrome[50] inflicted the most damage: everything outside the company was considered suspicious and unreliable.

The letters R and D occupied different worlds: the motivations and priorities of their researchers were different. Joining the two letters R and D into R&D in the 1970s was initially almost a wishful statement. To coordinate the connection between research and development, many companies set up a buffer between the two departments. One role of this buffer was to store an invention generated by the research department and then, when operations and the market were ready, to pass the invention to the development department. During the postwar golden age, many discoveries were shelved in this way for several years and sometimes indefinitely.

Most of the giant corporate research centers are now extinct. The flagship case, Bell Labs, dissolved gradually during the 1980s, the majority of its brilliant researchers finding jobs at public research centers. A recent study from the American Institute of Physics (AIP) reports that all blue-sky research in the United States is now done at universities and national laboratories rather than at companies.[51]

Open Innovation as a result of converging trends

The transition from closed innovation to open innovation has been slow but broad; open innovation, a collaborative approach, is used in a growing number of industries and countries. Gradually but inexorably, open innovation has become more efficient than closed innovation. The term *open innovation* was coined in a must-read book of the same name.[43]

Innovation Intelligence

We see the transition from closed innovation to open innovation as a Darwinian process: because the environment has changed and open innovation is, on average, more successful than closed innovation; companies must evolve, choosing to use this more collaborative approach to innovation, or be passed by. This is similar to mammals supplanting dinosaurs as planetary conditions changed. We have already explored some of key factors that drove the transition, but in this section we will propose a complete list of the factors. Although in many cases it is difficult to determine whether a given factor is a cause, an effect, or a concurrent change, each of these factors is certainly a part of the global transition we are witnessing.

Transition factor #1: Knowledge growth and fragmentation. We have already covered this factor in detail. The key points are that when knowledge is available, it is not efficient to rebuild it on your own, even for the sake of confidentiality. When knowledge sources exist already, dispersed in many different places, there is a good chance that in at least one of those places there is a potential partner who is willing to transfer it in exchange for a defined reward.

Transition factor #2: Job volatility. Job volatility, in particular for skilled personnel, has increased. The era of a lifelong contract between an employee and an employer has ended. This change began in the United States, where the concept of a free market extends to the job market. Experts who master a new field of knowledge with high economic value can easily demand a raise or leave for a better, higher-paying job. This personal mobility is making the metaphorical barbed-wire fence around research centers increasingly ineffective. Job switching has becoming common for young, educated professionals. By the 1980s, the average tenure for a process engineer at a firm in Silicon Valley was less than one year. The engineer would just cross the street, moving from, for example, Intel to AMD and sometimes back again. Ironically, industry in Silicon Valley did not suffer as a result of this employee behavior, but rather it was a key factor in maintaining leadership of the whole industry. The Silicon Valley companies progressed collectively along the experience curve and today they are

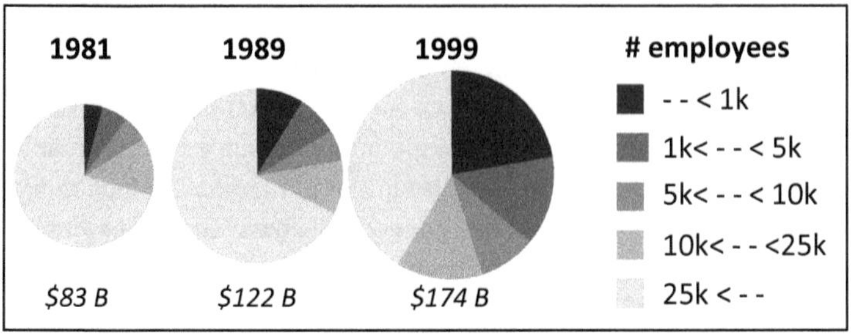

1981	1989	1999	# employees

Figure 4.13: Small companies' R&D investment. The pie charts show the increasing fraction of small companies contributing to R&D investment in the United States during 1981-1999. Source: Data extracted from National Science Foundation, "Science Resources Studies", Survey of Industrial Research (1999).

still leaders in advanced processor design and production. Job volatility is increasing in other countries. Europe is in a similar situation to the United States, especially with regard to young, skilled personnel. Asia, in contrast, is still dominated by a culture of employee loyalty. For example, it would be socially difficult for a South Korean engineer to switch from a job at Samsung to one at LG; surprisingly, however, he or she could easily resign and found a start-up firm. In Japan, more and more skilled young people are shocking their parents and switching employers frequently just like their counterparts in California. The corresponding knowledge leak across the tight barrier around corporate research centers is not likely to stop. In an ever-changing world, jobs are no longer guaranteed. Companies cannot guarantee that they will need a given class of expert forever. Finally, job mobility actually provides a company with useful fluidity in its workforce. This factor in itself is rendering the closed-innovation approach less effective than open innovation.

Transition factor #3: Emergence of venture capital as an alternative to corporate investment. During the period from the 1950s to the 1980s, large corporations were the only entities able to push innovation because they were the only ones willing and able to finance

Innovation Intelligence 101

it. Small and medium-sized businesses could not enter the competition, because innovation's inherent risk prevented bankers, which are risk-averse enterprises, from lending money for it. In the late 1970s and early 1980s, another breed of investors, venture capitalists, entered the game. Venture capitalists are not afraid of innovation, because they have learned how to manage the risk by keeping a close eye on their individual projects and distributing the risk across a balanced portfolio of projects.

As can be seen in figure 4.13, the effect of venture capital in the United States before the 1980s was very slight; corporate financing of R&D was dominant. During the next two decades, the situation changed dramatically. Today the distribution of R&D expenditure is relatively balanced between small companies and large companies. Venture capital has supported start-ups to such an extent that today start-ups are leading the way in applied research.

There is an interesting consequence of the emergence of venture capital as a source of financing for new firms: if an innovation project is at all viable, it is nearly impossible for a company to shelve it. If the company attempts to do so, the invention's champions are likely to leave the company and found a start-up to push the idea to market.

Transition factor #4: Improved protection for patent owners. Interacting with partners during the innovation process brings with it the risk of information leakage. A contractual non-disclosure agreement (NDA) can provide some protection if it includes an accurate description of the knowledge exchange. However, securing the key idea or ideas behind the project in a patent filing provides better protection; a patent also protects its owner from voluntary or involuntary leakage from the partners to a third party. Patenting is a good safeguard, provided that the patent does indeed protect you from infringers. It is a little-known fact that during most of the twentieth century, a patent was not an effective protection. The leading economy, the United States, was busy implementing its antitrust policy. As a result, patent owners that tried to enforce their exclusivity status were not well received by the U.S. justice system. The secrecy walls surrounding corporate

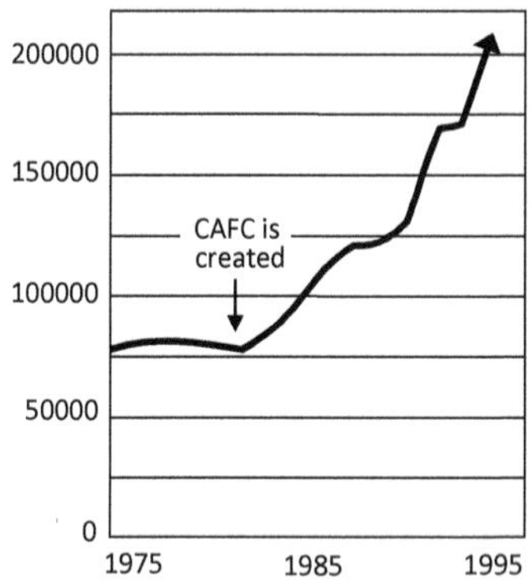

102   Chapter 4. Commoditization in a digital world

Figure 4.14: Change in U.S. jurisprudence. In 1982, the U.S. government made a move to enforce the legal protection of intellectual property rights. Local state courts were not often judging in favor of patent owners attempting to seek damages from infringers. A simple court of appeal, the Court of Appeal of the Federal Circuit (CAFC), was created. This court immediately changed the jurisprudence: before the change, two-thirds of such plaintiffs lost their cases, after the change, two-thirds won their cases.[52] This change in U.S. jurisprudence drastically increased the economic value of patents; the consequence was a hockey-stick change in rate at which patents were granted by the USPTO.

laboratories that conducted closed innovation were necessary during that time, because patents did not provide sufficient protection due to the lack of enforcement by the courts. The enforcement situation changed quite dramatically in the early 1980s. The United States was losing its industrial competitiveness to Japan, and several lobbies were explaining to the U.S. government that American inventions were being manufacture in Japan and then sold to American consumers. In October 1982 the U.S. government created the Court of Appeal of the Federal Circuit (CAFC).[53] This court would be the last resort for patent-infringement lawsuits. The CAFC changed the jurisprudence, shifting it in favor of patent owners. This strong legal statement was made very visible by several flagship cases, such as Polaroid v. Kodak[vi]

[vi] 1990 Polaroid won a marathon litigation case against Kodak for infringement of its many patents associated with instant photography. For Kodak it was a huge loss, summing up to approximately $3 billion including approximately $1.6 paid to Polaroid.

Innovation Intelligence 103

and Texas Instruments v. eight Japanese firms and one Korean firm[vii]. Because the United States was the largest technology market, its judges were at the forefront of nearly all intellectual-property conflicts and their jurisprudence set an international standard. The net result was that patent filing became credible insurance against the risk of unfair behavior in open innovation, and therefore patenting experienced a resurgence, as shown in figure 4.14. This sole legal factor was not, in itself, sufficient to trigger the shift form closed innovation to open innovation, but it did contribute.

Transition factor #5: Fragmentation of the value chain. Vertical integration is no longer the dominant business model for large companies. A prime case of an industry revisiting the organization of its value chain organization is the automobile industry. In order to become lean and flexible, the major players in the automotive industry split their value chains, spinning off parts production to subcontractors. Gradually, during the 1970s and 1980s, subcontractors moved further up the value chain, so that they now design and supply large subsystems, such as engines and power trains. Innovation often required that car design companies, called original equipment manufacturers (OEMs) companies collaborate with their suppliers. Part suppliers were also active further down the value chain, pushing innovation projects with the help of raw material suppliers. This fragmentation of the value chain in the automotive industry made open innovation a natural practice.

Open innovation: predatory vs. ecological behavior

There are several ways to perform open innovation, particularly for large, powerful companies. Open innovation starts by the action of seeking a source of knowledge, then entering into a relationship with the chosen partner with the objective of integrating the acquired knowledge into an innovation project. The relationship between what we will

---

[vii]Texas Instruments sued eight Japanese firms and one Korean firm for infringement of its patents associated with dynamic random-access memory (DRAM). The case was settled in 1987, forcing the Asian companies to pay royalties to Texas Instruments for several years.[54]

104 Chapter 4. Commoditization in a digital world

call the knowledge source and the integrator must be framed within a contract. The contract is drafted jointly by the partners during preliminary discussions, which are covered, at that point, by a mere NDA. The most important aspect of this early phase is that the two parties reach a mutual understanding of the strategic guidelines. Any hidden agenda will result, sooner or later, in a crisis that could damage one or both parties. Out of the many possible structures for cooperative research, we see a clear pattern.

Cisco Systems and benchmark in M&A

Cisco Systems is a benchmark in merger and acquisition (M&A) processes, successfully acquiring and integrating five to ten companies each year since 1994. They were aiming to become a one-stop source of sophisticated systems for the Internet and networking services. They acquired the design knowledge and manufacturing know-how for many components of their strategy, typically by acquiring the companies that were expert in those areas. In doing so, they developed highly respected expertise in the integration of acquired companies. Integration is the riskiest aspect of M&A.

In a predatory relationship, the smaller partner may exit the relationship in a weaker state than it entered or disappear completely, as when the larger company acquires the smaller company. Such an acquisition is a legitimate way to integrate new knowledge, and all of the people involved in the deal may go on to successful careers. This was the case for Cisco Systems, which successfully acquired and integrated many smaller companies. Sometimes the relationship ends badly; this is a common outcome when the related innovation project fails. Failure has a high probability in innovation projects, and the project's risk is not always managed properly during the enthusiastic phase when

Innovation Intelligence 105

the contract is signed. For example, Apple signed an agreement with GT Advanced Technologies to develop the process and capabilities of delivering sapphire-based screens for the next generation of the iPhone. As is often the case in innovation, ramping up production was difficult, the yield was poor, and screens cracked during phone-drop tests. The project's targets had been too optimistic. Finally, Apple decided not to use sapphire-based screens for the next generation of the iPhone. Because the collaboration contract had been set up as a strict supply contract with little acknowledgement of risk, GT Advanced Technologies ended up filing for bankruptcy. Apple, thanks to its large customer base and strong reputation, is in a position of advantage when negotiating with smaller companies. When such a large imbalance exists between partners, it is challenging for the smaller company to mitigate its risk.

Predatory open innovation does work in many cases. For example, it is actually one of the rosy dreams of most start-ups to be acquired as part of a collaborative innovation venture.

An alternative, non-predatory outcome is quite popular in active innovation centers such as Silicon Valley. The basic idea is that innovation grows best in a rich ecosystem full of biodiversity. When a large company engages in collaboration for open innovation with a smaller company, the goal is for both partners to survive the relationship and continue their own lives, richer from the shared experience but able to extend the value of the associated knowledge by applying it in other arenas. In such a situation, open innovation can be described as a networking process. The players know each other, or at least have a close recommendation, interact with one partner when needed for a given project, and then interact with other partners when pursuing other applications or business models.

Virtuous open-innovation ecosystem

This non-predatory, or virtuous, open-innovation ecosystem is probably the ultimate achievement in implementing open innovation. Many analysts are dissecting Silicon Valley's success stories in an effort to discover the magic recipe for a successful innovation culture.

Examples other than Silicon Valley may also prove the existence and effectiveness of virtuous open-innovation ecosystems: in technology, the Boston area, particularly around MIT; in painting, Paris during the roaring 1920s, in filmmaking, Hollywood during the 1950s through the 1970s.

These clusters share some key characteristics: a strong academic base, sufficient job opportunities to attract brilliant newcomers, a culture of freedom, and a critical size.

Many places around the world are trying to mimic such a dynamic environment: Munich, Germany; Berlin, Germany; Tel Aviv, Israel; Hsinchu, Taiwan; and Tsukuba, Japan, to name a few. In the inset below, we describe an ongoing example of the creation of an innovation ecosystem; this creation is symbolic of the transition from closed innovation to open innovation.

Philips and open innovation

Philips decided to make visible its decision to begin engaging in open innovation by orchestrating an ambitious urban-planning project. Philips Research Eindhoven is located in the High Tech Campus (HTC) Eindhoven in The Netherlands. The HTC was established in 1914, and the town grew around it. Eindhoven now ranks as the fifth largest city in The Netherlands. The R&D development zone, twenty-seven hectares of real estate, was initially fenced, with guards at the gate next to train station. It is now an open and vibrant community full of new projects housed in remodeled buildings. Philips lends space to start-ups and laboratories of all types – even its competi-

Innovation Intelligence 107

tors – and public life is welcoming, with cafes, gyms, and nursery schools.

Is open innovation just hype?

The answer to this question is both yes and no. Open innovation is the most natural and efficient way to perform innovation today, focusing on the company's core competency and acquiring all of the subsidiary knowledge by interacting with partners. The main virtues of open innovation are to the following:

- Effectiveness: no effort is wasted in building knowledge that already exists
- Response time: no time is wasted in slowly creeping up a learning curve

Open innovation is real, as illustrated by success stories such as Apple and Parrot. It became hype when some brilliant intellectuals such as Henri Chesbrough publicized the ongoing trend, putting words to something that was only vaguely sensed by many. The industry became aware of the trend and could observe the success of Silicon Valley with a general understanding. But then, as is often the case with new approaches to business, many players made the mistake of interpreting the phenomenon as a recipe that everybody could and should apply with a stroke of a magic wand. It is not such a recipe, for several reasons:

- Open innovation is an element of corporate culture. Changing corporate culture is a slow and difficult process requiring tenacious effort from the highest to the lowest levels of a company.
- Open innovation shifts the way R&D personnel, and indeed all innovation-driving personnel, should see their own jobs. Instead of creating valuable knowledge, they should search for value and conceive winning deals.
- For successful innovation, people must be encouraged to make preliminary contact with would-be partners.

Continuing to do closed innovation is a perfectly valid option, but only for businesses that do not need much knowledge, a nearly extinct

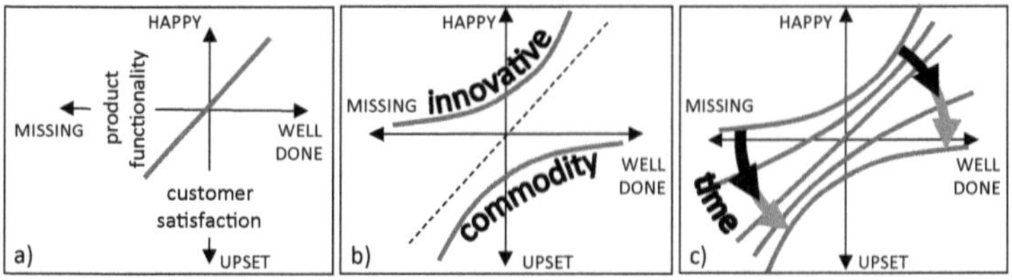

Figure 4.17: Kano model. Kano model linking customer satisfaction to implementation of features in a product.

world. Even businesses that are very sensitive to confidentiality, such as chemical or pharmaceutical industries, collect knowledge all around the world, although they prefer to operate in a predatory mode.

Some companies have behaved deceptively, declaring that they were willing to embrace open innovation but trying and failing to reshape the company's organization and processes accordingly. Unsurprisingly, the shift did not increase their innovation efficiency or response time.

We sense today a decline of enthusiasm for open innovation in the business community. The hype is cooling down, as it has for nearly all management hype throughout history. It is now time to manage reality, and reality is slow and tedious.

4.2 Permanent fight against commoditization

Let's now move from a discussion of knowledge to one of products. To gain a full understanding of the mechanics behind the current fast-moving trends affecting products, we should review the Kano model of product development and customer satisfaction developed by Noriaki Kano[55] as illustrated in figure 4.17 (a, b, and c).

The Kano model relates customer satisfaction (the vertical axis) to the quality of the technical implementation of a feature in a product (the horizontal axis). The simplest relationship is shown in figure 4.17a: if the product feature is missing or malfunctioning, the customer is

Innovation Intelligence 109

not satisfied; if the feature works well, the customer is satisfied. Figure 4.17b, the most important, shows this relationship for two product types. The innovative product includes a new feature, of which the customer was not aware and which he or she did not expect. If this feature is missing from a product, the customer cannot be dissatisfied, because he or she did not expect or demand it, but when the feature is integrated into a new product, the customer is happily surprised and very satisfied. For example, a label on a package of frozen food stating that the product has never been defrosted might pleasantly surprise the customer. A commodity is a must-have feature from a customer's perspective. The commodity is expected and required; its mere existence will not affect the customer's satisfaction. But if the commodity is missing, the customer will be very upset by the violation of a basic "rule." A classic example is toilet paper being present or missing. Figure 4.17c shows the typical downward trajectory of a given set of features over time, as features that were initially unexpected are gradually commoditized. A feature that initially simply provided the customer with a pleasant surprise gradually becomes a part of the customer's evaluation of the product, as competitors implement similar features in their products. Eventually all competing products will include the feature, and the customer will expect it. At that point, the feature has become commoditized. For example, consider the intermittent feature of windshield wipers. It was an innovative and a pleasing feature when introduced by Ford in the 1970s, but today this feature is a commodity because a driver would be very unhappy if it were missing from a new car.

In the fast-paced world of today, companies and their products are under more pressure than ever from the threat of commoditization. In fact, the threat of commoditization was a risk cited by all of the innovation managers we interviewed. They were all focused on mitigating the risk of their company being categorized as a commodity provider.

This fight against commoditization has always existed. In fact, the eternal purpose of innovation is to surprise and please customers with new features. When Leon Bel introduced the famous Laughing Cow brand of cheese, which has no shelf-life constraints, in the 1920s, the

110   Chapter 4. Commoditization in a digital world

intent was to escape the severe threat of commoditization that exists in the cheese industry. Innovation provides the customer with a higher degree of satisfaction, which makes him or her willing to pay a premium price for the product. A commodity, on the other hand, is just a generic baseline made by all competitors. As a result of commoditization, product profit margins are eroded to such an extent that they do not allow investment in innovation. Product commoditization is the beginning of the end for a company.

The perceived urgency of the commoditization threat today is related to the fast pace of the economy in general. It now takes much less time for a product to progress from a customer saying "aha!" to the same customer saying "so what?" We have seen that the knowledge flood is one of the drivers of this accelerated pace. Another driver is globalization: any company today must consider a large number of competitors in a variety of environments. The chances of a new product being rapidly duplicated, and thus commoditized, are much greater than they ever have been. However, the final straw is the digital wave. With its incredibly rapid response times, the digital wave has provided a significant boost to the commoditization process in many industrial sectors.

4.2.1 Products becoming increasingly complex assemblies of components

We have already described the impressive growth of knowledge. A direct consequence of this knowledge growth is the creation and availability of a multiplicity of technical solutions, including devices, tools, materials, and subsystems. As a way of sensing the degree of this ongoing change, try to list the different methods for measuring temperature that we have today in our engineering toolbox. The good old fragile, glass tube that was used by Galileo Galilei[viii] still exists, but there are many alternative solutions that are lower-cost, faster, more

---

[viii]Galileo Galeilei used water in his glass thermometer. Mercury was introduced by Daniel Gabriel Fahrenheit in 1714.

Innovation Intelligence

rugged, and more integrated. For example, a temperature measurement device can be introduced as a component in an integrated circuit. We can describe the same explosion of possibilities in nearly every field. In other words, the content of the grand catalog of all components, parts, and sub-systems that can be used to build a product has followed a parallel path of growth and acceleration to that of knowledge. A grand catalog of components also exists for service industries – tools such as credit cards, phone networks, the Internet, 2-D bar codes, and many other digital tools – and presents an increasingly rich number of combinations.

Diagram of an automobile transmission

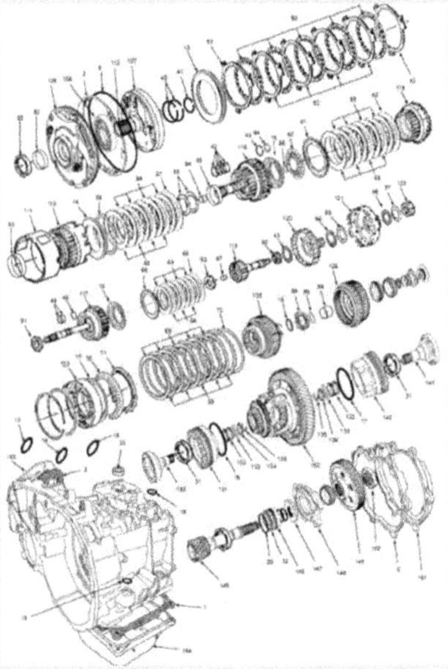

"The typical car contains about 2,000 components, 30,000 parts, and 10 million lines of software code." Despite this complexity modern cars are significantly more reliable than their predecessors. Indeed, the industry has developed – based on great effort over many years – the capability of assembling this intricate set of assemblies and parts, while achieving failure rates near zero. John Paul Mac-Duffie and Takahiro Fujimoto[56] continued: "Which companies are best equipped to

112   Chapter 4. Commoditization in a digital world

design the cars of the future? Those that have amassed the systemic knowledge to coordinate all the work and the many partners involved." (The diagram shows an exploded view of a portion of an automobile transmission.)

On one side, this toolbox is increasingly abundant. On the other side, companies are willing to provide customers with a superior answer to their need. If a customer wants a product to perform a given function, a basic solution exists, but to avoid commoditization, a company includes an additional feature in the product. Competitors soon copy the feature and perhaps even reply with another addition feature, escalating the race. If both of these features are satisfactory, they soon become standards from the customer's perspective.

Then the cycle of innovation continues, with the companies adding yet another feature to the product. Eventually, a product that initially performed a basic function is gradually wrapped with multiple layers of additional features. Piling on feature after feature is not difficult, thanks to the enriched possibilities offered by the ever-expanding toolbox. Adding a sensor, a motor, a logic circuit, memory, or a link to a product is now possible at reasonable cost, and if the additional feature will please customers, some company offer it.

As a net result, after many cycles of additive improvement, products are now bundles of features layered on the basic function. Products are becoming increasingly complex, combining layers of technology and offering multiple complementary functions.

This increasing complexity is visible when looking "under the hood" of almost any product or service in almost any industry: financial products, home appliances, professional software packages, air travel pricing, automobiles. The high end, at least, of each of these product lines is a complex assembly.

Moreover, this trend of increasing complexity has affected not only products but also production. Production lines have become extremely complex. Processes in service companies are also becoming complex. For the sake of control and optimization, they incorporate option gates,

Innovation Intelligence 113

feedback regulation, and artificial intelligence of many types.

The automobile is indeed the archetype of a product that has existed for more than a century and during that time has evolved from a somewhat complex system to an incredibly complex system. Like many other products, such as airplanes, specialized machinery, and robots, automobiles now incorporate elements from mechanics, hydraulics, electrical engineering, digital electronics, telecommunications, and so forth.

Somewhat simpler products have an even larger combination of knowledge packages that can be used to build their market propositions. For example the iPod, launched in 2001, has been updated through six generations thus far and has generated spin-off products in terms of miniaturization (iPod Mini and iPod Shuffle), video-player functionality (iPod Nano), and touch-screen functionality (iPod Touch and iPhone). Basically, iPod systems incorporate the following set of features (those that are core competencies for Apple are shown in bold font) to serve a customer's desire to listen to music:

- A case for protection and aesthetics
- Electronic components: processor, memory, antenna, and emitter/receiver
- A flat display and convenient touch interface
- **A friendly graphical user interface (GUI)**
- A battery and the means to charge it
- Sufficient data memory
- **Software, for both the interface and the decompression and decryption of music files**
- Earbuds
- Internet connection to a digital music bank (iTunes)
- **Customized formatting for presenting iTunes data according to each customer's taste**
- **Agreements with music distributors with regard to the commercial aspect of copyrights**
- A contract for access to rapid download of new music
- Purchasing and billing systems for iTunes downloads

114 Chapter 4. Commoditization in a digital world

This extensive list contains hardware, software, services, and a total-package business proposition enabling the customer to enjoy music. It is a perfect example of a rather complex system providing, to today standards, a satisfactory solution for music listeners. It was a success, although streaming alternative are now changing the odds.

The increased complexity of products and services has not affected only high-tech industries. In the inset below, we present the example of a new product, a pressure cooker that is much more complex than the copper pan used by our great-grandmothers.

Groupe SEB introduced NutriCook

Nevada, Groupe SEB introduced a pressure cooker. This is the same technological innovation show at which Parrot presented its famous drone in 2010. Among flocks of virtual-reality goggles, swarms of smartwatches, battalions of smart-phones and electric bicycles, Groupe SEB introduced NutriCook, an Internet-connected pressure cooker. The device downloads a recipe, follows a predefined temperature profile, and alerts the user when an ingredient must be added. The service also includes a forum for users to exchange recipes and to provide tips for using the device. For Groupe SEB, a leading appliance company, NutriCook is a first step in entering the future world of connected cooking and home management, making customer lives easier, more efficient, and more fun.

4.2.2 Product complexity's focus on service

We selected distance measurement in the construction industry to illustrate how products meant to serve a basic customer need are shifting from a mere tool for that basic function to a more complex product or service with a wider range of purposes. The product or service remains

Innovation Intelligence 115

centered on the basic need of the customer, but it now encompasses addition, peripheral needs, progressing from the initial basic functionality to a service-oriented package.

Measuring devices leaning toward services

Building measurement has evolved from the mere folding meter stick to the spring-loaded measuring tape. Recently, far more sophisticated devices that rely on ultrasound or laser echoes have become available, and they allow digital sensing, by a single person, of distances of several meters. These handheld devices have memory and are able to calculate surface. Today, sophisticated 3-D laser scanners are able to map, from one viewpoint, an entire building. The resulting large quantity of data can be transferred via Wi-Fi, and then software applications can transfer the data to CAD systems for generating drawings, 3-D models, or virtual reality. The product has evolved from a mere tool to a service that can provide much more information with much less effort.

One approach to achieving this progression, and therefore improve customer satisfaction, is for the company to focus on reducing the amount of consumer effort required to use the product. There are many types of effort and potential solutions for reducing each:

- Physical effort: solutions include motors in chainsaws and lawn mowers, electric engines in toothbrushes, and power windows in automobiles
- Adjustment effort: solutions include automated focus and anti-shake for cameras, and cruise control for automobiles
- Attention effort: solutions include cooking timers and spellcheck for documents

116   Chapter 4. Commoditization in a digital world

- Waiting effort: solutions include instant cameras, print-on-demand, and instant pain relief
- Repetitive-action effort: solutions include robotic vacuum cleaners and teaching machines
- Recordkeeping effort: solutions include additional memory, customized parameters, and automatic saving
- Carrying and storage effort: solutions include miniaturization

Another way of improving customer satisfaction is to provide ways for the product to be customized to each customer's preferences. This approach is particularly important for mass-produced products that run the risk of homogeneity. For a mobile phone, customization can include colorful cases, ringtone options, sophisticated parameter settings in the operating system and in individual apps, insurance against loss or breakage, and countless contract possibilities offered by phone carriers.

When creating a bundle by adding features to a product that is dedicated to performing a basic function, at each step the product designer must focus on customers' needs, attempting to meet more than the basic need. As a result, the feature bundle, accumulated over the course of many innovation cycles, gradually inhabits a wider space around the customer's basic objective, solving all possible ancillary problems. The product can then be seen as a full-service package around the product's main purpose.

This trend of turning a product into a service package is widely applicable. As stated by Jean-Christophe Simon, Director of R&D and Innovation at Groupe SEB, customers want a total solution. Thanks to the large selection of technologies available, delivering a bundle that approaches such a total solution is increasingly possible.

The shift from a product to a service package is also changing customer expectations, which has consequences for business models. Providing a broader and better service to the customer should enable the company to reap a greater reward than it does for less elaborate products. To this end, it is often wise to change the business model and adapt the marketing approach for the new product or service in order to differentiate it from the former one.

The example of Nespresso

A different business model for a more complex product that delivers a full-service package can be seen in the case of Nespresso. Nestlé was selling ground coffee in large packages. Then the company designed a new product for coffee drinkers. The machine, its compressor, and the sophisticated capsules of ground coffee form a bundle that provides quality single servings of coffee. Nestlé created a new business model, inspired by luxury shops, for its capsules. Machines were licensed to several high-end appliance companies.

The trend pushing industry players to innovate by enlarging the service aspect of their product is related to the permanent fight against commoditization. Development of service-oriented offerings is also occurring in B2B businesses. In the inset below, we recount the example of Air Liquide, a company that provides industrial gases to a variety of industries. Air Liquide has developed service-oriented packages around their basic product, industrial gases, with a different package for each industry. Oerlikon-Balzers, a company that provides hard coating for cutting tools for the mechanical industry, is another example of the transformation from product to service. Today, for large companies such as automotive plants, Oerlikon-Balzers' coating service has evolved to a full-service package that includes the following services for worn tools: collection, cleaning, removal of former coatings, sharpening, coating with a dedicated hard-vacuum coating, control, packing, and delivery. The service package also includes rapid response, because Oerlikon-Balzers' coating centers are located near

118   Chapter 4. Commoditization in a digital world

the large mechanical plants.

Air Liquide business model

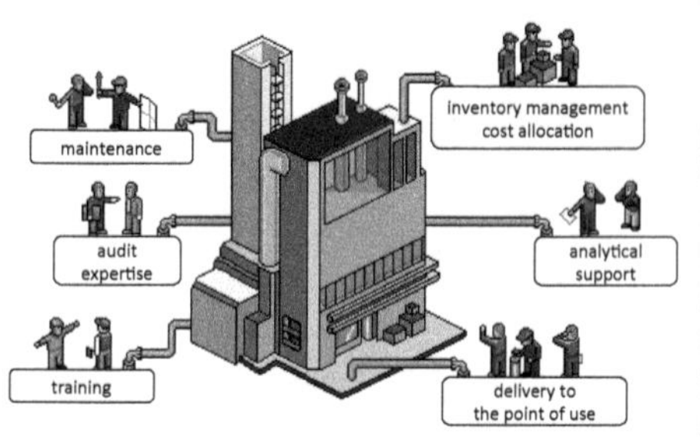

Air Liquide is one of the world's leaders in industrial gas distribution. Olivier Delabroy, VP R&D, explains with a smile that Air Liquide's business is based on a handful of very simple molecules that he calls small essential molecules (SEM), such as O2, N2, Ar, and so forth. Such gases are used along the value chain of nearly every industry, from medical to heavy industry and high-tech. Gas is used in quite different contexts by each of these customers, but a general trend is clear. Air Liquide's old business model was the delivery of gas in containers in response to customer orders, but that business model is changing. Air Liquid is changing its business model to instead provide service packages that are customized to each industry. If a customer wants the gas to always be available, it can choose to engage Air Liquide to handle all of the ancillary duties, such as checking the gas level, ordering on time, handling the gas, maintaining gas-handling systems, and ensuring safety of operations. More and more customers, particularly large companies, prefer Air Liquide to provide a full "gas always there" service package. Gradually, gas supplier is becoming a highly technical gas supply service. Gas-supply service packages are complex products, combining logistics, labor, control, and servicing, as well as the gas itself.

Innovation Intelligence

The complexity of the service package is also related to its customization to a customer's size and industry. The requirements of a semiconductor manufacturer are quite different from those of a polymer plant or a hospital.

4.2.3 Creativity in the art of assembly

melding art and engineering

A lot of value can be created by finding original ways of assembling bricks. Two young architects, Fabio Gramazio and Matthias Kohler (see photo at upper left),[57] from Zurich are masters of brick assembly. In addition to designing creative buildings from their firm's office, they lead a research team at ETH Zürich's architectural school. That research team creates elegant structures by assembling bricks (see photo at lower left). The team is also skilled at assembling knowledge, thanks to their relationships with ETH Zürich's computer design and robotics departments. They have developed processes for assembling bricks very accurately by use of a robot (see photo at upper right). They are exploring extension of the concept, currently working on steel-mesh welding by robots and high-rise assembly of foam bricks by swarms of small quadricopter drones (see photo at lower right). This team, melding art and engineering, stands at the forefront of modern architecture.

Products and services are becoming increasingly complex assemblies. Low-tech products, high-tech products, and services are combined and blended to create the most attractive package. The objective of the game is to find the best compromise between customers' aversion to effort and cost and customers' desire for personalization. Although customers appreciate the performance and breadth of service resulting from complexity, they do not want to have to struggle with complexity when using the product.

Finally, designing a new product is a combinatorial problem of how to select the appropriate technology "bricks" and combine them to provide an innovative service package that addresses customers' needs and desires. In this combinatorial exercise, the most critical step is not a technical one, because the bricks are in the grand catalog and come with the required technology. The most critical step is selecting, from the countless combinations, the best offering from the perspective of a customer so that the offering addresses the customer's basic and ancillary needs and desires while being simple to use. The creativity is in the act of selecting the right bricks and binding them to perform the desired service.

We believe that, surprisingly, in the current world of complexity, the brightest act of creative innovation is much closer to artistic skill than to technological engineering. Let's consider poetry, for example. Poetry is simply the assembly of words in order to convey emotion. Words are just small bricks of knowledge with definitions; the value of a poem is in the combination of words.

In this art of performing innovation, there are rules and guidelines to be respected, the most important ones related to customer satisfaction and profitability. The winning innovation offers the most elegant combination of bricks, seemingly simple, almost obvious (after you have seen it), and as elegant as flowers arranged according to Ikebana. Steve Jobs can be described as an art designer, and, according to many Apple customers, it showed in his products. We will return to this point in chapter 6.

4.3 Disruptive digital tsunami

In chapter 3 of this book, we introduced the concept of innovation waves sweeping across markets and industries and giving rise to intense innovation activity. We are currently experiencing one these waves, the digital wave, which includes innovations made possible by information and transmission technologies, namely the Internet, wireless communication, fast computing, and memory storage. This wave has been called by various names, but everybody recognizes it as a phenomenon; in this book we will call it the digital innovation wave or simply the digital wave. In fact, the digital wave is such a tall wave that we should call it a tsunami. It gave birth to what is called the new economy, but has also affected, often in an extremely disruptive way, traditional brick-and-mortar businesses.

The digital wave in dates

- 1947 First transistor (Bell Labs)
- 1956 First hard disk (IBM)
- 1964 First geostationary satellite for telecommunications
- 1971 Release of the 4004 processor (Intel)
- 1977 First personal computer (Apple)
- 1985 Internet formed
- 1989 Launch of the twenty-four GPS satellites
- 1991 First GSM mobile phone network in Europe
- 1994 Founding of Yahoo and Amazon.com
- 1996 Founding of eBay / In twelve months the number of host computers jumps from one million to ten million
- 1998 Launch of Google search engine
- 2003 Launch of WordPress, a personal publishing service
- 2006 One billion songs purchased from the iTunes Store / Founding of Twitter / Internet reaches 1 billion users
- 2010 Internet reaches 10% of the world's population
- 2010 Internet reaches 2 billion users

122   Chapter 4. Commoditization in a digital world

- 2014 Internet reaches 3 billion users

Young people think they are living in an exceptional time and that the digital wave is a unique, revolutionary event. However, we are inclined to think that the digital wave is not the first event of its kind. For example, traditional industries of the 1920s through the 1940s experienced another innovation tsunami, the electricity wave. At that time there was a severe shortage of executives who recognized the consequences of every home being connected to an electrical grid. The pioneers, the Apples of that era, designed appliances. Industrial success shifted from heavy industry to consumer goods. Eventually, industries adapted, but there were many casualties along the way. Even further back in history, another highly disruptive innovation wave was the steam wave. During that era, many riverside steel mills and paper mills disappeared, as did the successful stagecoach business.

The digital wave has enabled communication and information processing from between any two locations. This new set of bricks has entered the grand catalog, opening up possibilities for new features and new functions in designing innovative products. In fact, most products can benefit from the potential add-ons enabled by digital technology. The spectrum of possibilities is vast; indeed, information is an appealing aspect of the bundle of features a customer would like to see attached to any product, especially a total service.

4.3.1   Digital barbarians: threat to the customer relationship

Fifteen years ago, Apple changed the way we listen to music. While the major participants in the music industry were fighting Napster and CD burners, Apple launched the iPod, iTunes, and the iTunes Store. Suddenly, a newcomer, an alien, a digital barbarian had decided that we no longer needed to buy CDs to listen to music, and worse, that we didn't need to buy entire albums. We just needed to download the songs we liked. This change had significant consequences for the music industry. First, the era of the album containing one or two hits and 12 "filler" tracks was at an end. People would only buy the

Innovation Intelligence   123

songs they liked, each for 99 cents. Artists who rejected the new rules were not required to make their music available in the iTunes Store, but they would miss what became the leading sales channel. Second, major participants in the music industry were disintermediated. For an extremely profitable industry, this was game-changing and, for some, game-ending. After Apple was comfortably installed in its dominant position, it was disrupted by the entry of the even younger digital barbarians, Deezer and Spotify. The new rules of the game according to these newer digital barbarians? We no longer need to buy music at all. We can either rent music or buy a monthly plan to listen to as much music as we want. Even better, the monthly plan is built into our mobile-phone plan. Unlimited music, legally, and with the impression that it is free or nearly free.

A few years ago, the retail sector was also attacked. Amazon, founded in the United States, and Alibaba, from China, to cite the major barbarians, have written the new rules. We can order anything on the Internet, without living our homes. No shipping cost. Fast shipping. Secure payment. Buy with one click. Consumers save time and money. While the retail industry was shaken by these barbarians for a few years, a new balance between online retailers and traditional returns seems to have been found.

Like Deezer and Spotify have changed the way we listen to music, Netflix has changed the way we watch films. We can buy a monthly plan and watch as many films as we want.

Uber has changed the way we hire cabs (recall this example from chapter 1). BlaBlaCar is changing the way we share cars. Airbnb has changed the way rent lodging.

Price-comparison search engines represent a major development. A few years ago, a number of search engines were created to help consumers compare prices for flights, hotels, insurance, and so forth. Companies providing such services include Booking.com, Hotels.com, Travelocity, and Priceline.com, as well as many others in various domains. When these search engines debuted, everyone was happy. Let's consider the example of hotel rooms. Consumers were happy, because

124　　　　　Chapter 4. Commoditization in a digital world

they could compare prices among hotels and then make a reservation, all with just a few clicks. Hotels and hotel chains were happy, because these price-comparison search engines offered an easy new communication channel. Even a two-room bed and breakfast in a small village could get traffic. Suddenly, filtering a long list of hotels was possible. This enthusiasm was present at the beginning, but the hotels' opinion changed over time. The price-comparison search engines became hubs, taking over all of the industry's booking traffic. Hotels realized that they had to pay these search engines if they wanted to be visible to consumers. The hotels' opinion of the search engines soured. Don't want to pay the search engines? OK, then you will have no customers. So the hotels pay to be listed and they pay a fee for each booking made on the search engines. Finally, who has the relationship with the consumer? The hotel does not. What does all of this mean? Prices are imposed by the search engine and profit margins are captured by the search engine. With so much at stake, the French multinational hotel group Accor has recently announced that they will invest EUR 225 million in it digital strategy over the course of the next five years, in an effort to "reinvent the client experience." Price-comparison search engines have focused mainly on B2C industries thus far, but, as we write this book, the first B2B ones are appearing. Let's prepare for a new revolution.

The Laughing Cow: When traditional players are faster than digital barbarians at customer relationship

The famous French cheesemaker Bel Group (the manufacturer and distributor of the Laughing Cow, Babybel, Kiri, Leerdammer, and Boursin brands) is very active with regard to digital innovation. The first of the company that were affected were accounting and receiving, followed by ordering, production planning, and logistics. In parallel, the Bel Group built an attractive, interactive website. The company's product development team was highly

Innovation Intelligence 125

involved in the effort. The company has even used its website to solicit active feedback of customers; the product development team continues to work with customers of the Apericube product. Bel is one of the few cheese companies today that are driving innovation by collaboration with a social network of customers. There is more to come in the future: one day, cheeses will have radio-frequency identification (RFID) tags that allow automatic dispatching and communication with the refrigerator. In the future, your home refrigerator will most likely be connected to Internet, enabling easy ordering but also providing companies like Bel with information about their customers.

Apple has recently announced that the SIM card for future generations of the iPhone will be embedded. What does this mean? That Apple wants to save space in the iPhone? Yes, but it also means that the SIM card will soon be owned exclusively by phone carriers. In other words, Apple will soon play a role similar to that of a price-comparison search engine, enabling its customers to switch, in almost real time, between phone carriers in order to obtain the lowest price for a given service.

In 2014, Google acquired Nest Labs, a 200-employee company that makes smart thermostats, for $3.2 billion. Panic ensued among the major players in the energy sector. Yes, Google has deep pockets and it has acquired many companies, but $3.2 billion is a lot of money. Why did Google make this acquisition? It followed the same strategy as digital barbicans do in any sectors: forging a relationship with the consumer by offering a Trojan horse (a free service, a free product, or just something fun). Why smart thermostats? If consumers use Google's smart thermostats, Google knows when the consumers are at home, how they use energy, what our habits are, and so forth. Armed with all of that new information, Google's next step is obvious: provide new services to help consumers optimize their energy consumption. They capture the relationship that consumers previously had with energy providers, along with the associated profit margin. The energy providers are being

126   Chapter 4. Commoditization in a digital world

either commoditized or, even worse, disintermediate.

> An analysis of the major innovation waves through-
> out history shows that their curves appear very sim-
> ilar to one another. They each begin with a sci-
> entific revolution that leads to new technologies.
> Then comes the creative synthesis: the whole soci-
> ety (engineers, entrepreneurs, artists, and so forth)
> integrates these technologies. With regard to the
> digital wave, this is exactly where we are: after a
> technology-centered period, we are now entering
> the creative-synthesis period. Information technol-
> ogy is not such a new concept. Although the first
> computer is generally attributed to the polymath
> Charles Babbage in the early nineteenth century,
> the principle of modern digital computers was first
> described by Alan Turing in his seminal 1936 arti-
> cle. The digital wave is not limited to Internet tech-
> nologies. More than twenty-five digital-technology
> fields have been identified. They are all evolving
> extremely rapidly.
> **Based on remarks by Marc Giget at a confer-
> ence**

4.3.2 Digital innovation: reshuffling the cards

Digital technology is quite different from most of the earlier technologies that contributed to the grand catalog. As such, it is taking by
surprise many of industrial players. Let's examine the aspects of digital
technology that are changing so dramatically the innovation process:

Very low entry cost

Compared to the earlier technologies that drove innovation a few
decades ago, digital technology is very affordable. Beginning a devel-

Innovation Intelligence   127

opment project based on digital technology costs little – with a few desktop computers and a reliable Internet connection, your development team is flying. The capital expenditure can be reduced to nearly nothing, because most of the equipment can be rented and the cloud offers considerable computing and storage capacity.

Very low risk

The risk we are discussing here is the combination of the probability of failure and the cost of the project. Such innovation risk is much lower for the digital sphere than for previous technologies. The probability of success, however, is not necessarily higher for digital ventures than for other types of ventures. The success rate is similar to that for in traditional innovation. The difference lies in the amount of money that must be invested in a digital venture up-front. This smaller investment, less money at risk, is what makes venture capital firms so fond of digital innovation.

Focus on service

Digital technology is about information, and information is brain food. Customers are very fond of this aspect of a product and they like the control and awareness provided by information. As we have already discussed, products are being transformed into bundles of functions and sometimes even into service packages. Digital technology has entered the grand catalog at the perfect time; it provides an efficient way to add a layer of service-related features to products. Most of the recent disruptive innovations of the digital wave are services. Instead of buying CDs, you now get a full music experience. Instead of renting a car, you now get a full transportation experience. And the list goes on. Digital barbarians focus on the human experience. They reach out to individuals to offer the best services. They disintermediate traditional players and capture the profit margins. Digital barbarians are reshuffling the "cards" of value chains at an incredible speed.

128 Chapter 4. Commoditization in a digital world

Easy market entry

Launching a digital product or service does not require building a sales network or educating of army of salespeople and skilled workers. It can be done by simply using a laptop computer to create a web site. Although creating the desired buzz is not easy, the cost of launching the product or service is very low. Furthermore, a digital offering can be launched as a working prototype when it is not yet finished. Most physical products would entail a high cost of recall, but digital offers have no such barrier. Repairs and improvements can be made while the product is flying. In fact, an experienced digital expert can make such changes in real time, benefitting from immediate market feedback.

Big Data as a secondary benefit

Nonphysical items like data and knowledge can be used without being destroyed. Most digital projects collect data while providing whatever service they are designed for. Such data is accumulated, and experience has shown that this massive amount of data (known as Big Data) contains valuable information. The data could include statistics on the reasons for a component breakage, the consumer habits of a segment of the population, you name it. Exploiting the value of Big Data is at the heart of most digital industries. The associated business models are not yet well defined, however.

Faster, faster, faster!

The digital economy is moving at an incredible speed. Development time and time to market are an order of magnitude shorter than traditional industry was accustomed to. As digital becomes the driver of the pace in an increasing number of sectors, the sudden change of response time is taking by surprise many players who have not yet adapted their corporate cultures and organizations.

The speed associated with the digital economy has spurred the entire economy. Digital-driven companies respond rapidly and grow rapidly. Table 4.2 shows the top-ten fastest-growing companies in the United States between 2011 and 2014; they all experienced growth

Innovation Intelligence

Type	Company	Growth (factor)	Rate	2014 Revenue	Business
B2C	Fuhu	x 1600		$196M	Cloud-based services and software for children
B2C	Quest Nutrition	x 570		$83M	Protein bars and other healthy foods, as well as an online community
B2B	Reliant Asset Management	x 550		$85M	Online rental of modular space solutions
B2B	Superfish	x 260		$35M	Visual search and image recognition
B2B	Acacia Communications	x 200		$78M	Fast telecommunications hardware and software
B2C	Provider Power	x 200		$138M	Residential electricity supply with an online portal
B2B	Crescendo Bioscience	x 180		$27M	Diagnostic tools for use by rheumatologists
B2C	Plexus Worldwide	x 160		$160M	Diet food sold on the Internet
B2C	Vacasa	x 160		$26M	Online vacation rental property management
B2B	Go Energies	x 160		$33M	Online fuel management

Table 4.2: The top ten fastest-growing companies in the United States, 2011 – 2014

of more than a factor of one hundred during the three-year period. The companies are all still relatively small; such incredible growth is impossible with a large base. Still, each company generated revenue of $25M to $200M in 2014. Except for one company, Crescendo Bioscience, in the advanced medical service business, all of them are in some way part of the digital economy. Half of the companies are B2B, disproving the idea that digital business can be only developed on the consumer mass market.

The stars of the economy are digital. In 2014, among the top five market capitalizations on Wall Street were Apple, Microsoft, and Google, elbowing their way to success alongside major oil companies and other industry giants. Google was incorporated in 1998 – it was a fast rise!

Again, we emphasize that, in the digital world, the success rate for innovation projects is the same as it was for historical innovation projects. Ironically, digital hype may be reducing the probability of success. Indeed, there is a growing crowd of candidates working on digital innovation projects; the combination of buzz generated by success stories and the goodwill of venture-capital firms is attractive. Yet, the digital industry is demonstrating, also very quickly, that the rule of the game is winner take all. With only one winner among so many contenders, maybe the odds are not so good in the digital industry. Not so long ago, around the year 2000, hasty speculators created the Internet bubble. We may be living in a softer and slower rebound of the same bubble. The future will tell us.

Xavier Niel: the digital barbarian who disrupted traditional telecommunications operators

As of 2011 all telecommunications operators had very complex offerings. Aware that there was a strong risk of a digital barbarian entering the market with a much simpler and cheaper offer, the traditional operators all tried to simplify, without success. All of

Innovation Intelligence 131

the complex offerings were being developed by poor management. Some of the executives had good intuition, but there were too many other people around the table for decisions. Then the digital barbarian, Xavier Niel, entered. With his company Free Mobile, he simplified the offering, like Steve Jobs did when he returned to Apple in 1998. Free Mobile differed from the traditional operators in three main ways: focused resources, a simple offering from the customer perspective, and lower prices. At Free Mobile, decisions are made by small groups and command chains are short; there is hardly any middle management. As a result, top management cannot ask the rest of the team to implement much complexity. This structure and approach yields simple solutions and their associated lower cost, which was Xavier Niel's objective.

4.3.3 Global shortage of digital skills

We cannot entire blame traditional industry for the difficulties those companies are experiencing in the digital wave that can properly be called the digital tsunami. In fact, these traditional companies are trying to adapt but are encountering severe challenges.

First, they must adapt not only to new technologies but to an entirely new world of management. To ensure faster response times, command chains must be shorter. R&D must be closer to and more integrated with marketing. Feedback from customers and users must be the product or service almost in real time. Projects must be managed by multidisciplinary teams. Agility is key. As we will see in chapter 6, large companies that want to gain such agility for disruptive innovations tend to create dedicated structures separate from the rest of the company. We will revisit this notion of internal, but separate, innovation labs later. Since the environment is changing constantly at an incredible speed, traditional companies are facing not one digital transformation, but a series of constant transformations. They need to reevaluate their positioning in the value chain in almost real time. Second, these traditional companies are challenged by the shortage of digital skills, a

132   Chapter 4. Commoditization in a digital world

problem faced in most countries. The UK Digital Taskforce's report *Digital Skills for Tomorrow's World*[58] published in July 2014 explains that in the United Kingdom, "as of August 2012, the digital economy accounted for 14.4% of all companies and 11% of jobs. It's not just the technology sector that needs digital skills but all sectors." The need for digital skills is expected to continue to increase significantly in the coming years. Despite a number of alarming reports, most countries are not ready to meet the demand for these skills. As Isabelle André, head of digital activities for the French newspaper Le Monde, told us, "the problem is that young professionals in IT find it more exciting to work at Google than at Le Monde." The skills shortage is not so much at the young entry level. The critical skills shortage is at the executive level, among people who need a combination of expertise in digital technology and sound business background. These decision makers need to gain an understanding of the digital wave's potential, the fruitful, innovative options it could open up for their companies. Some people have this combination of digital knowledge and business experience, but most of them prefer to live in the new economy, in companies that can experience double-digit growth, and it is difficult for companies in traditional industries to attract them. This shortage of traditional-industry executives who have digital skills can also be partially attributed to passive reluctance from the executives who are already in place; they remember fondly the good old days and are not prepared to accept that the value of their traditional business is being diluted by the new opportunities presented by the new economy. Remembering is one thing; living in the past rather than not reacting in the present is a sign of slow and certain decay.

Recall that we mentioned the electricity wave as an earlier innovation similar to the digital wave. There is, however, a significant difference between the two. Evolution is taking place much more rapidly today, in part because the capital expenditure associated with digital innovation is much less than what was needed for designing appliances.

Point of view of an expert in the digital transformation

This section was written by Philippe Letellier. Philippe was R&D General Manager at Technicolor before becoming the Innovation Director of the Institut Mines-Télécom. He is currently Digital Fellow at Presans, Vice Chairman of the ITEA3 EUREKA program, and is launching an innovation accelerator. His perspective is balanced between technology and business.

Digital, smart, data, software, services, command, and control are words that express the revolution business world. Key to this digital transition is that it also effects our daily life: entertainment, health, energy, transportation, tourism, and on and on.

Digital is valuing data. It starts with data acquisition, data transmission via networks, and ends with data interpretation. It includes production chain automation and user communities. Step-by-step, all businesses are generating data about their processes and about customer usage of their products and services.

This data has tremendous value, because it follows along the production, distribution, and use of the product or service. It enables the company to redesign the product or service, for enhanced features and quality management, by a continuous, real-time adaptation. Digital is a means for all businesses to optimize their processes and become therefore more efficient and more profitable. Germany has taken the lead in this movement by setting up the Industry 4.0 program. The target of the program is to support German industry by helping companies to interconnect all of their machines to facilitate more agile production processes and improved quality management. This revolution, initiated in

134	Chapter 4. Commoditization in a digital world

2013 at CeBIT, the world's largest and most international computer exposition, intends to put Germany on the top of industrial countries despite its very high labor cost.

Access to digital data is also a way for a company to reinvent its business model. For example, Michelin was selling tires, a pure product. The company had optimized the design of its product, and its relationship with its customer had been stable for many years. Michelin has been able to take the risk of reinventing itself by no longer selling the product alone but instead as part of a bundle that includes a service component. The transformation from selling a product to providing a service bundle changes the entire company. Data exploitation is the tool that can help a company make this kind of transition. The company must analyze its product, gathering and managing the acquired data to ensure that the product provides the quality of service required by its customers. This movement from product to service is inexorable. Companies that do not make the transition will be attacked on the cost front by the countries that have low labor costs and on the composition of the offering (quality, features, and service) by companies such as the participants in the Industry 4.0 program. The digital wave is not a choice but rather an opportunity, which can become a killing threat to companies that don't move.

Digital data also provides an opportunity to continuously invent new businesses. Google, Apple, Facebook, and Amazon.com (GAFA) analyze industries looking for any that generate good profit margins but have weak relationships with their customers (for example, music, video, banking, retail, telecommunications, utilities, and other traditional industries have been attacked by these digital giants). GAFA focus on user demands and reinvent a high-value service for the user. They then often provide this service to the user for free in order to acquire the associated data. Because they have a rich understanding of the users, they are then in a good position to become intermediaries, providing customers

Innovation Intelligence

with access to the more traditional industries in exchange for a portion of the profit margin (such as the 30% revenue share earned by Apple's iTunes Store) and oftentimes even setting the price of the product or service such as streaming a song or owning an e-book (note, however, the price battle between Hachette and Amazon, which was settled in November 2014). Such a business transformation represents both a risk and an opportunity – at least, for the companies that take the lead. This transition is not a single step but rather a series of revolutions. By enabling companies to focus on users and gather information about them, digital opens the door to any kind of imagination. By tracking and analyzing user demands, creative people can develop new offerings tailored to the user feedback. For example, Pascal Nègre, CEO of Universal Music France, explains that the company is managing its fourth digital revolution in recent years: piracy, ringtones, the iTunes Store, and now streaming. The music production company hopes it has found the solution after experiencing a 65% decrease in value in less than fifteen years!

Digital transition is associated with a major social trend. Companies were accustomed to advertising their products to consumers who were waiting for this information so that they could consume even greater quantities. The reality of this digital era is the proliferation of communication channels. The Internet gave people the opportunity, and therefore the desire, to access information from various sources: the community effect. In some case, the customers are now more informed than the sales associates. These community tools have demonstrated an important consumer demand: people want to have deeper relationship with a product, service, or the company providing it. An advertisement is no longer sufficient. This customer preference is clear to retailers when their customers have already searched on Internet for information on their products before going to the store. It is also clear to companies that no longer have to be the lone voice boasting about

136 Chapter 4. Commoditization in a digital world

their brand; they can now foster direct communication among consumers on the brand's social networks (Facebook, Twitter, and so forth). The consumer demand for a deeper relationship forces companies to reinvent their communication strategies. Doing so often strengthens the value of the brand.

Digital is characterized by continuous innovation and access to the crowd. Some of the digital barbarians have become digital giants, pervading society. Google was founded in 1998; Apple, the most profitable company of all the time, was founded in 1976; Facebook, with more than a billion users, was founded in 2004. The digital transition is not a game we can just check on later. It is a challenge which can affect all businesses – and, indeed, everyday life – now, and when a company's position is taken by a digital barbarian, it is already too late. From a technology point of view, we are confronted by a series of waves: analog to digital information, compression, digital transmission and watermarking, pattern recognition, matching and statistics, service bundling, cloud computing, Big Data, high-performance computing, and real-time computing. We cannot master all of these new technologies. That is why platforms, open source, and reusability are so crucial in the digital era. They allow companies to follow and catch up to the technology waves. In this new world, the key is speed. The developer community has created new tools around reusability, agility, and test automation that enable companies to deliver continuously new versions of their products and services. In this digital world is has become more and more difficult to follow the traditional V-model process, because the specifications themselves cannot be stable if no one by the market itself knows exactly what the product should be.

The most recent hacker attack on Sony (data on forty-five thousand employees was published), the hacker attack on Target (it cost the company $1 billion and the CEO his job), and many other cyber attacks have put pressure on companies' security and

Innovation Intelligence 137

opened the door to additional investment in R&D in pursuit of more effective methods of cybersecurity.

The digital economy has spurred innovation by start-up firms. The digital giants that have had incredible success were created as start-ups. In addition, many successful start-ups have been integrated into more traditional companies and have continued to innovate from the position of insider (this is particularly true inside companies like Cisco Systems and Facebook, as well as Dassault Systems, a French software company). Many of the large industrial companies are now creating their own venture capital firms, incubators, or accelerators (examples include Orange, Alcatel-Lucent, Novartis, and Qualcomm) to manage innovation inside their own structures. It is not always easy for them to attract the key people, since such people typically have entrepreneurial spirit and a desire for freedom. This movement is not a cycle but rather a structural shift. Innovation requires freedom and risk. Because the digital economy has made innovation possible for everybody, the large players must adapt in order to remain on the forefront of innovation.

Digital transition is a risk for a sleeping company, but it is an incredible opportunity for an agile one – it opens up opportunities to reinvent the business and thus create new value.

Be optimistic – innovate!

4.4 Conclusion

This was a heavy chapter, wasn't it?

We have seen an old megatrend, knowledge growth, taking a runaway acceleration and exploding due to the digital innovation wave. We have seen knowledge becoming commoditized. Open innovation has become the natural approach.

We have gained an understanding of how this faster pace is also affecting innovation cycle time and product commoditization. The defensive path for product developers consists of permanently providing extra features in every product. This is possible thanks to the great potential offered by the ever-expanding technology toolbox. As a result, products have become increasingly complex, and now some are transitioning from products to total service packages. The innovation genius of today is no longer in the creation of basic knowledge. Instead, it is in the intelligent assembly of existing technology "bricks" into products and services that meet and adapt to the changing needs of users.

We have focused on the repercussions of the digital innovation wave's loud, forceful splash. Nearly everybody will get soaked. Digital barbarians can insert themselves between many traditional companies and their customers. Digital technology is a fantastic tool, presenting a superb opportunity. Traditional businesses will have to learn (quickly) and change their processes to become leaner, more agile, and faster.

In chapter 5, we will explore how experts can help traditional business to adapt.

Chapter 5
Expert and expertise

Happy, the man who finds sweet journey's end,
Like Ulysses, or he of the Golden Fleece,
Returning home, well-travelled, wise, to Greece:
To live life out, among his own again!

JOACHIM DU BELLAY

In Short. . . Experts are individuals who have made a personal choice to master a field of knowledge, taking about ten years to reach a high level, and two hours per day thereafter to stay at the top. We distinguish between the silo diggers, those who focus on one field, and the chipmunks, those who make multiple, interconnected burrows. Chipmunks are more adapted to our time. An expert's key value lies in his or her network; it extends reach capability, and enlarges coverage. The role of an expert has changed over the past sixty years. Today, the trend is for experts to be knowledge scouts, capable of outlining roadmaps and scanning world knowledge to identify interesting knowledge bricks that can serve a company's innovation projects. Due to rapid technological change and proliferation, the trend will increasingly move toward outsourcing of expertise. As

Chapter 5. Expert and expertise

such, companies must develop meta-expertise, becoming expert on experts, how to find them, coach them, be understood by them, and understand them.

In Wikipedia, an expert would be defined as "someone widely recognized as a reliable source of technique or skill whose faculty for judging or deciding rightly, justly, or wisely is accorded authority and status by peers or the public in a specific well-distinguished domain." For our purposes, let's limit the definition to the domain of knowledge, excluding such highly respectable people as musical instrument masters, magician virtuosos, and golf champions. An expert masters a piece of knowledge and is often an important mediator for the process of introducing this knowledge into the design of innovation.

In this chapter, we examine the two types of characteristics that could be considered necessary for an expert: the individual (personality and knowledge) and the collective (knowledge transmission, corporate culture, and professional network).

5.1 Definition of expert and scope of this work

K. Anders Ericsson,[59] professor of psychology at Florida State University, is an expert on experts. He defines an expert as a person who, in resolving problems related to his or her field, will:

- Provide consistently superior answers compared to his or her peers. The word *superior* implies that an expert has reached a very high level of knowledge and agility with the topic. As we will see, this also implies hard, constant work. An expert is, by necessity, a person who is willing to dedicate a significant amount of time and energy to learning and mastering a field of knowledge.
- Produce concrete results. Concrete results are key. It is not sufficient to perform a brilliant analysis of a situation to be an expert. An expert leaves a trace: the situation is different after the expert has provided input, the situation has progressed, the

Innovation Intelligence 141

degree of uncertainty has decreased, or some of the potential solutions have been considered and discarded.

Ericsson and his peers include in their analysis all types of experts, individuals who have achieved a high level of mastery in intellectual and physical art, such as cello virtuosos and talented surgeons. They all have in common the same long, never-ending path of learning.

However, the subject of this book is innovation. Experts bridge the gap between an innovation project and a field of advanced knowledge. The dialogue between an expert and an innovation team is, as described in C-K analysis (see Chapter 3), a purely intellectual game of ping-pong. As a result, we will not include in our discussion highly skilled individuals who express their art in a solely physical manner.

As a complement to Ericsson's two-pronged definition of an expert, we can follow Olga Lelebina's detailed description of an expert's output in his or her field of excellence:[60]

- Solutions: proposing the best solutions, faster and with more accuracy than do other individuals
- Spotting problems: efficient in detecting problems and determining their causes
- Qualitative analysis: focused on qualitative analysis and novel points of view
- Monitoring: acute observers, thanks to their error-detection capacity
- Strategy: efficient in selecting the best strategy for solving a problem
- Cognitive effort: extracting key messages from complex knowledge with less effort

However, this list of virtues has a corresponding list of limitations:

- Breadth: limited to the specific field of expertise
- Presumption: possibly overconfident in his or her knowledge
- Details: possibly neglectful of details, preferring a high-level perspective
- Context: performance may depend on context
- Rigidity: possibly stiff in manner, especially when moving out

| 142 | Chapter 5. Expert and expertise |

of his or her comfort zone
- Non-experts: may have difficulty in relating to non-expert members of the team
- Horizon limit: may have difficulty in thinking outside the box of his or her field

Let's summarize with a quotation:[61] "Nobody's perfect."

Given this book's focus on companies' innovation projects, we will also exclude from our analysis our society's use of experts for a service typically called *testimony*. An expert is often called upon for testimony when a judge or a political leader needs to support a decision with deep knowledge:

- Should we evacuate the town near an awakening volcano?
- What should the leaders of the town have done to limit the consequences of a flash flood?
- What is a reasonable estimate of the financial damage suffered by this arson victim?
- Does this product really infringe on this patent?

The list of situations in which experts are called upon for testimony is long. In many cases, the expertise is being used as a political shield by the decision maker. We exclude testimony from our analysis in this book, because its purpose is not innovation.

Indeed, experts involved in testimony must source that testimony from their most solid knowledge, facts, and scientific laws that are proven and accepted by their peers. In contrast, experts who deal with innovation are welcome and, in fact, encouraged to explore the nascent fringes of their knowledge and to take some risks in inferring the most probable consequences of their observations.

5.2 Becoming an expert requires a strange mindset

Experts are not born

Benjamin Bloom was a famous educational psychologist who taught at the University of Chicago. In his later years, his research focused on the education of children, particularly those who develop exceptional talents. He performed a very deep analysis of the early phase of creating a future expert. "Consistently and overwhelmingly, the evidence showed that experts are always made, not born."[62]

Nobody knows what trait in a future expert triggers the quest for knowledge. As demonstrated by Benjamin Bloom and his research team, there is no "gene" for expertise. We tend to think of experts as similar to collectors, but instead of accumulating postcards or luxury vintage cars they collect knowledge. There is no between a specific personality trait and the identity of a collector; the same is true for the identity of an expert. We know that about 30% of the population are collectors in some fashion (and a small percentage are compulsive hoarders). The fraction of the population who have dedicated themselves and pursued a calling for expertise is probably smaller, perhaps 10% (note that this estimate varies depending on the definition of *consistently*. Bloom also demonstrated that neither sex nor IQ was significantly corrected with vocation or success in expertise. Brain agility is certainly of great help in achieving superior expertise, but it is apparently not a determinant of an expert's initial vocation.

A future expert does not decide suddenly one day to focus on a specific field and acquire knowledge until achieving mastery. Rather, the future expert undergoes a gradual journey, beginning with small, unnoticeable events in which the reward of knowing generates more interest. A virtuous, self-reinforcing loop can eventually lead to the

144   Chapter 5. Expert and expertise

birth of a novice expert.

Although no rationale can be attached to the triggering mechanism for an expert's calling, environment can play a role as either a stimulator or inhibitor. In most cases, support by family, colleagues, or a benevolent tutor plays a strong role in the creation of an expert. Counterexamples, in which experts developed in very adverse conditions, do exist, however. A famous case is the criminal Robert Stroud. While serving a life sentence in U.S. prisons, he managed to feed and save baby sparrows; he gradually became a respected ornithologist. Stroud's interest in learning was probably compulsive; indeed, when he was transferred to Alcatraz Federal Penitentiary and forbidden to continue rearing birds, he shifted his interest to law and wrote a titled, *Looking Outward: A History of the U.S. Prison System from Colonial Times to the Formation of the Bureau of Prisons.*[63]

K. Anders Ericsson wrote about the making of an expert: "The journey to truly superior performance is neither for the faint of heart nor for the impatient. The development of genuine expertise requires struggle, sacrifice, and honest, often painful self-assessment."[64]

What is the personal reward that justifies such effort and dedication? Could it be curiosity and the satisfaction of a desire to know? Could it be the need to create a virtual security blanket? We do not know, but it is probably a mixture of both of these plus other ingredients that we leave to experts in psychology.[65] What counts is the result: experts do exist, and some of them reach a superior level of mastery in their fields of knowledge.

5.2.1 Concentration, self-training, and self-education

As the would-be expert accumulates knowledge, he or she gradually exceeds the knowledge level of his close environment, and in order to progress further, must learn from more distant repositories. The barrier to doing so is considerably lower today, due to the reach of the Internet, than it was historically. Previously, novice experts who were in the process of accumulating the knowledge to become full-fledged experts had

Innovation Intelligence

to struggle and be creative in ways to access superior knowledge. The eighteenth century so-called philosophers, who actually spanned many fields of knowledge, traveled on season-long journeys and exchanged letters via horse post. The young Michael Faraday, who became one of the best experimentalists of his time, had very little formal education. He was an apprentice in a bookbinding shop; he grew as a scientist by reading the books he was supposed to bind.

Ericsson points to a critical mechanism that enables further progression when an expert is already at a superior level: deliberate practice coupled with systematic self-evaluation. A high-level expert may find it difficult to evaluate his or her own performance, however. There are no obvious benchmarks. A scientist can perform a self-evaluation by reading a research paper about a new topic in the field and determining whether he or she understands it or, even better, whether it inspires him with new derivations. Even so, maintaining objectivity for this self-evaluation is challenging. In any case, it is obvious that the acquisition of expertise is a never-ending endeavor. In any field, an expert must continue to progress, otherwise the expert is going backwards, falling behind. There are many examples of famous experts who, despite the fact that they were already at the summit of their field, challenged themselves in new areas, such as playing many chess games simultaneously or struggling to play a violin with fewer strings.

It is fair to assert that personality traits such as introversion and extroversion are not correlated with a craving for expertise, which means that among mature experts such traits are about equally represented. We do observe, however, that those two personality types tend to result in somewhat different patterns of cultivating expertise. We illustrate the difference between these two approaches by using an analogy of digging animals; this analogy is provided in figure 5.2. An introverted expert will tend to push expertise deeper and deeper and become trapped in a silo. An extroverted expert, typically driven primarily by curiosity, detours, changes topics, and, if talented, creates a number of burrows that are interconnected by a network of galleries, as chipmunks do. A deep digger is usually among the best experts in

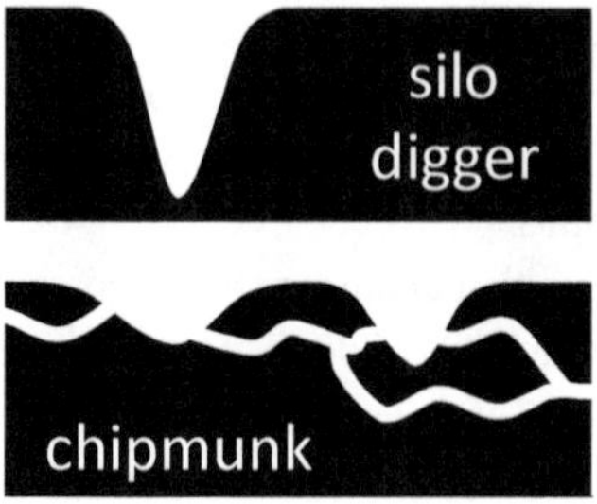

Chapter 5. Expert and expertise

Figure 5.2: Silo digger vs. chipmunk. These illustrations contrast the two main approaches to cultivating expertise. A silo digger digs deeply in their specialty but tends to lose contact with the rest of the world. A chipmunk[a] builds a network of burrows, each burrow a specialty; although each burrow is shallower than one that would be dug by a silo digger, the chipmunk's burrows are all interconnected.

---

[a]The zoology of thinkers was explored by the philosopher Isaiah Berlin in his essay, "The Hedgehog and the Fox."[66] For Berlin, hedgehogs have narrow but deep knowledge, while foxes pick and combine from many places.

that sole field, but is less likely to be useful in an innovation project unless he or she has the precise knowledge required. A chipmunk's expertise may not be as deep as that of a deep digger, but it covers a larger territory. Because a chipmunk can make connections and guide the search for knowledge across a wider territory, more fields, this type of expert is the partner of choice in innovation teams.

Both types of experts must, in any case, continuously working to improve their expertise. This discipline, this permanent dedication of time and energy to knowledge, is the main difference between experts and ordinary people. The happier experts make a living from their expertise and skills, but there are many others: such as experts in botany who use their skills only to cultivate their own gardens, banking clerks who, at night, become masters of obscure art, and retirees who become expert in medieval history.

Innovation Intelligence   147

Everything about nothing

"An expert is someone who knows more
and more about less and less, until eventually he knows everything about nothing."
This anonymous quotation is repeated at
many occasions by action-oriented people
who are irritated by experts when their knowledge does not provide a straightforward response to an urgent need. To further
batter the expert's ego, let us also quote Winston Churchill, who
said that "an expert is the one who complicates simplicity." These
quotations provide good material for reflection by experts.

5.2.2 Maturity of an expert

Ericsson's publications and similar scientific analyses have estimated
the typical amount of time required for the making of a high-level
expert: approximately ten years. Some of this time can be put in during
the novice expert's basic education. To be clear, ten years is not the
end of the expert's development, but rather the moment where the
expert has reached a sufficiently high standing. In his book *Outliers*,
Malcolm Gladwell quotes[67] the impressive number of 10,000 hours
of practice to reach a superior level. Assuming the novice expert is
enjoying life outside education and work to some degree, that figure is
roughly equivalent to ten years.

Maintenance of expertise

When the expert has reached this high level, the effort must be continued by permanent updating, enlargement, and refinement of the secured
knowledge.

For the expert, applying expertise in daily practice is not sufficient
to maintain its standing. It has been proven that experienced doctors
are more likely to overlook rare symptoms or diseases than are junior
doctors. An experienced doctor may have never encountered this

rare case, so the relevant knowledge was gradually stored in deeper and deeper memory until it faded away. A true expert would act differently, always evaluating and challenging the completeness of his or her knowledge. One humorous example is Dr. House.[68] A misanthropic character in the television series *House*, he is brilliant, obsessed by his own expertise, and, here's the kicker, severely lacking in empathy.

Studies on the maintenance effort required of experts were done by Ericsson and his peers. The result of their research was an estimate of two hours per day. That is an enormous amount of effort, but the estimate is likely accurate. An expert must pay this price to remain at the top. As we will see, employers are not happy with this aspect of expertise. However, what is most impressive is that experts are gladly willing to pay that price – this is what makes them different from ordinary people.

The thrill of changing topic

Now let's consider an expert who has already spent ten years mastering a topic and, for some reason, wants to change focus and engage in a new knowledge conquest. If the new topic has some minimum relationship to the former one, the knowledge-acquisition time is considerably less than ten more years. There are several reasons for this. One reason relates to learning agility. When first becoming an expert, one also learns about learning. Already having been through the journey of mastering a field, the expert has already progressed along the experience curve in terms of learning how to learn, so is better at learning. Hence, learning in the new field will be easier and faster. Second, part of the making of an expert is the development of personal discipline, both for concentration and for continuous benchmarking; having already developed discipline, the expert can simply apply it to the new endeavor. Finally, even if the new topic has little relationship to the former one, any common basis between them can be recycled. As explained by Sternberg,[69] while mastering a first field, an expert develops metacognitive skills. For example, an expert knows in advance approximately how much

Innovation Intelligence   149

time it will take to make perform a calculation or to read carefully a book. The typical amount of time an expert spends in reaching a decent level of expertise in a third or fourth topic is typically closer to five years and possibly even less than five years if the expert stops cultivating the former topics. Of this book's authors, one of us is a serial topic switcher (actually, both of us are switchers, but one has switched fewer times, simply because he is younger).

Surprisingly, plenty of experts have changed topics at some point in their lives; in some cases, they were not even forced to do so by external influences. The main reason for the switch was probably the strong curiosity that drives most experts. When a topic has been deeply explored, the satisfaction of learning further about it becomes slow and uncertain, while another topic may offer more opportunities to discover intellectually rewarding new concepts.

This step of changing topic is a key step for an expert, because for a certain period, a few years, the expert is vulnerable, having voluntarily become an apprentice to experts far superior in the new topic. Some experts give up in the face of such risk; they will be deep diggers. Switching to another topic, then, may be, what makes chipmunks. They enjoy the thrill of being vulnerable during the switch. Selecting a topic somewhat connected to the previous one provides some degree of security, but even more reassuring is the expert's learning agility.

Polymath

The word *polymath*, of Greek origin, it is not found in all English dictionaries. Even less common is the equivalent word *polyhistor*. Both words designate a person who has superior knowledge in a multiplicity of domains. Polymaths, able to switch easily from one domain to another, have built up expertise in several fields. Being a polymath was a standard for educated people in several eras, first in Ancient Greece, then during the fantastic era of the Umayyad and Abbasid Caliphates stretching from the seventeenth century to the eleventh century, and finally in Europe at the onset of the Age of Enlightenment. Figure 5.4 provides some historical examples of polymaths.

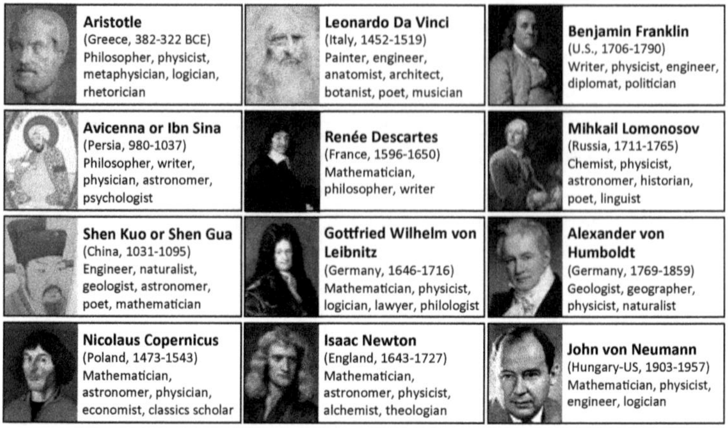

Chapter 5. Expert and expertise

Aristotle (Greece, 382-322 BCE) Philosopher, physicist, metaphysician, logician, rhetorician	**Leonardo Da Vinci** (Italy, 1452-1519) Painter, engineer, anatomist, architect, botanist, poet, musician	**Benjamin Franklin** (U.S., 1706-1790) Writer, physicist, engineer, diplomat, politician
Avicenna or Ibn Sina (Persia, 980-1037) Philosopher, writer, physician, astronomer, psychologist	**Renée Descartes** (France, 1596-1650) Mathematician, philosopher, writer	**Mihkail Lomonosov** (Russia, 1711-1765) Chemist, physicist, astronomer, historian, poet, linguist
Shen Kuo or Shen Gua (China, 1031-1095) Engineer, naturalist, geologist, astronomer, poet, mathematician	**Gottfried Wilhelm von Leibnitz** (Germany, 1646-1716) Mathematician, physicist, logician, lawyer, philologist	**Alexander von Humboldt** (Germany, 1769-1859) Geologist, geographer, physicist, naturalist
Nicolaus Copernicus (Poland, 1473-1543) Mathematician, astronomer, physician, economist, classics scholar	**Isaac Newton** (England, 1643-1727) Mathematician, astronomer, physicist, alchemist, theologian	**John von Neumann** (Hungary-US, 1903-1957) Mathematician, physicist, engineer, logician

Figure 5.4: A selection of famous polymaths throughout history.

Many people believe that polymaths do not exist today. This is false. Polymaths still exist. For example, Umberto Eco, Jared Diamond, Douglas Hofstadter, and Roger Penrose have all been described as polymaths. Polymaths are definitively not ordinary people, particularly if they achieve mastery in their many domains of interest. In fact, they represent the highest level of what we call chipmunks.

In ancient and medieval times, if someone was to become a polymath, at least one artistic domain was included in the fields of interest. Either poetry or music was considered a must in China and Persia; Europe as also encouraged painting and sculpture.

While we are touching the relationship between art and expertise, we should mention the extensive research on U.S. Nobel laureates in scientific fields, which was conduction by Robert Root-Bernstein, a professor at Michigan State University.[70] He and his team studied all of these Nobel laureates from a one-hundred-year period and counted how many of them had some active interest in art. The results were then compared with those for other segments of the U.S. population. The average number of people involved in art, per capita, is about 0.3

Innovation Intelligence   151

for the U.S. population in general, 0.55 for members of the National
Academy of Sciences, and 0.95 for these Nobel laureates. We will
leave to the psychologists a debate of the direction of cause-effect
relationship. Regardless, this finding confirms the impression from
ancient polymaths: art is very interesting to minds that are prone to
become talented chipmunks.

5.3 Experts in the enterprise

5.3.1 Expert pool

Companies do care about having experts on staff. These experts are
either hired as such or subsequently developed in-house. In both cases,
an implicit value is attached to this asset, the expert. In order to properly manage and benefit from this asset, both top management and the
rest of the organization must be aware of the expert's existence. This is
very easy in small companies but increasingly difficult in larger organizations. In such cases, the first task is to identify and list the experts,
making the list available to the entire company. Indeed most companies make an effort to generate and maintain an expert-pool inventory,
which they then use to ensure a policy of performing regular valuations
of the expert pool. This expert pool, or knowledge base, is utilized for
putting out the "fires" of urgent technical crises and for contributing to
innovation efforts. From our experience, the existence of a mere list
of the experts does very little to improve internal communication in
an organization. We will return to this point when we discuss expert
networks later in this chapter.

The knowledge distribution among the experts at a company always reflects the history of the company. This is normal. Experts are
long-lasting; they contributed to the development of former products,
and they are probably still supporting them, possibly pushing incremental innovation. Moreover, due to the normal delay in knowledge
acquisition, the internal pool of experts is inevitably weighted toward
former innovation activities. This weighting of in-house experts toward
history means that, in a world of continuous and accelerating change,

152   Chapter 5. Expert and expertise

there exists a mismatch between the pool of in-house experts and the strategic avenues the company may need to consider. Such a mismatch can be managed by introducing management of the knowledge capital at a strategic level, consistent with Thomas Stewart's observation that "knowledge assets, like money or equipment, exist and are worth cultivating only in the context of strategy."[71] As the tempo of innovation beats faster and faster, the issue becomes more critical and strategic anticipation alone may not be sufficient to ensure that the company is fast and agile. Most companies today, particularly the front-runners in the innovation race, are solving the problem – at least in part – by relying on external experts.

Most expert-pool lists that we have seen have another downside: they are mainly comprised of scientists and engineers. Yet we have seen that products are becoming increasingly complex, in many cases transitioning to a service package. Therefore, innovation is dependent on not only technical experts but also experts in marketing, human resources, business development, strategic planning, legal, and so forth. Yet these non-technical typically are not listed as experts alongside the engineers. This technical-only list reflects the old way of thinking about innovation. We are not saying that one should build up an exhaustive list of experts, including those in sectors such as tax optimization or health security, but it is time for many companies to reassess the position of innovation activity in their organizations and to send a clear message to all company functions. One possibility would be to assemble a pool of experienced innovation contributors, a mix of engineers, a patent attorney, an expert in market analysis, and other non-technical experts. Stirring communication among these experts, motivating young, envious, would-be experts to join the pool, may be a good way for a company to gradually shift its culture away from the old way. We have seen spontaneous networks emerge in subgroups, usually comprised of veterans from former innovation battles, but we are not aware of a methodical application of the principle in a large corporation.

Innovation Intelligence

5.3.2 Coincidence and/or conflict of interest

> Experts create problems...
> **Hervé Arribart, former Scientific Director of Saint-Gobain**

Companies love their experts when they are key contributors to winning a superior market position. In such an environment, the fact that an expert is spending about two hours each day bettering his or her expertise is seen as a good investment. But times and priorities are changing rapidly. Let's follow, for example, an expert in mechanics, a key contributor to designing a system such as components of a piece of machinery. The expert is a hero when the parts are designed on CAD systems and during the assembly of the prototype. Then other experts enter the game. The software expert implements many lines of code for the machine. Then the process expert takes over, fine-tuning parameters and testing the machine's performance. If, as it always does, something goes wrong, the innovation team enters crisis mode, with everybody joining the brigade to fight "fires." But if the problem is the software's inability to cope with an unexpected process requirement, the mechanical expert will feel useless, and the other team members will be upset at him if they see him or her reading the proceedings from a conference on mechanical engineering. We tell this short story to illustrate a clear fact: it is impossible for a typical company organization to keep an expert at peak efficiency. In this example, the scheduling problem responsible for an expert having no assigned task can be fixed by assigning to each expert a set of projects, each project at different levels of maturity and with different degrees of urgency.

The problem becomes more serious when the company's technological demands are changing. Experts become insecure when forced to operate outside their comfort zones, the need time to acquire new expertise, and because in-house experts are employees, their salaries are fixed costs for the company. When a company's business slows or becomes unprofitable, maintaining a pool of in-house experts becomes a challenge. In that situation, experts may lose their jobs.

An observer of the interaction between technical experts and businesspeople inside companies cannot miss the love-hate relationship. The conflict comes mainly from experts having a secondary agenda. An expert's primary agenda is to serve diligently the company's purpose to the best of his or her ability. The secondary agenda is hidden: it is the continuous update of the expert's knowledge, which we discussed earlier in this chapter. Managers are perfectly aware that this extra activity, learning, is the price to the company must pay to have in-house the best possible expertise for serving its projects, but they cannot help occasionally being irritated by the balancing act. Indeed, an expert's extra activity includes some inflexible elements, such as participation in conferences. We have witnessed a crisis resulting from a scheduling conflict between a company event and an international symposium in an expert's specialization. Experts who are loyal to their employers may stint themselves with regard to continuous learning, especially conferences which provide opportunities for them to benchmark themselves against their peers in the field. If the expert decides to go to the conference, the manager will imply that the expert made the wrong choice and prioritized the secondary agenda above the primary one.

On the other hand, from the perspective of an entrepreneur, an in-house expert is slow: slow to acquire new expertise and perhaps not interesting it making a burrow in a different field. (Recall that the tedious effort of self learning requires that the expert have a real appetite for the new knowledge.) Experts can be rigid, slow, and unreliable when change is required, and businesspeople do not like it.

This love-hate relationship has existed for ages; still, the expert and the entrepreneur together make a winning pair when they develop mutual respect and a good understanding of their respective roles. Many successful start-ups were and are driven by such pairs. Some of those pairs are famous, including Bill Hewlett and Dave Packard, the founders of Hewlett-Packard, and Steve Wozniak and Steve Jobs, the cofounders of Apple.

5.3.3 Human resource management challenges

Experts are generally difficult to position in a company's organizational chart. They have made the choice to cherish knowledge, and they are consistent in that behavior. In most cases, this choice is not compatible with managerial responsibilities. However, this statement is distance generalization; there are exceptions. Industrial history abounds with examples of former technical experts who became excellent managers.

Social pressure is very high for experts to continue their careers by climbing the managerial ladder. However, a significant proportion of brilliant experts are not willing or able to become managers. The vocation for expertise is sometimes correlated to either fear of responsibilities or weakness in leadership. Human resource (HR) management experts have addressed this problem. Among the many solutions proposed, the dual ladder, a system introduced in the United States in the late 1970s, has had some success. As explained by Rick Lamont,[72] there are clear upsides to the dual ladder system, mainly that it provides talent experts with a career path. However, the results of such a system range from fair to disappointing, and the downsides of the concept are well explained in a rather old paper by Thomas Allen and Ralph Katz.[73] Whatever complex HR management approach is used, no company has yet invented a magical solution to the problem. Managing experts remains difficult; it is straightforward and rewarding when their assigned tasks are within their expertise, but it may become as difficult as herding cats when the company's priorities are only marginally related to those of the experts.

We recommend addressing the problem up-front. At the time of hiring, select experts who have shown signs of being or becoming chipmunks. This can be done as part of the interview: discuss the expert's fields of interest, and gauge his or her response when presented with a challenge outside those fields. Experts in psychology may be able to help in designing and formalizing a screening process for young experts.

A complementary way to treat the problem at the source is to man-

156 Chapter 5. Expert and expertise

age anticipatively the experts' interests. For example, the company's most valuable experts should be either directly involved in or consulted about formulating the company's strategy and critically evaluating the options.

5.3.4 Expectations from innovation experts

Innovation managers expect experts to make decisive contributions to their most important task, reducing the level of uncertainty associated with a project. Uncertainty is extremely high in the early phase of a project and, similar, in the development of an innovation strategy. Experts are often of great help in defining the main trajectory of future innovation efforts and outlining a development strategy to achieve it. Later in a project, when it has gained momentum, experts implement their knowledge to incorporate their part of the solution. Experts are also important in helping to collect, read, and interpret all relevant information from around the world.

An expert can make a decisive contribution to a company's innovation process in three ways, as illustrated in figure 5.5:

- Strategy development (including roadmapping)
- Innovation-related intelligence (networking, knowledge collection, and knowledge screening)
- Technology implementation in future products

These three ways are applicable to all experts, both in-house experts and external consultants.

Solid knowledge versus expert' opinion

From a company's perspective, an expert should be able to state an opinion even if it is not yet fully confirmed by a solid set of experimental facts. When discussing innovation with an executive, a project manager, or other team members, the expert should outline the contours of the future based on his or her expertise, including any speculative insights. By definition, scientists are trained to accept only well demonstrated hypotheses; their papers should avoid any statement that has not been rigorously proven. Asking a scientist to extrapolate and elaborate on

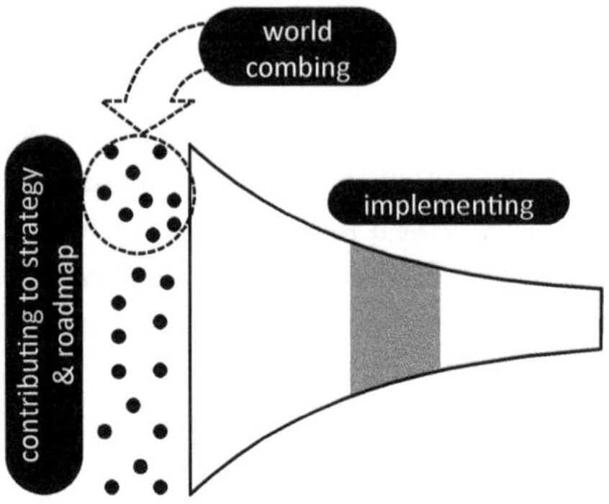

Figure 5.5: Experts' contributions viewed as a funnel. Experts' main contributions during the innovation process can be represented by the famous funnel. Experts' actions are represented by the black bubbles. The multiple small dots entering the funnel represent innovative ideas. Some of these ideas may be inspired by the experts' survey of world (which we call world combing) knowledge via attending conferences, reading articles, or consulting a network of peers. Inside the funnel, the gray band represents the stage of the innovation process during which an expert may implement his or her knowledge by contributing directly to the project. The bubble at the far left indicates that strategic guidelines for the project are established up-front based on roadmapping and then regularly revisited if new knowledge dictates it.

158 Chapter 5. Expert and expertise

possibilities that have not yet been proven is contrary to the expert's training and perhaps natural tendency. However, for the benefit of innovation guidance, the expert is expected to do such extrapolations, provided he or she also describes under what conditions the extrapolations would be confirmed, elaborates on the uncertainty that needs to be eliminated, or lists alternative scenarios.

An expert should provide two types of information:

Confirmed knowledge. Confirmed knowledge is more than welcome during the planning phase for implementation of a technology in a product: How long will this battery last in extremely cold weather? How can we analyze five thousand customer-feedback e-mails? How difficult is it to paint or print a logo onto this new composite? How much cooling does this LED lamp require? Answering such questions is bread-and-butter work for experts. The answer should be straightforward and documented. If there are several possible answers, the expert should provide a comparison, with a focus on solutions which are the most appropriate to the company's business. Indeed the same expert may give somewhat different answers to a low-cost mass producer or a high-end luxury-product designer.

Insights and opinions. Expert input also includes insights and opinions. These may touch on the still unstable fringe of knowledge, particularly during the early phase of an innovation. Both the questions and the answers are about the future: How would electrical motors perform if rare earth elements were missing? What can we expect from future generations of pattern recognition algorithms? For which products will nutraceutical food gain momentum? Can we imagine a cleaner way of extracting shale gas? Only high-level experts who regularly visit international conferences in their fields can provide thoughtful answers to these forward-looking questions like these. Even imperfect and surrounded by a cloud of uncertainty, educated insight and opinion from an expert will help the company. Innovation is about exploring an uncertain path; any input capable of lifting some of the fog is more than welcome.

Innovation Intelligence

Serendipidy

The word serendipity is an old neologism; coined in 1754 by Horace Walpole, it was inspired by an old Persian tale, The Three Princes of Serendip, in which the heroes make discoveries by observing their environment and making shrewd deductions based on their observations. The word is applied to unexpected and accidental discoveries, such as Fleming discovering penicillin by examining an old Petri dish that was contaminated by mold. Serendipity requires luck, breadth of thought, and shrewdness. Unfortunately, the word's meaning is losing strength; it is increasingly being used to mean just the luck aspect. In fact, serendipity is a manifestation of creativity in which inspiration comes from outside. It is the ability to see connections – even among needs not on today's agenda. As such, serendipity is a necessary virtue for experts when they are combing the world.

One aspect of expert insight is the screening of new ideas. Experts who know the company and product strategy and have contributed to its roadmapping are better able to scan and screen the complex world of new ideas, new tools, recent results, and unexpected discoveries. By serendipity (see the inset above for a detailed explanation of this term), they are able to detect interesting connections, and then decide whether a new concept is opening up opportunities and whether those opportunities have a good probability of becoming fruitful. This screening activity is of extreme importance for companies living in our new world, which is flooded by knowledge that is constantly being renewed. This *world combing*, a key responsibility of experts, is a major contribution to a company's *innovation intelligence*.

Roadmapping

Roadmapping the silicon industry

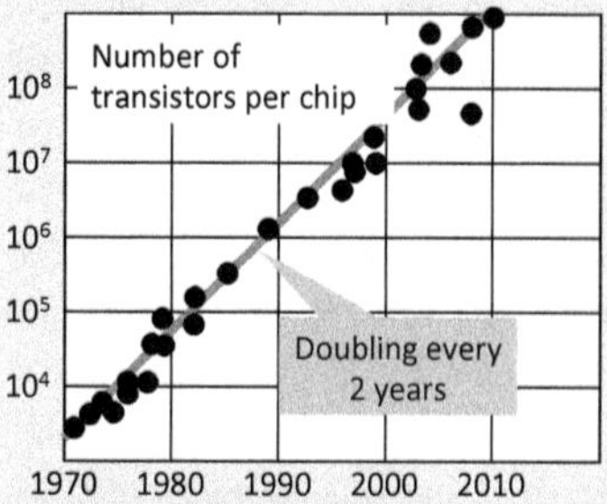

Number of transistors per chip

Doubling every 2 years

Gordon Moore

in 1965 (left) and recently (right)

We mentioned Gordon Moore and Moore's law briefly in chapters 3 and 4, but here we provide additional details about the law's performance and its implications for the silicon industry's roadmap. Moore worked at Fairchild Semiconductor during the pioneering times of the silicon industry. He wrote a paper in 1965, speculating that the transistor density in future integrated circuits would grow exponentially, doubling every eighteen months. His predictions turned out to be quite accurate, although the doubling rate was closer to two years. Moore's law is not a law but rather a prediction for technological progress. It became the backbone of the silicon industry roadmap, which managed to maintain that doubling rate for approximately forty years, achieving a millionfold increase in transistor density on a chip. Moore predicted an end to this rapid progress when critical sizes approach the size of an atom. Indeed, gate oxide thickness is now down to only a few atoms. The doubling rate predicted by Moore's law is now stalling, mostly due to the cost increase associated with a technology pushed near its limit. The roadmap now must explorer new directions of research. Gordon Moore was cofounder and president of Intel.

Several of our interviewees mentioned the importance of experts' input in their companies' roadmapping efforts. Experts have insider

Innovation Intelligence 161

knowledge of both ongoing research and preliminary results in targeted fields. This enables them to predict innovations and sometimes even to estimate the length of time until significant progress will be made in a specific sector. For any company, a roadmap consists of the deployment of various technologies in its product lines. To create such a roadmap, the company must be able to forecast what will be available and what will be obsolete in the future.

In the above inset, we offer the example of Gordon Moore. In the mid-1960s, he was an expert in integrated semiconductor devices, which was frontier knowledge at that time. Still, he made a prediction that became known as Moore's law. This prediction became the roadmap for the entire silicon industry for over four decades. Moore's law is a striking example of how an expert can provide a decisive contribution in predicting the future; however, we warn that his example is a somewhat misleading, because its having been so accurate for so many years gives an impression that such predictions are easy to make. In fact, Moore lived in exceptional conditions, and we freely admit that most roadmaps, even those developed by the best experts, are rarely so ambitious. Still, even if sketchy and tainted with uncertainty, a well-prepared roadmap provides valuable guidelines, and experts are better qualified to outline roadmaps that is anybody else. Roadmaps should be continuously updated as knowledge develops and uncertainty gradually fades.

Experts are generally good at listing possible scenarios and assessing their comparative strengths and weaknesses, but they often struggle when trying to list the sequence of events on a timetable: When this innovation will be launched in the market? How long will it take to qualify this invention? Which applications of this technology will come first?

It is often pointless to try to assign a date to a forecasted event, because there is such a high degree of uncertainty. Even if the outcome of a technology is almost certain, the best experts can rarely estimate the time it will take to fix all the problems that will appear along the way.

162   Chapter 5. Expert and expertise

To counter this timing uncertainty, experts can propose early warning flags along the progress curve. The following are a few examples
of early warning flags:

- Wait until RFID technology penetrates this market, then consider
  adopting it
- Initiate R&D on this molecule when the U.S. FDA begins debates
  on its approval
- Regularly survey progress in this lab to keep an eye on quantum
  cryptography
- If this company starts sampling, consider this subsystem for your
  products

5.3.5 Experts in the knowledge flood

The role of experts and the nature of experts have been changed by the
ever-growing knowledge flood that our society has been experiencing
for decades. Experts who are close to innovation operate close to
the very active frontiers of knowledge, so are more affected by the
knowledge flood.

Experts must make choices

As most experts tend to seek perfection in their knowledge, learning
today has become a rat race, with knowledge expanding in a runaway
mode. This is a challenging situation for experts. Permanent learning has become a heavier and heavier task just to keep afloat in this
knowledge flood.

Truly ambitious experts must make choices. Let's consider the
example of a specialist in dating for paleontology and archeology. She
knew bones, mineral chemistry, photoluminescence, isotope extraction,
and fine nuclear measurements. A decade ago, genetic code analysis
became an important new tool for dating and interpreting samples. At
that time our expert had to face the question of whether to expand
her knowledge toward genetics. Learning genetics would not be a
small step, and if our expert did so, she would also need to refine her
knowledge of other dating methods, such as amino-acid dating. Our

Innovation Intelligence   163

expert had to choose how to direct and focus her expertise.

Such choices are common for experts in most sectors today, whether digital electronics, biochemistry, renewable energy, medical imaging, or data mining. Nearly every field is expanding, branching out toward either new applications or new technical methods. Because it is impossible to keep track of every new branch and interconnections in these fast moving fields, the expert must choose which branches to monitor. If the expert is working for a company, the chosen branches will usually be the ones most adapted to the company's present and future needs. If the expert is an independent researcher, the chosen branches will be the ones most fertile for his or her own research. Making this choice is sometimes difficult for deep diggers. It is easier for chipmunks, because their choices are somewhat reversible – if the chipmunk starts digging in one direction and is disappointed by the outcome, he or she will simply move to a different place. Facing the knowledge flood, today's deep diggers are easier to convince to start behaving like chipmunks, because their personal knowledge flood can become a burden.

Even chipmunks need to make choices, albeit somewhat reversible ones; their networks of galleries cannot cover a territory as large as all accumulated knowledge. The real, small, stripped rodents select the location of their burrows where there is the maximum chance of collecting food and where they can hide quickly. Because experts manage their knowledge according to their understanding of the company's orientation and strategy, their guidance is far more efficient if they are fully aware of the company's non-technical constraints, business, financial, or political.

One consequence of experts distributing their knowledge in the ever-expanding flood is that, like knowledge itself, experts are forming a widespread, fragmented distribution of expertise. Some central fields such as thin films, iron metallurgy, and molecular modeling, have a high density of experts mastering them. On the other hand, the distribution of experts in small, niche fields, such as orphan diseases, liquid lithium handling, and RFID security, are in the long tail part of the distribution. In such niches, the number of experts is very limited. When we speak

164   Chapter 5. Expert and expertise

about hard-to-find experts, we are referring to the very top experts in central fields and all of the experts in niche fields. Historically, experts in the long tail were often lonely; since the advent of Internet communication, they can communicate with fellow experts and are more easily identified and reached.

An expert's key asset: the network

Experts and graph theory

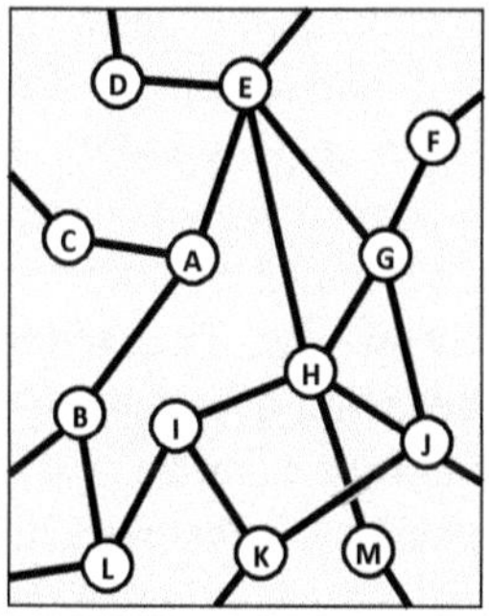

Graph theory[a], a branch of mathematics, is the study of graphs, collections of nodes or vertices possibly attached in pairs by links or edges. In this graph, a circle is a node and the black lines are links. The degree of a node is the number of links attached to it. A path is a way to connect two nodes via links. The distance between two nodes is the number of hops on the shortest path linking the nodes. For example, the degree of node **A** is 3, of node **C** is 2, and of node **H** is 5. The distance **A-B** is 1, while **A-H** is 2, and **A-K** is 4. A graph diameter is the longest of all of the distances. Graph theory is often applied to the study of human related networks, using link definitions specific to complex social relationships. The famous relationship "**A** once shook hands with **B**" leads to the surprising conclusion: "world population is a small graph," because any one of us is at most only six or seven handshakes from anybody else in the world. Another surprising fact about real-world networks, human or not, is that they often contain highly interconnected subgroups (often named cliques or small worlds). Most humans belong to several cliques, such as family, neighbors, colleagues, tennis club, and so forth. Any two cliques are, at least,

Innovation Intelligence

weakly connected to each other thanks to the few nodes they share. Nodes of high degree are critical in creating network connectivity; they are called hubs and play a major role in connecting cliques. Graph science is experiencing a boom today, because it is highly applicable to the Internet, websites, social media, and so forth.

[a]is many books on the topic of graph theory, enough for a would-be expert to spend ten years mastering; this summary is adapted from just one brief but dense website.[74]

An expert's network enables the expert to grasp a much wider base of knowledge than just his or her own field. Networks are common among experts: experts in the same field know each other, they read each other's papers, they meet at conferences, and they often visit each other when traveling. Experts are the nodes of an important knowledge exchange network. If we use graph theory (see inset above) to describe this type of relationship, we can define the linking edge between two experts **A** and **B** as follows:

- **A** and **B** know each other and have mutual respect
- **A** knows what type of knowledge is in the expertise of **B**, and vice versa

It is not necessary for **A** and **B** to be experts in the same field. If an expert (**A**) wants to answer a question outside his or her own expertise, the expert may ask a person (**B**) who he knows to has that type of knowledge. Let's assume that the average degree of a node in this graph of experts is, say, about 10, meaning that a given expert has a tenfold increase in his or her available knowledge at short distance (actually, the increase would be slightly less than tenfold due to expertise overlap among adjacent experts). Imagine that when the expert (**A**) asks the other expert (**B**) the question, **B** replies, "I may know a bit in this field, but the true expert is one of my colleagues, Dr. **C**. I'll introduce you and he may give you the answer." In that case, the knowledge is available at a distance of 2 – not 1, as it would have been if **B** had known the answer to the question, but still very short. To our knowledge, the chain distance for information access is not much longer than two in real life.

The value of a recommendation decays rapidly with distance.

In our global environment, experts in the same field tend to know each other, members forming a small, highly connected community (a clique). The most valuable connections for extending knowledge coverage beyond this field are the nodes that connect this field, or silo, to other fields. Chipmunks are such nodes, connecting experts in their various fields.

The numbers in the example above are rough estimates. Without a detailed calculation, we all understand that in an expert network the key players are hubs, experts who have far more contacts than the average expert. The best experts to contact for knowledge gathering are these hubs, in particular hubs connected to hubs. Hubs are usually easy to identify in a technical community; they are valuable contacts but always busy.

Most experts know that their network is valuable and are keen to maintain it (keeping contact with other experts) and extend it. The value of an expert is as much in the expert's network as it is in his or her direct knowledge. With the present knowledge flood and globalization, building a sufficiently wide network is of paramount importance. Companies should assist their experts by letting them know how highly their networks are regarded and helping them to expand their networks in directions of strategic interest to the company.

Experts and knowledge of what matters

Let's consider an example about home decorating. Imagine that you have a problem: you have one painting on a large wall and it looks lonely, so it would be nice to have a second painting on that same wall. You also have many

Innovation Intelligence 167

other home improvement projects mind, none yet well defined. You decide to invest in the effort of visiting a huge flea market nearby and several antique shops downtown. Maybe you will find the second painting that you want, but if you are particular about its size and style, the probability is low. At the same time, if you have a strategic vision of your home, you may, by pure serendipity, return full of good home improvement ideas to discuss with your spouse. You may find readymade acquisition opportunities, such as a huge travel trunk that could decorate the attic and save the effort of building a storage closet. You may steal an idea: you may see a renovated wardrobe that has an inner lining of fresh, colored foil, and you could use the same concept in the drawers of your grandmother's chest. You may take a photograph of a collection of antique cooking pans, because you know that your spouse is searching something along this line. The chance that your big tour pays off will depends very much on the breadth and richness of the set of problems you have in the back of your mind when you go.

Knowledge gathering and world combing. One of the most important tasks for an expert is world combing. This activity consists of searching for pieces of knowledge that can be either solutions to problems already identified or opportunities for the company to develop new products or consider new businesses. The scope of a world combing is vast, and it should be.

Following the example of home decorating (see inset above), let's consider a similar story in which an expert travels to San Francisco, California for a weeklong gathering of the Material Research Society and then some visits to large laboratories on the West Coast. The more this expert is aware of the ongoing problems and the business expectations back at his company, the greater the chance that he will return with relevant ideas and opportunities.

In a knowledge flood what counts most is not drainage of the maximum amount of knowledge (we have Google for that). The most

168   Chapter 5. Expert and expertise

important task is the screening of this conglomeration of bits and pieces of knowledge, identifying those that could possibly be of interest for the company. This screening requires an acute vision, a deep understanding of the company's present and future needs, and a good seasoning of creative thinking.

Give and take in knowledge exchange. Whether activating the network by contacting another expert or drinking a beer next to the conference hall with a new, interesting contact, an expert will, one way or another, have to enter into a give and take ritual. Experts love knowledge and will be happy to share a piece of their knowledge with a fellow expert, but the quality and durability of the relationship will depend on how well the taker pays back the giver with other knowledge. Managers are often concerned about their experts talking and exchanging information with other experts, but experts do have to give some information. This situation is indeed frightening if managers treat their experts like children so that the experts are not in a position to understand whether a piece of information is strategically important to the company. In contrast, if managers treat their experts with respect and brief them on the competitive situation, both technical and business, the experts will understand what information is strategically important. Experts who are treated in this way can safely exchange knowledge with other experts, without even a hint of important, confidential information.

This exchange of knowledge is a well-established ritual when an expert visits another expert. A classic session is what we could call "family" news: What happened to your brilliant Russian postdoc? Did you contact the person I recommended? Which research field is Professor Suzuki involved in today? Did you fix the problem we discussed last time? Have you visited the new facility at KAIST? Why did Dr. Doe and his team move to that big company? Questions and answers will flow back and forth, and the quality of the exchange will depend on the subtle balance of give and take.

Chipmunks also have an advantage in this situation. A chipmunk can feed the other expert plenty of knowledge from adjacent fields. The other expert will appreciate the information if it has value for him

Innovation Intelligence   169

or her. In this exchange, as in many other situations, knowledge is practically a commodity. The knowledge the chipmunk provides is public and known by experts in that field, but in our exchange scenario its value lies in the selection of the right pieces.

5.4 Expert role shifting with rapidly changing trends

5.4.1 Three shifts in the expert role in recent history

By looking back at history, we can see how the role of the expert has changed in parallel with the trends that affected industrial research, which we discussed in chapter 4.

Concentration and focus era (1950s' through the 1970s')

Expert of the concentration and focus era

We propose Dr. John E. Karlin as an example of an expert in industry during the 1950s through the 1970s. He was one the first scientists to tackle the issue of the human factor in the use of electronic devices. Karlin was a polymath, a violinist, electrical engineer, and expert in ergonomics and psychology. In today's terminology, he would be called a slasher rather than a polymath. At Bell Labs, he led a group working on the early stage of push-button telephones. He had little to learn from outside the company. The discipline did not exist, he was creating it. He designed the first nine-key pad for digital telephones, initiating the future science of human-machine interface.

We as an example of an expert during this era a leader at Bell Labs (see the inset above), the archetypal research center of this period (see chapter 4). In that era experts were asked to concentrate and focus on the progress of their own projects. They regularly visited their library, scanning the latest issues of the few science and technology journals. (During that period, well before our current knowledge flood, reading all of the new, relevant articles was easy.) Then they returned to their labs for their key task: pushing their research projects. Bell Labs, with its famous long hallways, was designed by the building's architect to promote contact between researchers. But the long hallways did not have the intended effect. The scientists at Bell Labs knew their few competitors overseas better than they knew their neighbors who occupied the same hallway[i]. You could find the same working atmosphere at the Siemens Research Center in Ottobrunn, Germany; at the Thomson-CSF in Corbeville, France; and at the Philips R&D center in Eindhoven, The Netherlands.

Cross-fertilization era (1970s' through the 1990s')

Expert of the cross-fertilization era

Top: Buildings at Xerox PARC. Bottom ; An informal meeting, at Xerox PARC, of a subset of Bob Metcalfe's team that was inventing Ethernet. Xerox PARC place was lively and open; coffee places were filled with people communicating. Many cross-disciplinary seminars were held and accompanied by tea and incredibly tasty cookies.

---

[i]This is a personal experience from one of the authors of this book who did a few consulting jobs in Murray Hills, New Jersey in the mid-1970s. Guess which one of us?

Innovation Intelligence   171

During the 1970s, innovation observers realized that the most fertile areas for innovation were the cross-border zones between the various scientific fields. Breeding two sciences – mathematics and computing, biology and molecular chemistry, or thin-film electronics and liquid crystals – was found to lead to creative encounters. At that time, there were few silos than there are now. But when the barriers between two or more silos were lowered, creativity was boosted. Many laboratories were organized to take profit from this effect: researchers from various fields were put together under the same roof and communication and collaboration among them were stimulated. We choose Xerox PARC as the flagship of this breed of research center; it was founded in the early 1970s in Palo Alto (PARC stood for Palo Alto Research Center). A large, modern building, located very close to Stanford University, Hewlett-Packard, Variant, and Fairchild Semiconductor, among others, it hosted about two hundred researchers of various origins who had one common objective: design the office of the future. The idea was to invent by learning while interacting and bouncing ideas off one another. Experts from various fields were digging laterally for a common objective. The concept was perfect – PARC created many of the technologies that we all use today.[75] Unfortunately, Xerox's business development office lacked business model flexibility, so Xerox, as a company, did not profit from much of the value created at Xerox PARC.

During the same period, several important innovation waves, including nuclear magnetic resonance imaging (NMRI) for medical purposes, arrays for rapid sequencing of DNA, multiparametric feedback control, and graphical user interfaces (GUIs), triggered the creation of cross-disciplinary research centers.

The trend for cross-disciplinary research, which began in the 1970s, gained momentum in the 1980s, and peaked in the 1990s. Experts were expected to interact with experts from other domains and build bridges that could be fertile in periods of innovation. Because the flow of knowledge was already impressive by this time, it was difficult for an expert to keep up with all of the new knowledge being generated by at least two fields. Most experts started to organize their knowledge bases by focusing on the technology set that most closely match their application. For example, an expert in sound propagation had to choose a specialty from medical ultrasound imaging, cognitive hearing science, electroacoustics, building design, and underwater sensors.

During this era, a new breed, system-oriented experts, began to emerge.

Connection era (1990s' through the present)

Expert of the connexion era

Left: Three visitors at a booth during a Consumer Electronics Show in Las Vegas, Nevada. Right: A rendering of Apple Campus 2, a research center currently in construction in Cupertino, California. Today's experts are scanning the knowledge flood and screening it in search of relevant pieces of knowledge that could contribute to their innovation projects. We consider Apple the flagship example of pioneering this approach to innovation. The information technology community is leading the trend toward this new approach to innovation practice, but most industrial fields have been or will be affected.

Apple led the entry in the new era of innovation. The trend has been driven by both the knowledge flood and fast connection speed, thanks to the Internet. Industry has realized that it is cheaper and faster to identify and retrieve new knowledge from outside the company's walls. Experts are knowledge scouts who can scan and screen an impressive volume of knowledge; the rule of the game is to connect the experts' findings with their companies' projects. When they have identified an opportunity, they can shift gears and enter that new sector of knowledge with speed

Innovation Intelligence 173

and talent. Experts are comfortable changing topic and evaluating the relevance of a piece of knowledge before mastering it. Experts are primarily navigators and explorers who are experienced at landing in new countries and mapping their potentials.

A task for experts when they return from their travels, often virtual travels, is to evaluate the multiple combinations they can assemble from the various bricks of knowledge they collected. The creative part of product design is in finding the right combination, a process that implies the scanning of a very large number of combinations.

5.4.2 New requirements for expert knowledge and skill

Nani gigantum humeris insidentes

Standing on the shoulders of giants. This Latin metaphor of dwarfs standing on the shoulders of giants expresses the fact that new discoveries are always built on the foundation of previous discoveries. The metaphor is generally attributed to Bernard of Chartres. It is also found in a letter written by Isaac Newton in 1676: "If I have seen further it is by standing on the shoulders of giants."

From the 1950s to the 1970s, the best experts knew all of the theoretical foundations of their fields and all of the basic properties of the objects they were manipulating. Mathematicians knew how to prove the theorems they were using, experimentalists could open and repair the sophisticated measurement systems they were using, chemists knew how the compounds they were using had been prepared. In the years since, this deep basic knowledge has gradually eroded. Experts may have been taught those basic elements when they were at school, but they are no longer operating knowledge. Today's experts are too busy dealing with the latest layer of knowledge to make sure they can explain in detail the principles of their phase contrast microscope or the exact logic of a convergence algorithm. The best experts remain conscious that whatever tool they use has limits and that, if operating in nonstandard conditions, they must double-check its basics, at the cost of significant intellectual effort. Finally, even though they are experts, they must accept as given a large amount of foundational knowledge. By doing so, they can focus solely on using these sophisticated tools. In order to remain agile, experts must understand completely the best uses of these advanced tools, but they can afford to be somewhat light on the details of all the parts inside the tool. For example, an engineer can invert a matrix using MATLAB or a similar software application, without having to rework the inversion algorithm. Similarly, a forensic expert can analyze a sample without having to learn the working principles of the mass spectrometer.

As a result, modern experts are more conceptual, in a fashion, than were their predecessors. They use sophisticated tools, whether theoretical concepts, computer modeling, or equipment, but they set aside the details of how the tools work until they have pushed a tool beyond its limits.

Expertise today probably requires a greater capacity for abstract thinking that did expertise of the past. The knowledge required today is itself more abstract than the knowledge of the past. Imagine using a theorem that you know is valid but whose proof you learned in college and have forgotten. This theorem is more abstract than the solid chain of proof that backs it. Experts must be skilled at and comfortable with using black boxes.

Experts and mental agility

Successful completion of a jigsaw puzzle requires one of the key skills needed by modern experts who contribute to innovation. An expert must scan a large collection of "knowledge bricks" and determine if any match one of the needs of their innovation

Innovation Intelligence 175

projects. This scanning and screening process is very similar to a person scanning puzzle pieces to determine which piece fits where and thus complete the puzzle. The mental skills of the two tasks are also similar. Educational experts are aware that jigsaw puzzles are tools for improving children's spatial skills. For today's experts who contribute to innovate, the problem is a bit more complex than a jigsaw puzzle, but the mental agility and cognitive skills are the same.

As we have already emphasized, due to the knowledge flood, one of the key skills for an expert is the ability to quickly screening many pieces of knowledge and determine if any of them match the present or future needs of the company's innovation portfolio. This process is serendipity at work.[76] The chaos of a modern expert's daily life lies in exposure to many pieces of knowledge but mastery of few of them. Without mastering a specific piece of knowledge, a skilled expert can recognize whether it is relevant. In fact, this recognition is an inventive step. Most brilliant inventions were, after analysis, no more than joining two pieces of knowledge together. We reject the idea of emphasizing the luck aspect of serendipity. It is not luck to recognize the potential of a given piece of knowledge that just happened to pass by – there is a spark of genius in the recognition. Most ordinary people, if exposed to the same flood of knowledge, would simply be blinded by cognitive jamming.

5.4.3 Toward meta-expertise

Networking and judging knowledge quality

In monitoring new knowledge in his or her field an expert cannot rely solely on searching the Internet. We live in such a fast-moving world that when a piece of knowledge becomes available, the winner of the game is the one who is first to gain access to the piece of knowledge, first to analyze its potential for innovation, and first to develop a strategy for incorporating it into a company's product and service portfolio. By the time the new piece of knowledge is published in a blog or online journal, it's already too late. Moreover, data on the Internet data is rarely accurate or sufficiently complete to enable an expert to form an opinion on the quality and applicability of the new information. Yes, we said information – not knowledge. The use of the word *information* is intentional. A mention on the Internet is not yet knowledge, it is just information. It must be examined before it can become knowledge.

Experts and network

Conferences are network operation in real time. If an important piece of news about an invention is released, a conference is a perfect place to observe the reaction of a network. During the ritual coffee breaks, experts soon gather in small groups discussing the news, compiling all related information, and finally trying to form opinions on the invention, its importance, and its likely consequences for the future. Keep in mind that in a discussion group, the value of what an individual says depends on the person's expertise and distance from the information source. In just a few hours, a consensus emerges, usually of high value, because it summarizes the input from a large group of high-level experts. Expert consensus is often maligned for its historical errors. Errors are possible, and this risk must be incorporated, but in most cases expert consensus is very valuable.

The best route for an expert to gain access to new pieces of knowledge is via his or her network. If the network is strong, our expert's contact will know that our expert has interest in a given field and will inform our expert of any important news. Important results usually are known by a close community of experts in the field before the data are published. This is normal, because results must be confirmed and

Innovation Intelligence

sometimes even reproduced, before they can be published. Meanwhile, the author's local community is highly excited and the finding is often leaked. Our expert's contact may have access to this community; if the contact hears about the new knowledge, he or she will inform our expert. Then begins the most important phase for our expert: gauging the credibility of the new knowledge and judging to what extent the promises behind the hype are real.

Here again, our expert's network is extremely important. A robust network will convey the news via more than one channel. Then the network can be activated to collect the maximum amount of complementary information about the new knowledge. Finally, our expert will be able to decide if the new piece of knowledge should be fed into the alert system of the company's innovation pipeline.

Critical to this process is our expert's reliance on other experts for a large part of the evaluation process. This reliance requires that our expert be able to judge whether a given expert is sufficiently knowledgeable or needs independent confirmation. This is another talent required of today's experts: they must be able to judge another expert and determine to what extent the other expert can be used as an extension.

Today's expert must extend his or her own coverage via use of a network. The extension should be both geographic (in particular, having strong, reliable nodes in Asia is critical) and thematic (covering fields adjacent to that of the expert). Building the network requires the ability to judge the capability of each potential contact. In other words, we are asking our expert to develop sufficient knowledge about other experts to enable sound judgments about them.

Presans and meta-expertise

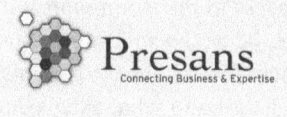

Presans is our company, a young operation assisting industry innovation managers in seeking specific knowledge. If we dare use ourselves as illustration, it is because we have experience in enrolling and coaching would-be meta-experts. We call our meta-experts Fellows, and they are headhunting and coaching experts for addressing specific problems. We enroll Fellows who match the following guidelines:

- Senior specialist of the chipmunk expert type
- Has maintained his or her expertise according to knowledge expansion process
- Broad knowledge with skills in making connections
- Free from any ties bearing a potential conflict of interest (company, lobby, agency)
- Balanced career, including both academic research and practical industry innovation
- Natural, innate empathy for the problems of others

Most of our Fellows are retired former CTOs. In our experience, Fellows are difficult to find. Moreover, even with such a complete set of selection guidelines, we still need to coach new Fellows through a learning curve. One of the dangers is that a new Fellow will begin by trying to solve the client's problem on his or her own instead of searching for the best expert. Fellows create value at several stages of Presans' processes: when rephrasing a practical industrial problem into a set of generic knowledge-seeking projects, when selecting the best expert from a set of candidate experts, and when assisting our clients in interpreting the expert input.

Innovation Intelligence 179

Expertise about expertise

Meta-expertise is not a neologism per se. Adding the prefix *meta* to a field, as in metaphysics, implies that it is a science about a science, but it also implies a loop around a given knowledge. For example, metadata is data about data, and metacognition is cognition about cognition. This explains what we mean by meta-expertise: it is the expertise one could develop about experts and expertise. This chapter is definitively meta-expertise. In previous chapters, we have visited many areas that could be termed meta-knowledge, or knowledge about knowledge. The concept of meta-expertise is one level more abstract than is mere expertise.

The following is based on an excellent blog post by Stephen Turner,[77] a professor of philosophy at the University of South Florida, in which he listed meta-expert skills:

- Knowing the broad parameters of and requirements for attaining expertise;
- Being able to distinguish a genuine expert from a pretender;
- Estimating whether expertise is and when it is not attainable in a given domain;
- Possessing effective criteria for evaluating expertise, within reasonable limits;
- Keeping awareness of the limitations of specialized expertise.

In that blog post, Turner was discussing experts in climate change. We think we should add a few complementary points to his list, so that it can be adapted for use in identifying meta-experts who provide support to innovation.

- Identifying which expert profile is best suited for treating a given problem
- Reshaping a problem to be generic and palatable for experts
- Coaching experts in their quests for knowledge
- Assisting innovation drivers in their quest for value

Meta-expertise also implies the ability to go one level above one's own expertise and consider with an open mind all the possible options that could contribute to the solution for a given problem. At Presans

180   Chapter 5. Expert and expertise

we are fond of the story of John Harrison showing that Isaac Newton was not, after all, a meta-expert. An expert will always be victim to the street light effect: whenever confronted with a problem, an expert will tend to search for a solution within his or her own small world. A meta-expert is expected to gain altitude above the problem and give experts from all fields a chance to find the best solution to the problem.

Even Newton could be wrong!

Although ships exploring the world during the seventeenth and eighteenth centuries could easily measure their latitude, nobody knew how to measure longitude. No clock was able to keep the proper time through the hazards of transoceanic journey. England, the dominant marine nation, was eager to maintain its leadership. In 1714, the British Parliament passed the Longitude Act, establishing the Board of Longitude and offering a Prize of £20,000 (more than EUR 3.5 million in today's terms) to whoever could find a practical method of measuring longitude to within 30 nautical miles (56 kilometers). Among the initiators of the project were astronomy experts, including Isaac Newton. These experts were convinced that only celestial mechanics was sufficiently precise and delocalized to provide a solution. In their defense, we should mention that the jury was also influenced by the opinion of the deceased polymath Robert Hooke (1635-1703), a highly respected expert in clockwork who invented the anchor escapement used in pendulum clocks, who had declared that a clock would never be accurate enough for solving the longitude problem. John Harrison worked from 1730 to 1761 at refining a series of improved chronometers. In 1761, al-

Innovation Intelligence 181

though Harrison's timepiece was demonstrated by real navigation tests to provide a sufficiently accurate measurement of longitude, the Board of Longitude continued to delay recognition of a solution developed by a mere ironsmith. Harrison had to go to court and enlist the support of the King George III to finally get credit and be awarded a fraction of the prize in 1773. The official prize was never awarded to anyone.

A meta-expert must be a former expert. He or she should know from personal experience what it means to become an expert and what it costs to maintain expertise. The coach of a soccer team is nearly always a former high level player. The difference is that here we are dealing with intellectual matters. Although the soccer coach can no longer play in the league, our meta-expert can remain an expert in a few topics. However, a meta-expert will typically gain altitude with respect to the expertise battlefield, because the meta-expert's main interest is now above, dealing with processes and generic laws that direct the creation and flow of knowledge.

Industry in now entering a new world in which innovation performance will be driven primarily by the capability of innovation drivers to rapidly scan, screen, and digest a flood of knowledge. For this, the company will need to rely on a multiplicity of experts, both internal and external. Engaging and coordinating this effort is essentially a meta-expertise job. As a result, meta-expertise is likely to become an important component of innovation performance in the future.

5.5 Conclusion

We have seen that experts are special people who dedicate a significant amount of their time and energy to building a high level of knowledge. Driving innovation requires the assistance of experts who closely follow the frontier activity in relevant fields of knowledge.

We have gained an understanding that experts are not all alike: deep diggers are extremely focused on what can become a mental silo, while chipmunks are more curious and versatile, branching into multiple, interconnected burrows. Although companies need experts, in-house experts are difficult to manage, the key point being the amount of time they require for switching topics. We have predicted that, in today's rapidly changing environment, expertise must become a flexible resource, often in part externalized.

We have measured the importance of quality and breadth of the expert's network. The expert's capacity to reach out to other experts and to set up a focused global alert network is of extreme value. We have found that experts contribute to three phases of an innovation: they assist in developing the roadmap in the planning phase, they continuously comb the world collecting ideas and inspiring bricks of knowledge, and they assist in implementing new knowledge or technology in a product or service. The first two actions are part of the innovation intelligence effort.

Because innovation takes place in an environment of agility and lean innovation, in the future the meta-expert will be a key player. The meta-expert, an expert on experts, is an experienced expert who coaches other experts and acts as a mediator between the innovation team and external knowledge.

The environment in which a meta-expert will operate in the future will be examined more closely in the following chapter.

Chapter 6
Toward Innovation Intelligence

Innovation has nothing to do with how many R&D dollars you have. When Apple came up with the Mac, IBM was spending at least 100 times more on R&D. It's not about money. It's about the people you have, how you're led, and how much you get it.

STEVE JOBS

In Short... In this chapter, we address the issue of disruptive innovation in present and near future enterprises. We introduce three new levers companies are using to redesign their approaches to innovation in our rapidly changing environment: The Chief Innovation Officer, a new executive figure, is migrating closer and closer to the CEO. This person injects into innovation management both business and customer value components, in addition to technology. The Chief Innovation Officer drives disruptive innovation and fosters innovation intelligence. The Innovation lab is one of the materialization of a commando style of managing disruptive innovation. This cross-functional entity is one of the key valuation nodes for innovation intelligence results. The innovation lab should

184   Chapter 6. Toward Innovation Intelligence

perform creative synthesis and find fast, lean experiments to sort out the most valuable ideas and transform them into business propositions. Innovation intelligence is a network collecting information, not only technical, but also from business and customer value areas. It also sorts and recombines the pieces of information into knowledge. The innovation intelligence network is valued by innovation drivers and becomes a part of the company's overall competitive intelligence.

6.1 Introduction

In chapter 2, we presented an example of disruptive innovation: Parrot's drone project. The project was disruptive in the sense that drones were very far from Parrot's core business. We saw how the direct involvement of the CEO, Henri Seydoux, was critical to the project's success and how his strategic vision integrated various disparate areas of knowledge (market, trends, and technologies). Finally, we saw how Parrot's ability to generate and rapidly test ideas eventually led to the project's success. We know that knowledge and innovation are tightly interwoven and that the spiral is whirling faster and faster. A relatively small company like Parrot can be agile, so it is well suited to this environment.

For a large company, being agile is a challenge. In this chapter, we will discuss how large, multinational companies can succeed in today's rapidly changing environment. We will first examine the processes that large companies are implementing in efforts to improve their agility and extend their reach in terms of multiple market segments and multiple technologies. We will recognize some patterns in these companies' adaptations, although the current situation is far from stabilized and some essential pieces of the puzzle are missing.

6.1.1 Three levers for facing disruptive trends

We begin this chapter with a brief overview of innovation in today's environment, perform a case study of the multinational oil and gas company TOTAL SA, and then introduce three levers that are emerging to

Innovation Intelligence 185

help large companies adapt to the disruptive trends described in chapter 4. The first of these levers is a new figure, the Chief Innovation Officer (CINO), who is described in detail in section 6.3. After introducing the CINO, we turn to the other two levers, both of which are important activities of the CINO's team. The next lever, idea generation and rapid experimentation, often conducted by the fashionable innovation labs, is the focus of section 6.4. Finally, the third lever, innovation intelligence, is covered in section 6.5. Although it is still emerging and not yet fully structured in most companies, innovation intelligence is essential – and probably the most important activity conducted by the CINO's team – because it is the starting point of the innovation process.

6.1.2 An aside: what is meant by *innovation* in our time?

> There has been a strong push over the last 10 years to align what you do in R&D with what you do in the business.
> **Oliver Nussli, Head of Project & Portfolio Management at Nestlé**

Let's review some highlights from earlier chapters before we focus on how large companies are adapting to today's environment:

- Knowledge is growing at an accelerated rate and has become highly fragmented
- Knowledge itself is becoming a commodity
- The art of innovation is in collecting, sorting, and assembling pieces of knowledge
- The digital wave has accelerated the innovation cycle
- The combination of rapid change and globalization has boost the threat of product commoditization

186 Chapter 6. Toward Innovation Intelligence

> Dream is at the root of everything, not technology. People do not love Wi-Fi! Dream is powerful strong and always renewed. But passing from technology to dream is very difficult.
> **Marc Giget**

All these changes contribute to economic turbulence. Innovation capability has become a key differentiator for a company and, in many cases, a key attribute for the company's survival. The stock market reflects this important fact: the stock prices of companies that are able to adapt and innovate in this new environment are performing much better than those of their competitors. This is a fact. The best companies are innovating more and better than are their competitors. Innovation is rarely only technological; it also requires questioning the company's business model and culture. When innovation becomes a decisive factor in company performance and a key shaper of company behavior, it must be driven from the very top of the organization. The stars of the new economy, players such as Apple, Google, Amazon.com, Parrot, Tesla Motors, SpaceX, and Alibaba, are driven by top executives who are directly involved in steering of their innovation. This does not mean that every company should search for and hire as CEO a clone of Steve Jobs, it just means that companies must adapt. Innovation is becoming a highly competitive race among companies; it is not sufficient to create a research lab with smart experts and a proper environment and let it run, waiting for happy surprises. Innovation is an activity that now affects nearly all the functions across a company:

- marketing and sales, for market intelligence
- human resources, for ensuring that employees have the proper skills
- legal, for drafting the appropriate contracts with potential partners ensuring the protection of intellectual property
- finance, for aligning ambition and resources

Innovation Intelligence 187

- R&D, for providing technology intelligence and feasibility assessment
- purchasing, for integrating suppliers into the company's innovation process
- communications, for presenting a coherent picture of the company's strategy
- top management, for steering and coordinating the ensemble

To avoid ambiguity, let's first review what we mean by *innovation*. In the *Oslo Manual*[i] we find the following definition: "An innovation is the implementation of a new or significantly improved product (good or service), or process, a new marketing method, or a new organizational method in business practices, workplace organization, or external relations." We find here two key notions: newness (but not necessarily from within the company); and value, the driving purpose. Innovation is not about ideas; it is about what you effectively do with the ideas. Without ideas to start with, innovation is not possible, but there are plenty of ideas, especially other people's ideas.

Marc Giget likes to give different definition: "An innovation consists of integrating the best state of knowledge into a creative product to improve the satisfaction of individuals." This definition is quite good, because it features the three important points: knowledge, creative synthesis, and satisfaction of individuals. As we have seen, today's explosive growth and fragmentation of knowledge make the task of creative synthesis extremely difficult.

Both definitions encompass incremental innovation and disruptive innovation. Incremental innovation is business as usual. It is generally taken care of by the classic business functions within companies: strategy, marketing, research and development, production, and so forth. Large companies are optimized for operational efficiency including incremental extensions of what they are already doing. However, these

---

[i]The *Oslo Manual* is the principal international reference manual related to innovation. Published by the Organisation for Economic Co-operation and Development (OECD), it is available in French, English, Spanish, and Russian. The first edition appeared in 1992 and the third, the most recent, in 2005.

188   Chapter 6. Toward Innovation Intelligence

same companies usually lack the flexibility to explore new territories, to make movements laterally (like's Parrot development of drones).

That is where the three levers, which we will discuss later in this chapter, come in: they enable these large companies to engage in disruptive innovation. The goal is to create the extra 30% of revenues that are required for growth but that business as usual and incremental innovation cannot produce. Most recent initiatives are inspired by the notion of an ambidextrous organization, a company that has *organizational ambidexterity*.[78,79]

6.2 TOTAL: organization vs. agility

Among the companies that we have met in various industrial sectors, TOTAL is a very interesting case[ii]. Over the past few years, among numerous initiatives to improve the company's innovation performance, TOTAL created a Scientific Directorate at the corporate level and an Innovation Directorate in the its Marketing & Services branch. TOTAL has also reorganized its entire R&D organization. This multinational company is a prime example of a company in perpetual transformation and that, despite its large size (more than 100,000 employees around the world) has managed to be agile and cope with the diversity of its activities, the maturity of certain parts of its industry, and disruptions that can come from anywhere.

6.2.1 Even for TOTAL, danger is everywhere

TOTAL is one of the world's five super-major oil companies; in terms of revenues it is the number one company in France and the eleventh largest company in the world. Its activities span the entire value chain of the oil and gas industry, from extraction to energy generation, refining,

---

[ii]This case study on TOTAL SA was based on numerous discussions with people involved in innovation and R&D in the four branches of TOTAL. These informal discussions were capped by detailed interviews of Jean-François Minster (Scientific Director), Christine Halliot (Innovation Director of the Marketing & Services branch) and Jean Parizot (R&D Director of the Marketing & Services branch).

transformation, and commercial exploitation. TOTAL has presence in approximately 130 countries. In addition to a number of support functions at the corporate level, the company is organized in four branches:

- Exploration & Production
- Refining & Chemistry
- Marketing & Services
- New Energies

> We need to collaborate with players we are not used to working with, to get out of incremental innovation and be faster. It is by looking at what L'Oréal was doing for Shampoo that we discovered certain molecules interesting for motor oil.
> **Jean Parizot, Research Director, TOTAL**

Activities related to innovation and R&D exist within each branch and at the corporate level.

Despite its size and scope, TOTAL is under pressure from a number of recent trends, including the rise of China, new sources of energy, shale oil and gas, and the current oil crisis. In chapter four, we described three important trends that have affected companies: growth and fragmentation of knowledge, risk of product commoditization, and digital transformation. TOTAL is facing all of these trends. Like other companies, TOTAL must adjust the way it creates and accesses knowledge, as well as the way it integrates that knowledge. The company also needs to become more flexible, more agile, to meet increasingly volatile demand.

Non-core technological renewal

Even for TOTAL's Refining & Chemistry branch, a business operating in a mature industry, there is a strong need for innovation to differentiate its products from the competition and thus sustain profits. New business lines must be envisioned as extending far into the future, and new technological bricks must be continually introduced. The main challenge lies in the fact that some of these bricks of knowledge (digital technologies, biotechnologies, high-performance computing, nanotechnologies, drones, and others) are historically very far from TOTAL's core business. Even if it does not develop most of these new technologies in-house, the company must know them well enough to select and guide their suppliers and partners. Keeping up on a very broad range of technologies is even more complicated when technologies are being improved and replaced more and more quickly. The acceleration of the innovation cycle is even more important for the Marketing & Services branch; the least industrial of TOTAL's branches, it produces and sells lubricants, fuel, and so forth. Historically, new molecules for lubricants were introduced every seven or eight years; today's market expects new molecules much more frequently – every three to four years.

Acceleration of innovation cycles and real-time evolution of needs

According to Jean Parizot, the main challenge that he is facing, as R&D Director of TOTAL's Marketing & Services branch, is not only the accelerating innovation cycles but also real-time evolution of the specifications. The following is a typical situation that he now encounters regularly but that did not exist ten years ago: The R&D department receives a request from the Marketing or Strategy department, an R&D team begins working on the request, and then before they reach the objective, the specifications of the request change! Researchers hate that and find it extremely demotivating. Moreover, researchers often make an unexpected discovery, finding a promising molecule, while working on a chartered project, but the discovery cannot be introduced in the new product because Marketing puts too much pressure on getting the shortest time to market. In the end, the product that is put on the market is not as good as it could have been. The big question: how can TOTAL incorporate unexpected opportunities within the desired time to market?

Innovation Intelligence 191

6.2.2 Organizational and innovation shifts

In order to overcome these disruptive trends and respond quickly to changes in the environment, TOTAL needs to integrate a lot of knowledge – far from its historical core business – and become extremely agile. This transformation is all the more challenging for a diversified company like TOTAL; with businesses ranging from mature heavy industry (oil exploration & production and oil refining), to rapidly evolving businesses (chemistry and photovoltaic), TOTAL cannot take a one-size-fits-all approach to innovation. Given this background about the company's challenges, let's review briefly a number of initiatives that the company has put in place during the past few years.

Corporate scientific direction

A few years ago, in 2006, TOTAL created the Scientific Directorate (DS) the corporate level. It is headed by Jean-François Minster, who reports directly to the CEO of TOTAL. One of the roles of the DS is to build medium- and long-term what-if scenarios predicting the effect on TOTAL of various potential disruptions. The following might be a what-if scenario: What would happen if Chinese growth fell from 7% to 3%? The DS is composed of a small team of Deputy Scientific Directors who each have a broad understanding of both the science and technology and the potential business applications. Like the Fellows at Presans, these Deputy Scientific Directors are a rare breed. The DS has close interactions with the company's branches, in terms of both technology and business. The DS is also focused on acquiring knowledge from outside the company: each year members of the DS team visit approximately 150 laboratories around the world and animate a network of external scientific advisors who act like small antennas deployed outside of the company. One might think that visiting labs and participating in international conferences could be replaced by simply reading scientific articles. Maybe this was true not so long ago, but today the pace is so fast that reading scientific papers is looking toward the past rather than toward the present or the future. Speaking to experts and getting their opinions is looking into the future.

192   Chapter 6. Toward Innovation Intelligence

Corporate expert network

The corporate expert network is an important topic at TOTAL, and it was one of Jean-François Minster's personal interests. Over the past few years, the company has made significant progress in expert management, in large part due to learning from the work carried out by Olga Lelebina during her PhD (recall her definition of an expert that we cited in chapter 5). The leaders of TOTAL, like those in many other companies, felt that experts were the source of the problems. The vast majority of companies define an expert based on the recognition of the superior knowledge an expert holds compared to a non-expert. This definition is limiting, because it does not emphasize what the company can expect from the expert, and it does not provide criteria to evaluate the expert (since, by definition, the expert know that field best). At TOTAL, experts are now managed according to their defined role:

- Develop knowledge: experts must develop new knowledge and, in particular, address aspects of the knowledge management system
- Transfer knowledge: experts are not guardians of their own knowledge temple; they must transfer the knowledge to others in the company
- Apply knowledge: experts are at the service of the company and must apply their expertise to support troubleshooting, strategic thinking, detection of opportunities, and other projects assigned by their managers
- Communicate knowledge: experts are also the vehicles to carry messages outside the company

As soon as TOTAL decided to manage experts according to this definition of their role, evaluating experts became much easier. TOTAL has setup a jury that names and revokes experts. Top-ranked experts at TOTAL are called Fellows. In selecting Fellows, the jury even considers feedback from people outside the company, which was a revolution in terms of approach.

Innovation Intelligence

Toward more open R&D and platforms?

As mentioned above, TOTAL's R&D department has difficulty matching the accelerated pace of the market and the need to put new products on the market faster and faster. Jean Parizot explained us that he had recently reorganized the R&D department, attempting to clearly separate long-term research from short-term development. The Management Committee of the Marketing & Services branch has set the goal that the branch put ten disruptive products on the market by 2017. Ten new products is a lot, and 2017 is almost here. Parizot is well aware that, given the tight timeframe and limited resources – even in the Marketing & Services industry – the branch cannot do everything in-house. In 2014, the Marketing & Services branch's R&D department began a comprehensive review of the knowledge and technologies the team needs to master in order to succeed. The goal of this ongoing review is to decide which technologies can be safely outsourced and which ones are core so should remain in-house. We cannot provide any further details, for confidentiality reasons, but we know that similar reviews are taking place in the other branches of TOTAL. There is also an ongoing strategic initiative to develop strong international partnerships with leading academic researchers.

Outsourcing some R&D would address the acceleration aspect; however, is would not address flexibility: Parizot admits that TOTAL needs to set up robust product platforms, like has been done in the automobile industry, to which disruptive innovations can be added in a plug-and-play approach. The strategic thinking is progressing, but platforms are more difficult to conceive when products are relatively simple.

Toward a Chief Innovation Office?

At the time we are writing this book, TOTAL has no Innovation Director at the corporate level. The Marketing & Services branch established an innovation team in August 2012, and the Refining & Chemistry branch is currently trying to build one. The main motivation for creating the innovation team at Marketing & Services was to accelerate

194   Chapter 6. Toward Innovation Intelligence

time to market. As previously explained, the silos of a traditional company are at the root of inefficiencies, posing a mismatch between the organization's structure and the fast-paced environment, and they are no longer sufficient to enable the company to compete with the faster and more agile newcomers. This innovation team, composed of just a few individuals, plays the role of internal consultant: the team members benchmark existing innovation practices and make the results available to other entities (countries and business functions) within the branch. Aware that innovation is not a question of only technology but rather should pervade all functions of the company, the General Secretariat of the branch oversees the innovation team. Ideally, the innovation team would like each entity within the branch to develop its own innovation roadmap. To this end, the small innovation team has created a network of 170 correspondents in all areas of the branch. The ideal traits of these correspondents are curiosity and entrepreneurship. Their role is to animate and develop a culture of innovation deep inside the branch. This networking approach allows the innovation team to have an efficient and well-structured presence in all areas of the branch.

Embracing and leveraging the digital revolution

As explained in chapter 4, the digital wave is both a disruptive factor and a powerful toolbox. For both aspects, TOTAL has put in place a number of initiatives.

While other groups in the energy sector are only today (in 2014) creating their digital office, TOTAL Marketing & Service created its digital office back in early 2012 – three years ago. Considering the pace at which things evolve these days, three years was a long time ago! By creating its digital office, the branch had an opportunity to explore completely new worlds: the first, digitizing and the second, the consumer decision-making process. Exploring this area early enough could, perhaps, prevent TOTAL from being disintermediated by digital barbarians.

On the toolbox side, let's discuss Big Data. As we explained previously, one of the main challenges for TOTAL Marketing & Services

Innovation Intelligence 195

was to put on the market new products (new mixtures of molecules) faster and faster. Today, experience and intuition enable TOTAL's chemists to discover the right "recipe" of molecule for the company to obtain certain properties with its products. A large volume of data is generated at each step in the conception of a new recipe, but the data is not yet being analyzed. Big Data could be used to accelerate the conception of new recipes: if the researchers could use models based on this data predict the performance of molecules, a lot of time would be saved. According to Parizot, the problem is currently well formulated: Now the company needs to develop the right tools to relate molecules, properties, and performance.

6.2.3 Challenges remain

Despite TOTAL's many initiatives, its approach is still not optimal. Next we give a few examples for areas of improvement that will most likely be addressed by TOTAL in the future.

Innovation everywhere: a dramatic cultural change

The first issue brought to our attention by Christine Halliot, Innovation Director of TOTAL Marketing & Services, is that it is still very hard for her innovation team to make the voice of innovation heard throughout the branch. A form of conservatism still exists; although the top management is convinced of the necessity for innovation, there is still much resistance among the rank and file of the organization. According to Halliot, engineers tend to think about technology and product before thinking about value for the client. Our opinion is that the resistance among the rank and file results from the lack of a strong mandate from top management. The tone is always set by the top. You can be asked to think outside the box (for example, the head of the bitumen department thinking about connected roads), but if it is not part of the company's culture, if it is not part of yours and your annual bonus does not depend on it, why bother?

Adapting the pace of research to the fast pace of the market: toward platforms?

Earlier in this chapter, we mentioned the potential benefit from developing product platforms to which innovations could be added. This may not be so easy for comparatively less complex products, as compared to automobiles and airplanes. One approach may be to blend the fast screening techniques used in the pharmaceutical industry (see chapter 7) with platform-like shortcuts (perhaps pre-mixing of compounds), and then incorporate a massive effort in data acquisition and modeling.

Obtaining an integrated overview of knowledge

The main challenge that came through in the TOTAL interviews concerned the gathering of integrated knowledge. Most of the interviewees admitted that they and their teams are not yet very good at that game. They analyze patents, read scientific publications, watch for technology trends, analyze markets, analyze megatrends, and so forth. There are three main issues with their current approach to knowledge gathering. First, all of these tasks are led and conducted by separate teams in the company. The various knowledge-acquisition activities are not coordinated or integrated, therefore they do not feed innovation. Second, knowledge acquisition intrinsically suffers some loss in translation. For example, a request from the Innovation Director is summarized into keywords by the person in charge of the search. This person will most likely not have a full understanding of the question and what is really at stake. This person will not think about who the client is or who ultimately will benefit if the search is successful. Keyword searches return results that are then filtered and interpreted by the person in charge of the search. And last but not least, traditional knowledge searches rely on published data, which by definition is outdated; the outdated information is no longer sufficient, given the fast pace of knowledge renewal. The knowledge "market" is similar to a financial market: it is efficient, meaning that everybody has access to the same data. An anticipative and creative examination of all data is needed.

Innovation Intelligence   197

6.2.4 Conclusion of the TOTAL case study

TOTAL was chosen as the introductory example for this chapter, because in some ways its approach to adapting its innovation process is mature, and yet it still has many challenges to address. It is interesting to note that despite the TOTAL's maturity regarding innovation organization, process, and tools, it has decided not to have a corporate-level Chief Innovation Office, likely due to need for such an Office to ultimately hand off any innovation that it might conceive via experimentation to operational development departments within the branches and their individual businesses. However, it would probably make sense to establish and strengthen innovation teams at the branches, perhaps raising them to a higher level called Chief Innovation Office. In addition, TOTAL does not have an innovation lab, which we will see later is now in the toolboxes of many large corporations. Indeed, to really think outside the box, one may be need to be outside the operating branches.

6.3 Rise of the Chief Innovation Officer (lever #1)

The number of hits returned by a Google search for the term "open innovation" shows a rapid increase from 2006 to 2010, and then a slow decrease since then. In 2010, we began to see interest in the term "Chief Innovation Officer." The term was coined and described by Miller and Morris[80] in 1998, but it seems to have only received interest in the past three years or so. Another proxy for estimating the increased attention given to this new C-level function is the number of recent (blog) articles,[81] studies and reports[iii], or even upcoming books[82] on the topic. Many of them are just a few months old and they have titles like "the rise of Chief Innovation Officer."

Some C-level functions are well defined: the Chief Executive Officer (CEO) is in charge of the overall business and strategy, the Chief Information Officer (CIO) is in charge of IT, the Chief Finance Officer

---

[iii]Deloitte conducted a survey of more than 700 companies regarding the evolution of the Chief Information Officer (CIO) into a Chief Innovation Officer (CINO).

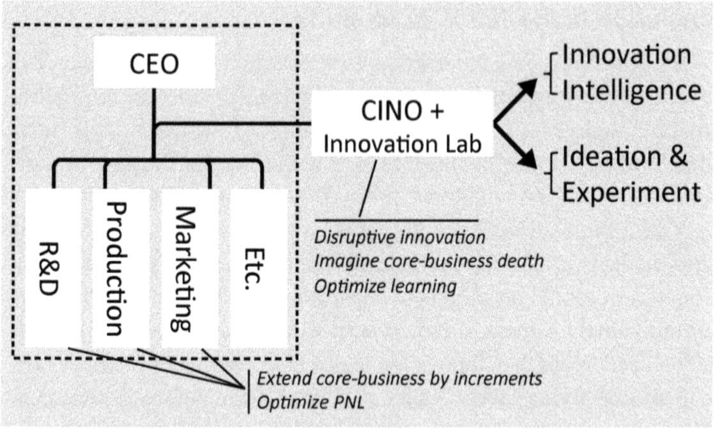

CEO

CINO +
Innovation Lab

R&D Production Marketing Etc.

Innovation
Intelligence

Ideation &
Experiment

Disruptive innovation
Imagine core-business death
Optimize learning

Extend core-business by increments
Optimize PNL

Figure 6.1: Chief Innovation Officer (CINO) role. The Chief Innovation Officer (CINO) and team explore new territories by leveraging innovation intelligence, ideation, and experimentation.

(CFO) is in charge of financial aspects of the business, such as cost management, budgeting (see figure 6.1). The concept of Chief Innovation Officer (CINO) is new; actually, as we have seen in our interviews, even the specific title is not yet stabilized. We have used the acronym CINO to avoid confusion with the Chief Information Officer. While CINO's function is becoming increasingly strategic, its description is still in its infancy and varies among companies. However, the ideal profile of the CINO is clearer.

6.3.1 Chief Innovation Officer: a role in its infancy

The challenge for large companies is to be agile despite their size. Because the feedback loop between knowledge and innovation must be fast and tight, R&D, Production, Marketing, Strategic Planning, and Finance are interdependent around the cradle of innovation. For a traditional company in which the team of CEO and CTO are performing well with regard to incremental innovation, the role of the

Innovation Intelligence

CINO is to redefine what is possible for the company. The CINO is not necessarily an innovator, but he or she understands how to get things done: the CINO must create an environment that fosters innovation, values innovators, and enables innovators to be as efficient as possible.

Before entering the debate about the details of the CINO role, let's face the variations on the title itself. The Chief Technology Officer cannot just change his or her title to Chief Innovation Officer and suddenly improve the business value of R&D. When the former CTO of Groupe SEB retired a few years ago, the company revamped the role, replacing it with a Chief Innovation Officer. When Jean-Christophe Simon took on that role, the company experienced a real transformation. In some other companies, however, the R&D Director simply became R&I Director – the I standing for Innovation, but that was it. The change in title didn't change the scale or scope of the company's innovation. In other companies, there is a person in charge of driving disruptive innovation across the silos, but the title is not necessarily CINO. This is the case at Pernod Ricard, where the Breakthrough Innovation Group (BIG) was created a few years ago (see section 6.4 in this chapter for a discussion of on innovation labs). The General Manager of this entity has a significant budget and reports directly to the company's Executive Committee. Although it is not stated in his title, Alain Dufossé is acting as a CINO.

The CINO is, first of all, in charge of disruptive innovation. At least, we have seen this in most companies, but CINO and CTO sometimes overlap (Airbus Aircraft in an example). In such cases of overlap, both the CTO and the CINO can look at both incremental and disruptive innovation, with the main distinction being that the CTO is mostly concerned with technologies and the CINO is mostly concerned with new business models.

> Until quite recently the growth of the group was ensured mostly by a geographical extension. Now that we are implanted everywhere, sustainable growth can only be ensured with disruptive innovations that will solve new problems.
> **Olivier Delabroy, R&D Director, Air Liquide**

The role of the CINO is to drive innovation across the whole company, across the silos, across the functions, across the business units, across the geographical areas, and possibly beyond the company's traditional borders. Ultimately, the CINO must ensure that innovation delivers business results. Because the CINO function is still emerging and every sector, company, and country is different, we do not pretend to provide here a detailed, comprehensive overview of all the functions of a Chief Innovation Officer. Moreover, the following should not be taken as a grand truth of what a CINO should do in a company but rather as a common base for the CINO role in most mature companies:

- Focus on business value
- Define the language of innovation and foster a culture of innovation
- Organize and leverage innovation-driven intelligence
- Foster idea generation and rapid experimentation
- Ensure that innovations have business propositions
- Bridge the gap between the innovators and the rest of the company

6.3.2 Focus on business value

Innovation is business oriented, and so is the CINO. The CINO ensures that innovation initiatives are designed for business value creation. An innovation project should not be undertaken just because it is fashionable (nanotechnologies, drones, 3-D printing, and so forth). To ensure that innovation is focused on business value, the CINO is in

Innovation Intelligence 201

charge of defining and monitoring the metrics of innovation performance. The CINO's business focus is mainly new territories, areas not currently covered by the company. The purpose of the CINO to identify disruptive threats and opportunities based on emerging trends.

6.3.3 Defining language and changing culture

The first function of the CINO is to develop a culture of innovation in the company. All of the CINOs who we have met insisted that it is the most important. To be able to create such a culture, the first key is language. A common language for innovation must be defined across the entire company. It is then important to distinguish between core-business innovation, also known as incremental innovation, which is covered by the standard functions of the company, and disruptive innovation, which cannot be covered by standard functions. This is crucial, because the very reason the CINO exists is to lead disruptive innovation, the exploration of new territories to ensure sustainable growth of the company. A shared language is essential, because it prevents potential conflicts, such as an employee asking, "What is the role the CINO? We already have a CTO." Moreover, once there is agreement on the definition of innovation (specifically, disruptive innovation), determining how to evaluate its performance becomes easier. Core-business innovation is generally a matter of executing the standard processes of the company, and adequate metrics already exist for measuring its performance. On the contrary, evaluating the performance of disruptive innovation, although it is driven by business, cannot be done with the traditional indicators.

Once the common language has been agreed upon, another job of the CINO is communication. By communication, we mean both internal and external. Internal communication shapes the company culture. It is the only way to make the residents of the business silos aware that innovation can happen everywhere in the company. External communication can be a means to develop the innovative spirit of the company in such a way that it attracts creative talents and partners

202   Chapter 6. Toward Innovation Intelligence

from horizons far away from the core business. Among communication tools, innovation contests have gained some importance in the last few years (see chapter 7), as both tools to generate innovation intelligence and powerful communication tools.

Another important mission of the CINO is training. The CINO should set up the most appropriate environment to train the company's experts in the art of innovation (see the Airbus case in the inset above).

6.3.4 Leveraging innovation intelligence

Knowledge is the CINO's main key. This was underlined in almost all of the interviews we conducted. The issue is that encyclopedic knowledge is no longer possible. The good old days of the Age of Enlightenment are over. It is no longer possible to stuff in one brain all the knowledge of the universe. Flooding and dispersed, knowledge represents a real – unsolved – challenge for CINOs. An unsolved challenge, because the volume of information is enormous, it is not only technological but rather begins with the unstated dreams of people. Creating an integrated synthesis of the required knowledge is the CINO's key challenge. And yet, the CINO must also anticipate and build a long-term strategic vision for the company. Moreover, based on the knowledge and vision, the CINO must take actions.

Intelligence is not a new task. All companies have teams dedicated to technology watching, market analysis, trend analysis, and so forth. The main issue with this current approach is that traditional companies are built in silos, and these individual intelligence tasks are performed by various teams that hardly communicate with one another. Moreover, the people performing these tasks may not have a good understanding of what really matters for the company. Most importantly, these tasks are not synchronized, coordinated, or synthesized to focus on innovation. Intelligence-driven innovation should be concerned with both established knowledge on technologies, markets, and trends and new knowledge generated by the CINO who dedicate most of his or her actions into transforming assumptions into knowledge.

Innovation Intelligence   203

Based on innovation intelligence, the CINO determines the company's innovation strategy and aggressively manages the innovation portfolio. The CINO has a budget to fund promising ideas that are too risky or out of the scope of the business units.

6.3.5 Fostering idea generation and rapid experimentation

Chief Innovation Officers are not themselves responsible for idea generation, but they are in charge of setting up an environment that fosters idea recognition and rapid experimentation. Such an environment includes the physical place but also the people, tools, and resources. The tools may include hackathons, crowdsourcing, and innovation challenges, – all situations in which collaborators can post ideas, enrich other people's ideas, and provide feedback about ideas. Beyond idea generation, the CINO is also in charge of what happens to the ideas afterward: their final evaluation, selection, incubation, and maybe coaching their transformation into new products or services. The almost real-time and real-world evaluation has become critical. More details about the tools are provided in section 6.4, in which we discuss innovation labs, the playgrounds of the Chief Innovation Officers and his or her teams.

The innovation environment inside a company does not depend only on process and tools, but also – perhaps mainly – on people. Therefore, the CINO must cultivate the right talents. A CINO's team tends to become increasingly multidisciplinary over time, incorporating not only engineers but also marketers, designers, and sociologists, among others. The team members must all be capable of operating with minimal structure. They must be able to deal with ambiguity and learn from failures: one idea out of ten succeeds, but the lessons learned from the nine failures are as important as the one success. Managing learning is essential. While core-business innovation relies heavily on the extrapolation of established knowledge about technologies, markets, customers, and competition, disruptive innovation, or new-business innovation, relies on completely new knowledge generated by the CINO's team. Ideas

204　Chapter 6. Toward Innovation Intelligence

must be tested by rapid, small-scale experimentation. The low-cost "test tube" can be a specific geographical location or small customer group, and it should not be perturbed by the current core business of the company. These small-scale experiments are ways to evaluate rapidly the viability of an idea. These experiments are used to convert assumptions into knowledge of what works and what does not work, in terms of both technical feasibility and business model. The new, emerging knowledge is fed via a fast feedback loop into the innovation process.

Another way for a CINO to have one eye on reality is to participate in start-up firms. For example, Danone is using its Bridge incubator to be a partner in selected start-ups. Other companies pay, by participating in venture capital funds, for the privilege of closely observing start-ups. These are all approaches to learning what will and won't work.

Speaking of learning, the metrics to evaluate the Chief Innovation Officer's performance should reflect this notion of creating new knowledge. What did the organization learn? How? How much? How fast? By how much was the original risk or uncertainty reduced? These are the types of questions that should be asked about a CINO's performance.

6.3.6　Bridging the gap with the rest of the company

As shown in figure 6.1, new territories are explored by the CINO leveraging innovation intelligence, ideation, and experimentation. Once a new viable business opportunity has been identified (the CINO having transformed assumptions into new knowledge) and proven both technologically feasible and desirable for users, the project should be transferred to a business unit. The question is how to transfer? The answer is not obvious. Should the project be hosted by an existing business unit? Should an ad hoc business unit be created? Should it be spun off? The choice of approach depends on the situation. According to Jean-François Minster, for a CINO this is one the most difficult parts of the innovation process. The CINO is there to facilitate the transition,

Innovation Intelligence   205

the transfer, and to bridge the gap between the innovation team and the rest of the company. As we will discuss later, in the case of Valeo, the new territories that explored by the commando team of the CINO (who was not called CINO at the time) gradually replaced the historical business units.

6.3.7 Chief Innovation Officer: multidisciplinary and closer to the CEO

CINO: The case of Airbus Aircraft

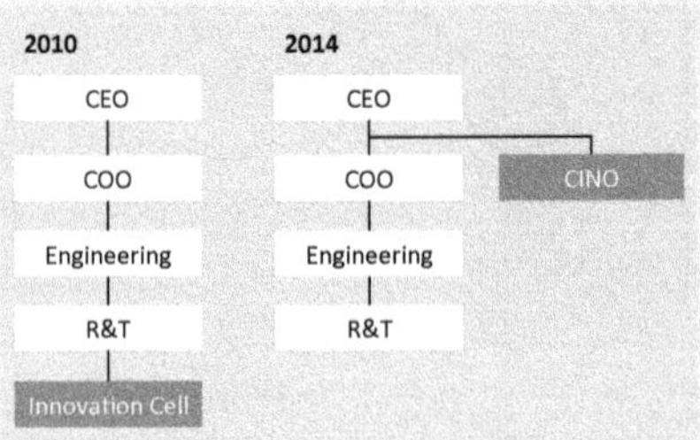

The Innovation Cell (later renamed Technology and Concept team) at Airbus Aircraft was created in early 2010. As shown in the diagram, the Innovation Cell was originally four degrees away from the CEO. In mid-2013, a powerful Chief Innovation Office (CINO), headed by Yann Barbaux, was established.

2010	2014
CEO	CEO
COO	COO — CINO
Engineering	Engineering
R&T	R&T
Innovation Cell	

A transversal organization: The CINO office is composed of approximately twenty-five people around the world, as well as a network of twenty-five Senior Vice Presidents in the various business functions and a network of seventy-five (the target is two hundred) Innovation Catalysts in various functions across the company.

One mission: accelerate innovation: The goal is to create new products and services for Airbus' clients (the airlines), with final customers (pilots, passengers, and airports) in mind.

The first action is training. Innovation is a key skill that must be in the company's culture and genes. Partners of the group must be trained to use simple yet agile methods. For example, the entire innovation network is trained in design thinking.

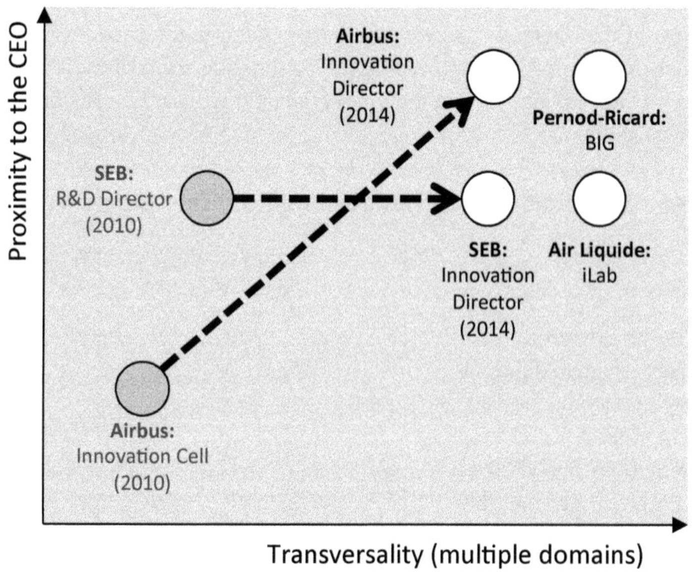

Chapter 6. Toward Innovation Intelligence

Proximity to the CEO

Airbus:
Innovation
Director
(2014)

Pernod-Ricard:
BIG

SEB:
R&D Director
(2010)

SEB:
Innovation
Director
(2014)

Air Liquide:
iLab

Airbus:
Innovation Cell
(2010)

Transversality (multiple domains)

Figure 6.3: Evolution of the CINO role. Estimate of the CINO position at various companies, in terms of proximity to the CEO and multidiscipline. The position between companies does represent reality – we wish to represent general trends in a simple way.

The second action is idea generation, filtering, management, and incubation. To that end, a number of initiatives were launched. As we write these lines, the Airbus BizLab has not been officially announced, but by the time the book gets out it will have been. Another initiative is co-innovation clients (for example, turnaround-time optimization or predictive maintenance) and suppliers; co-innovation is very new approach for Airbus.

In the 2014 report[83] "Proven Paths to Innovation Success." by Jaruzelski et al, the authors summarize the analysis they carried out after a survey of more than 500 innovation leaders across a wide range of companies. Although innovation expenditure growth slowed in 2014,

Innovation Intelligence

the companies' innovation leaders felt that they had made significant progress in the efficient use of R&D investments by better aligning innovation and business strategy. This conclusion is shared by a number of other recent studies:[84] the innovation function is rising in the hierarchy of a company and is moving closer to strategy. We conducted our own study of forty-four companies in twenty countries. One-third of the innovation managers who responded to our survey hold positions that were created within the past three years. The first remarkable conclusion is that the innovation function has moved closer to the CEO: as of 2013, approximately 20% of the CINOs were members of their company's executive committee (compared to 10% in 2010), and almost 60% have access to the CEO (compared to 40% in 2010). The role of the CINO has also become more closely aligned with company strategy: 70% of CINOs claim to have corporate strategy in their scope (compared to 56% in 2010). Finally, a major highlight is the progression of forward-looking innovation intelligence activities: 78% of the CINOs stated that it was the primary mission (compared to 59% in 2010).

Proximity to the CEO allows the CINO to take a holistic approach across the organization. At the beginning of the 2000s, there were just a few dozen CINOs in the world. There are probably thousands today, in early 2015. The European Institute for Creative Strategies and Innovation, headed by Marc Giget, conducted an extensive survey more than five hundred CINOs around the world to gain an understanding of how the function has evolved over the past few years. As of today, half of the large companies surveyed have established a CINO function. The role of the CINO is not yet uniform across companies and is still evolving. As illustrated in figure 6.3, it has generally started as a small cross-functional team, buried somewhere in the organization, evolve toward a powerful function in close proximity to the CEO. Good examples are Airbus Aircraft and Lafarge who now have CINOs who report directly to the CEO (see earlier inset regarding Airbus). In China, the country's most recent five-year plan requires every large corporate groups to set up an Innovation department. By the way, CINO is

208 Chapter 6. Toward Innovation Intelligence

increasingly regarded as the ideal position to hold before becoming CEO of a company. CINOs are not only for large corporations. Small and medium-sized enterprises, start-ups, and even public organizations are creating CINO positions. It may even become a hype.

As exemplified in figure 6.3, the general trend we have observed is that the role (and the team) of the Chief Innovation Officer is becoming more and more multidisciplinary and it is moving closer to the CEO of the company or business unit. As we will see in section 6.4, the trend is to assemble innovation teams that can think outside the box. Air Liquide's i-Lab, for example, has a team of approximately twenty-five people, including engineers, sociologists, designers, and business people. Innovation teams are also comprised of a balanced mix of thinkers and doers. These teams are transitioning from being a sample of the company to being a sample of the world.

The second trend we have observed is top-management support. To be effective, the CINO needs strong support and a clear mandate from the CEO. Because the CINO's role is to explore new territories, he or she must be able to be challenge silo residents and business as usual. The CINO should not be evaluated in terms of business value created, but rather in terms of the radically new knowledge created. Such a new piece of knowledge can be "we have looked at this trend, and although the company is suiting to tackling the problem, we have not found a technical way to address it." In core-business innovation – business as usual – failure is hardly acceptable. In disruptive innovation, it is. In this case, the CINO has demonstrated that an opportunity, though attractive, is not feasible, so the project should be killed. He or she has created new knowledge. The CINO should not be punished because an idea does not work but rather should be evaluated by how efficiently the project is determined not to be feasible and how quickly resources are redirected in more promising directions. Innovation is risk. A good CINO should not be so conservative that he or she fears the risk associated with trying out daring, new ideas.

Innovation Intelligence   209

6.3.8 Chief Innovation Officer: a unicorn?

Because most traditional CEOs cannot assume the function of a Chief
of Innovation, the CINO, with the CEO's mandate, is a person who
can apply multiple skills to a broad range of knowledge, knowledge of
not only technology but also markets, finance, and so forth. The ideal
CINO will know how to seek input from others, both within and outside
the company. The CINO is convinced that innovation is a necessity. He
or she believes in innovation and is not risk-averse. The CINO is not
necessarily a creative person or an innovator. Although many CINOs
have a technological bias (although a growing proportion of CINOs
are coming from digital, management, and strategy), the ideal CINO
combines traits which are very seldom embodied in a single person:

- **Business understanding.** the CINO has a good business understanding, which enables him or her to combine long-term
  strategic planning and short-term tactical operations. The CINO
  must have a thorough understanding of the company's competitive position.
- **Technological wisdom.** the CINO must a sufficient level of
  understanding of technologies as enablers of new products and
  services. Although not necessarily a specialist, he or she should
  be able to listen to and challenge technical people.
- **Communicative leadership.** The CINO must bridge the gaps
  among other C-level executives at the speed of light. The CINO
  is not the only leader but rather is able to bring other functions on
  board and invite them to contribute to in-house cross-fertilization.
  Even if the CINO is a born leader and a genius in communication,
  this can requires the support of the CEO.
- **Client-centric experimentation.** As discussed in Chapter 4, innovations must be tested as quickly as possible on users or clients.
  The CINO has therefore a strong taste for experimentation. He
  should have a natural empathy for the final user problems and be
  able to focus all his experimentation on this point.
- **Ability to connect small worlds.** The CINO must be able to

bridge disparate areas of knowledge. To do that, the CINO must have a large active network comprised of small worlds and be able to connect the dots.

Steve Jobs had probably all of these qualities, but he was also a very difficult person to work with.

6.4 Innovation labs: idea generation & rapid experimentation (lever #2)

A key role for the CINO is to create an environment that favors the emergence of ideas and rapid real-world and quasi-real-time experiments. One of the effective levers for doing this that have received attention over the past few years is what we call innovation labs. They are places of freedom where new territories can be explored in search of disruptive innovations. BIG at Pernod Ricard and i-Lab at Air Liquide are well known innovation labs that have received a lot of press coverage. They are not the only innovation labs: Unibail Rodamco, the largest commercial real estate company in Europe, has urLab, Airbus is about to announce its BizLab, and Groupe SEB has its SebLab.

Many other companies have structures similar to innovation labs, although they call them something else. For example, Danone's combination of the Bridge Incubator and the Ateliez could constitute an innovation lab. The Bridge Incubator is a small team focused on external knowledge without interference with and from the core business. The Ateliez is a laboratory for food prototyping where consumers can try new products in real time.

Another peculiar example comes from the multinational automotive supplier Valeo. To our knowledge, Valeo was the first company in France to introduce a structure like an innovation lab, in the early 2000s. Valeo called them domains rather than labs. At the time, OEMs were starting to outsource product development and product innovation to their suppliers. Valeo was organized in a way that was optimal for its financial reporting but not for innovation in a radical mode. The domains were created with the mission of to explore and demonstrate

Innovation Intelligence   211

new paths to value. They were composed of small teams, with a strong hierarchy. Each domain (driving assistance, powertrain, and lighting) included a leader, who reported to the company's top management, and a small team. They worked in an unusual way: armed with prototypes, they would bypass the traditional functions of company and make demonstration directly to clients' strategic marketing departments). If the client confirmed interest in the project, the project would transition to the more standard process involving the business units and the purchasing department. It is interesting to note that in 2010, a few years after the creation of the domains, Valeo's traditional business units (alternator, gear box, and so forth) were replaced by business groups that somewhat match the domains. The leaders of the domains became CINOs of the business groups, demonstrating the possibly transient nature of innovation labs.

6.4.1 i-Lab: the case of Air Liquide

R&D at Air Liquide has focused mainly on technologies. Over the past three years, Olivier Delabroy, Air Liquide's VP of R&D, strongly contributed to transforming the company's R&D approach by incorporating science and usage in addition to technologies.

try quickly, fail early, succeed big

The i-Lab

- Program directors are in charge of core technologies and applications.
- The scientific direction goes back to the science, the roots, of existing technologies to find new applications and new business opportunities based on existing know-how.
- The i-Lab is Air Liquide's laboratory for new ideas. It was

212 Chapter 6. Toward Innovation Intelligence

created in December 2013 by Delabroy, with a mandate from the CEO. The i-Lab's mission is to explore new territories, areas far from the traditional activities of the company and which would not be explored by a traditional extrapolation of current business.

The i-Lab is quite a peculiar place, very different from Air Liquide's main research center located in Les Loges en Josas, France. Despite the main research center's location relatively near a number of other large companies, excellent universities, and engineering schools, it feels somewhat isolated. To enter it, like most research centers, security is key: security gate, ID card, guests remain with hosts, and other standard procedures.

In contrast, visiting i-Lab is like visiting a rich start-up. The i-Lab is located near Bastille in downtown Paris. When you enter for the first time, you may wonder if you are even at Air Liquide. The building is a modern loft. There is no security. There is a bar with a coffee machine, people are sitting on sofas. A guy is sitting at a table – not a desk – with a laptop and headphones. He is Gregory Olocco, the head of the i-Lab.

Three areas are currently explored by the i-Lab team: a Digital World, Breathe in the City, and Responsible Food. To determine whether a territory has potential for Air Liquide, the i-Lab first addresses three questions:

- What is at stake, and is it a relevant topic?
- Is it already a business of Air Liquide?
- Is Air Liquide suited to address this question?

Let's consider the Breathe in the City area. What is at stake? Is it a relevant topic? "Obviously, yes, we are all going to die due to pollution," says Delabroy. Is Air Liquide already addressing the problem? No. Is Air Liquide suited for this new territory? Yes, absolutely. In fact, Air Liquide is already helping people to breathe in hospitals, for example. The company can therefore begin to invest in and investigate this territory. A start-up incubator called Breathe in the City was established by Air Liquide's i-Lab and Paris Région Lab in June 2014.

6.4.2 Common features of innovation labs

> If you want to increase your success rate, double your failure rate.
> **Thomas J. Watson, Founder of IBM**

The core functions of a company (marketing, R&D, production, and so forth) are designed to extend the current business (such as via incremental innovation) and to optimize the financial results. However, when the usual growth drivers (for example, geographic expansion) are no longer sufficient, the company needs to explore new areas. The role of an innovation lab is to find new opportunities, which will potentially disrupt – and possibly even kill – the existing core business.

Such structures require strong support, mandate, and control from the highest level of the company – they are source and part of the strategy. Let's explore how these labs work once top management's strong support is in place. In order to reach their goals, innovation labs share three features:

- **Place.** Although not always the case, mainly for budgetary reasons, the innovation lab is often hosted in dedicated location outside company headquarters or outside the company's traditional offices. The location is key to fostering a new mindset. Innovation labs are generally designed to foster creativity, therefore are often located in the central area of a city or town rather than in the outskirts like research centers typically area. The building itself is open to suppliers, clients, and partners. An open space where a person can grab a chair and a table, it is friendly and designed for interacting and sharing. Being physically outside of the company's traditional buildings is also a way to put some distance between the core business and this disruptive innovation team. The challenge remains to find the right balance between distance and alignment with the company's strategy.
- **Team.** The team at the innovation lab is generally quite small.

The largest teams we have observed were comprised of twenty members. Several companies were proud to say that their innovation teams were composed of an equal number of men and women. Even more important for outside-the-box thinking is a mix of functions (businesspeople, engineers, designers, sociologists, and so forth) and nationalities. The diversity of the team is critical. The small team should extend its reach and effectiveness by gathering together representatives from the rest of the organization. They know what is important for the company, what really matters. This new blood is also critical, because the representatives will bring a fresh point of view, perhaps triggering disruptive innovation. Many of the new areas to be explored lie at the interface of existing businesses.

- **Methods.** While there seems a consensus that these innovation labs should not be driven only by technology, the question of methodology is still pending. Although many companies adopt design thinking, others claim that there should not be any process at all. For example, Alain Dufossé claims that "algorithms prevent companies from being disruptive." According to him, innovation cannot and should not happen within a process. Some of the structures that we observed did not have key performance indicators (KPIO.

Although the innovation labs that we have studied are all very different from one another in terms of industry, size, and so forth, they all try to find the right balance between think tank and do tank. The think tank is in charge of innovation intelligence and serves innovation by ideation, and the do tank is in charge of transforming assumptions into knowledge. The tasks performed by the innovation team are as follows:

- **Understand.** The goal is to get a better understanding of the world. What are the mutations? What are the trends? The idea is to go far beyond traditional customer studies with more advanced sociological studies.
- **Map.** Given the trends identified above, what are all the possible

Innovation Intelligence 215

territories that can be explored?

- **Select.** The goal is to select the territories that are worth exploring, the ones with the highest potential. For that, three attributes should be considered: size of the opportunity, suitability for the company, and degree of newness.
- **Ideate, experiment, and feedback.** Given the selected territories, ideas are rapidly generated and tested. The goal of the experimentation is to kill projects as early as possible if the opportunity is not viable. Regardless of the methodology used for generating ideas (brainstorming, TRIZ, divergence and convergence, DKCP method, or an alternative approach), nothing should be forbidden. Innovation labs have their own budgets to support ideas and projects that would not otherwise emerge from the company.

Alain Dufossé insists that innovation intelligence is key: half of his staff is dedicated to collecting and analyzing knowledge to build intelligence. This intelligence is driven by innovation and serves innovation. Understand, Map and Select are the three key steps of innovation intelligence. Before we examine innovation intelligence in detail, let's first focus on idea generation and rapid experimentation.

6.4.3 Design thinking: innovation labs' favorite tool?

Idea generation followed by rapid experimentation enables the transformation of assumptions into knowledge of what does and does not work. Rapid experimentation allows the assessment of not only a technology or a combination of technologies but also of a business model and a market response. As shown in figure 6.5 this assessment incorporates analysis of the technology (feasibility), business profitability (viability), and human values (usability and desirability). As an example of rapid experimentation, a prototype is often used to evaluate potential clients' response to the proposed product or service, willingness to pay for it, way they use it, frequency of use, and so on. These real-world experiments provide the innovation team with quasi-real-time, real-world

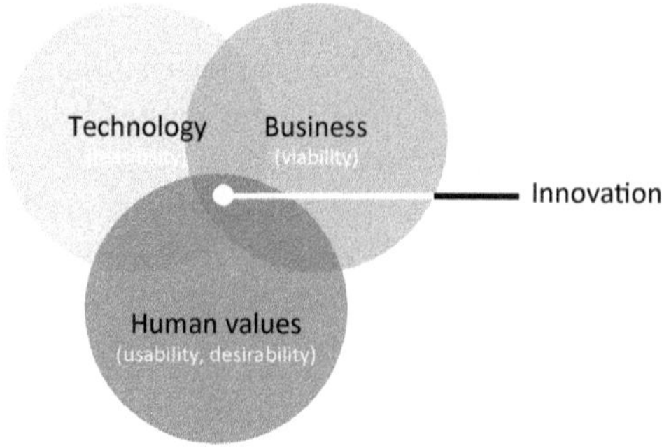

Technology

Business
(viability)

Innovation

Figure 6.5: Three dimensions of design thinking.

Human values
(usability, desirability)

feedback from customers. This generates new knowledge that is fed back into the innovation process.

Various tools can support idea generation and rapid experimentation. Most methods commonly used are inspired by design thinking, an approach developed at Stanford University by Rolf Faste. Design thinking seeks to combine analytical thinking and creative thinking. The description of the process of design thinking varies from author to author, but the main ideas are the same. The steps of the process follow a logical flow, but the process should be performed not as a linear process but rather as a series of fast iterative loops. Let's take a quick look at how the Institute of Design at Stanford (the d.school[85]) describes the design thinking as a five-step process (see figure 6.6):

- **Empathize.** The innovation team establishes empathy with users. This can be achieved by interviews. The goal is to understand what users do, think, feel, and say. What do users need and why?
- **Define.** In this second phase, the scope is defined: what problem are we trying to solve? How will ideas be evaluated?
- **Ideate.** In this phase, as many ideas as possible are generated. Various methods can be used to foster wild creativity, including brainstorming, mind mapping, Metaplan, divergence and convergence, analogies, TRIZ, DKCP method, and Six Thinking Hats.

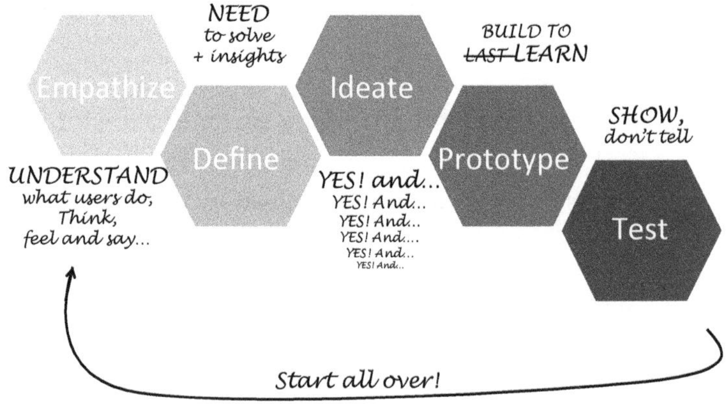

Innovation Intelligence 217

Figure 6.6: Sequence structure in design thinking.

At the end of this phase, the ideas are ranked and prioritized.

- **Prototype.** In this phase, the product or service is made concrete in order to increase empathy with the final user. For quick prototyping, anything is allowed, including 3-D printing, virtual reality, role-playing games, and bootstrapping. The prototype will enable the exploration of various options, laying the groundwork for tests and inspiring the innovation team members.
- **Test.** In this final phase the prototype is presented to the final user. Does the user like it? How does he or she use it? What would he or she be willing to pay for it? New knowledge generated by this test is then fed back into the design process, initiating the next iterative loop.

The concept of an innovation lab, lean and fast, is linked to the concept of *lean start-up*, advocated by Eric Ries.[86] This young, Silicon Valley entrepreneur is trying to formalize and possibly extend to adjacent businesses the ability of dot-com companies to put unfinished prototypes on the market and utilize user feedback to improve the final offering. This approach is indeed a way to conduct rapid experimentation. It is not straightforward to extend the approach to physical

218 Chapter 6. Toward Innovation Intelligence

products, however, though exposing a crude prototype may help in addressing key shortcomings.

6.4.4 A short history of the iPod: was there an innovation lab?

> Picasso had a saying. He said 'Good artists copy, great artists steal.' And we have always been shameless about stealing great ideas.
> **Steve Jobs, Triumph of the Nerds: The Rise of Accidental Empires, PBS, 1996**

We are Apple fans. Not because the products are so cool, but because Apple is a truly innovative company. Some claim that Apple is not innovative because it doesn't do R&D but rather it "steals" ideas and technologies. Our opinion is quite the opposite: Apple is not only one of the most innovative companies in the World, but is also an emblematic example of what we call the firm of the third era, the networked firm. Apple knows how to scout talents and technologies on-demand to put on the market a very successful product in almost no time. The birth of the iPod is amazing. The reason we speak about Apple here is that despite not having an official innovation Lab when Apple launched the iPod, the original team that worked on the iPod was an informal innovation lab: a small commando team, close to the CEO (actually, the CEO himself was highly involved in the project), including talents from outside, and so forth.

Let's put ourselves back in the year 2000. People are downloading music from Napster, and they are ripping and burning CDs like crazy. And guess what? The iMac has no CD burner! Steve Jobs realizes that Apple was about to miss the music-sharing wave: "I thought we had missed it. We had to work hard to catch up," Jobs said in a Fortune Magazine interview.[9] Adding a CD burner to the iMac would not be enough. This is when Apple put together its digital-hub strategy, which would transform the company and make it the most valuable one in the

Innovation Intelligence

world. Apple had to act fast. Faster than ever.

The first brick was iTunes. At that point in time, existing music-management applications designed by other companies were clunky and complex. Apple had to design its own. Apple bought SoundJam MP in July 2000, bringing the software as well as one of its developers, Jeff Robbin, who would transform SoundJam MP into iTunes in just four months. Apple unveiled iTunes in January 2001.

The next step toward Apple's digital hub strategy was to design the iPod and take it to market. Steve Jobs knew that, and he had started pushing for a portable music player in late 2000. We are now in spring 2001. Jobs wanted the iPod to be available for sale for Christmas gifts, which would mean unveiling it in October, eight months later. Jobs put together a small team in charge of creating the iPod. The first key member of the team was Jonathan (Jon) Rubinstein, who was put in charge of sourcing the right hardware. Rubinstein sourced a suitable small LCD screen, a rechargeable lithium polymer battery from Sony, as well as a key element for which he negotiated exclusivity: a tiny 1.8-inch, 5GB hard drive that Toshiba had just developed. The second key member of the team was Jonathan Ive, who was put in charge of design. The third team member, Tony Fadell, came from outside the company and would be in charge of putting everything together (hardware, software, and business model) based on an eight-week contract with Apple. The final key element of the iPod project was the exclusive partnership with the small Silicon Valley company PortalPlayer, whose hardware platform and software would serve as the foundation. This dream team, sourced partly from outside the company, put together technologies that were also outsourced and leveraged an exclusive external partner, to be able to release the iPod, as planned, for Christmas 2001, eight months after the decision to go for it.

Since Fadell thought of the whole thing in terms of a system, he also proposed the third brick of the digital-hub strategy, enabling customers to seamlessly acquire music. iTunes enabled music management. The iPod enables people to carry a thousand songs in their pockets. The system was not yet perfect, because acquiring new albums for use by

220 Chapter 6. Toward Innovation Intelligence

iTunes and iPod meant buying a CD and ripping it. In addition, the use of Napster-like platforms had to be stopped. In early 2002, Steve Jobs was in a good position to negotiate with Warner Music Group, Universal Music Group, and Sony Music Entertainment a content-licensing agreement allowing Apple to sell music tracks (songs) for 99 cents each on the freshly released iTunes Store, which would become the largest online music seller worldwide.

Apple caught up with the wave of music sharing.

6.5 Innovation intelligence (lever #3)

As we have already discussed, CINOs, and their innovation labs must set up an environment favorable to building intelligence, which is driven by and serves innovation. Let us now explore in more detail the content of innovation intelligence.

6.5.1 Learning innovation intelligence with Pernod Ricard

"GIGO. Garbage in. Garbage out." It is with these words that Alain Dufossé, the general manager of BIG at Pernod Ricard, started our interview. What he meant was that if the quality of the intelligence used to feed the innovation process was poor, then what comes out of the innovation process, the innovation itself, would also be of poor quality. High-quality intelligence is at the heart of the innovation process's success.

Let's look at Pernod Ricard's flagship Project Gutenberg. Project Gutenberg is a sort of connected Nespresso machine for making cocktails. A connected mixologist!

Alain Dufossé explained us that everything starts by defining the real métier of Pernod Ricard. The term does not have an accurate translation in English; it is a mix of job, business, mission, and motto. Saying that Pernod Ricard's métier is to sell spirits is far too narrow. To allow the company to explore new territories, its métier must be defined in terms of what it provides to people. What is the human value?

Innovation Intelligence   221

"Pernod Ricard enables conviviality." This is the métier of Pernod Ricard. BIG's is to invent new experiences of conviviality. Based on the company's métier, spaces of freedom for exploration can be defined – BIG calls them opportunity platforms. These opportunity platforms define the perimeter, or the playground, in which they will seek opportunities. Project Gutenberg was born in the opportunity platform called augmented home entertainment, or conviviality at home. This slogan, that C-K theory aficionados would perhaps call a projecting concept, aims to inspire people. What kind of conviviality experience could we organize at home, leveraging digital technologies. . . and spirits? The opportunity platform drives the intelligence activities.

Intelligence activities will seek phenomena that can affect conviviality. The three main classes of phenomena that the BIG considers are human, digital, and other technologies. For the human aspect, BIG would typically look at demographic trends, lifestyle trends, sociology, culture, gender evolution, and so forth.

For the digital aspect, BIG looks at emerging technologies, business models. . . and start-ups. The fact that thirty-five startups were created in that topical area in one year is a strong signal. Something is going on.

Finally, the other technologies aspect is less important for Pernod Ricard's spirit group, but there are still a few areas, such as nanotechnologies, that could provide disruptions.

Intelligence can be decomposed into several activities. The first activity is data collection. BIG follows approximately 800 sources of information, including blogs, newsletters, magazines, and dedicated studies. This desk research is supplemented by physical presence at a number of relevant events, interviews with experts, and a network of twelve scouts who act like small antennas in various locations around the world. After it has been collected, this information is then analyzed and archived. Archiving is currently done at BIG via an internal blog in which the content is hash-tagged. Both processing and analysis are performed by members of the team. Analysis consists of detecting the convergence of phenomena. The identification of these phenomena

222 Chapter 6. Toward Innovation Intelligence

enables the identification of a number of territories to be explored within the opportunity platform. At that point, ideation can begin, based on the intelligence. For Project Gutenberg's ideation phase, BIG worked with a company specialized in design thinking. As we write these lines, the project is currently entering the pre-series phase. New real-world, real-time knowledge will be used as feedback in the next iteration of the innovation process.

After three years of existence, BIG team has learned a lot, but Dufossé admits that many challenges are still ahead: How can BIG industrialize the process of intelligence, both for collection and analysis? How can it be faster and better? What tools can BIG use? How can BIG train its own personnel in becoming proactive in this innovation process? Qualified people to perform the critical part of innovation intelligence, the analysis, are hard to find.

6.5.2 Challenges of innovation intelligence

The majority of the companies we have interviewed admitted that they are not as good at innovation intelligence as they would like to be. Furthermore, it is likely that the companies that stated that are in fact the ones that care the most about the topic so are probably the most advanced about it. They have tried various approaches and identified the following challenges that remain to be overcome: integration, timeliness, skills, and digital.

Integration. In a large organization, silos pose a significant obstacle to integrative knowledge. All of the companies that we interviewed have teams each assigned to a different topic. Teams dedicated to market analysis. Teams dedicated to technology forecasting and roadmapping. Teams looking at trends. The main issue is that, in most cases, these teams do not communicate enough with one another. They belong to different silos. Most importantly, they are not coordinated and their reason for existing is not to feed innovation. Because the company has no integrative vision of business, technology, and human, there are blind spots. Because their innovation process implies a succession of

Innovation Intelligence 223

hand offs from one function to another, the process is slow, real-time, real-world feedback is impossible, and the lag between conception and customer feedback is too long. Multiple, diverse knowledge sources must be taken into account in a coordinated manner.

Timeliness. The second challenge for innovation intelligence is to look toward the future rather than toward the past. The majority of CTOs and CINOs we interviewed commented that it is not sufficient to rely only on desk research. Visiting research labs across the world in a systematic manner to meet and discuss with experts or opinion leaders in various areas may seem cumbersome and time-consuming, but it is necessary. Desk research deals with published information, but anything published is already old. Considering the faster pace of innovation, this reliance on outdated information is no longer good enough. In addition, because desk research is available to competitors, it does not give any company an edge. Published documents are also biased: they cover up failures, the most important part of learning. Searches only yield what the key words you plugged in were worth; the net is full of holes! Automatic searches by concept are not yet accurate enough. On day they will be. To improve the time-dependent aspect of innovation intelligence, the innovation team must search for insights directly in the heads of experts who are permanently scouting the active frontiers of knowledge.

Skills. Innovation intelligence requires people who can deal with the three drivers: human, technology, and business). The list of required skills is long and demanding: fast reader, rapidly grasping the big picture, understanding the company, team player, unwaveringly loyal, precise, concrete, concise, curious, driven by value, and above all, loving innovation. There's no need to panic – people like this do exist, and you already know some of them. When you've identified them, the next challenge is to recruit them and train them. A practical and unsolved issue, however, is that such a valuable person already has a job – in a specific functional area of the company – and the challenge will be to help them find a way to balance their responsibilities. Management must find a solution to this problem. Unless the company wants to

224 Chapter 6. Toward Innovation Intelligence

create another silo (innovation intelligence), innovation intelligence servants will not be full-time but rather shared with another function in the company. Sharing an employee's time and attention is never easy, but if innovation intelligence is properly valued in the company's hierarchy, negotiations may be simpler.

Digital. The final challenge for innovation intelligence is digital. Digital tools are discussed in detail in chapter 7, but here we provide a few high-level comments. Digital technologies can be used to support the process of innovation intelligence in various ways: leveraging external experts to collect their opinions, augmented archiving, and so forth. Many data handling tools have been proposed, but thus far none really embraces the full scope of innovation intelligence. An ideal innovation intelligence tool would have the following functions (let's dream!):

- Identify weak signals early: Such a tool would detect emerging trend, emerging technologies, and new, relevant start-ups
- Build a 360° panorama along the three driver dimensions (human, technology, and business), leveraging various data sources (scientific publications, patents, blogs, and so forth)
- Enroll two or three experts to provide opinions regarding the distance between the company and a topic of interest, evaluating delay and entry cost
- Design and construct a dashboard to facilitate the life of the CINO, who needs to convince or influence his or her management and the rest of the company

6.5.3 Innovation intelligence cycle

We are not specialists in other types of intelligence – we failed to get training from the CIA, NSA, or the French Army – but we do recognize that a lot of interesting know-how is probably hidden there. We limit our scope to intelligence driven by and in the service of innovation. In other words, we limit our scope to the collection, analysis, and use of knowledge, driven by innovation and intended to feed innovation.

Innovation Intelligence 225

The word *intelligence*, with the notion of information gathering and processing, is often combined with other words to indicate its application, as in the following examples: military intelligence, defense intelligence, economic intelligence, competitive intelligence, and innovation intelligence. Regardless of the field of application, the essence of the definition remains the same. In our own words, intelligence is the ensemble of activities for collecting, processing, and analyzing data, in order to guide or support strategic decision making or operational actions.

Without going into the detail, two main approaches to intelligence exist:

- Older approach: search for information on a given strategic topic, then analyze it
- Newer approach: collect information based on the environment of the organization, discern relevant information from a strategic standpoint, and structure it in a form of collective memory

The first, older approach was historically used by the secret services. Today, the second, newer approach is favored; because it focuses on perception and analysis of the relevant environment, it enables analysts to apply their serendipity skills to detect unexpected opportunities.

In the following, we attempt to outline the best way to match innovation and intelligence. We may use the word *intelligence* to refer to either the process or its outcome, the result of the collection, processing, and analysis of information.

Intelligence is generally modeled as a closed loop (figure 6.7a): decision makers define a scope; data is collected, processed, and analyzed; and then the resulting intelligence is leveraged to make decisions, take actions, and refine the scope.

It is impossible to capture the complexity of what happens in real life, in particular because practices are empirical and still currently emerging. We have tried to find patterns in the complexity, however, and now propose the following process for innovation intelligence:

- **Define.** Define the orientation of the receivers that will collect information. The scope is delineated based on the company's

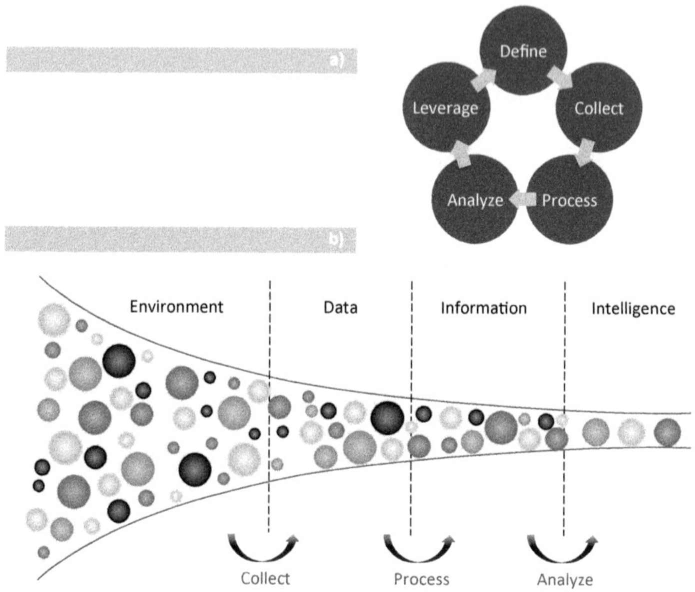

226 Chapter 6. Toward Innovation Intelligence

Figure 6.7: Innovation intelligence cycle. Data is collected from the environment. A first stage of processing is applied to transform the raw data into information. A deeper analysis is then performed to transform it into intelligence.

Innovation Intelligence 227

current strategy, positioning, legitimacy, mission, and so forth. The scope will serve as a foundation for selecting the data sources and tools to be used. Note that the narrower the scope, the less likely the data quest will detect unexpected things.

- **Collect.** Based on the defined scope, data is collected in a systematic manner, activating the network and utilizing available sources and methods. As shown in figures 6.7 and 6.8 and detailed thereafter, we have distinguished three drivers (human, business, and technology), three sources (desk research, investigation, and experimentation), and three types of knowledge (pre-established, on-demand, and real-time, real-world).
- **Process.** When collection is completed, the raw data is now available and must be processed into a usable form. Processing involves basic treatment, such as translation from foreign languages, and more advanced treatments, such as the verification of relevance and reliability. In this phase, data is transformed into information (see figure 6.7b).
- **Analyze.** The goal of this analysis phases is to transform information into intelligence. An expert[iv] of the organization screens information and integrates it with the three drivers. The expert identifies patterns, or phenomena, and establishes their significance and implications. The expert also challenges phenomena with newly developed knowledge.
- **Leverage.** The finalized intelligence results can take several forms, because they are then leveraged in three main ways: refinement of the scope (feedback loop back to the beginning of the innovation intelligence process), definition of territories to be explored, and ideation.

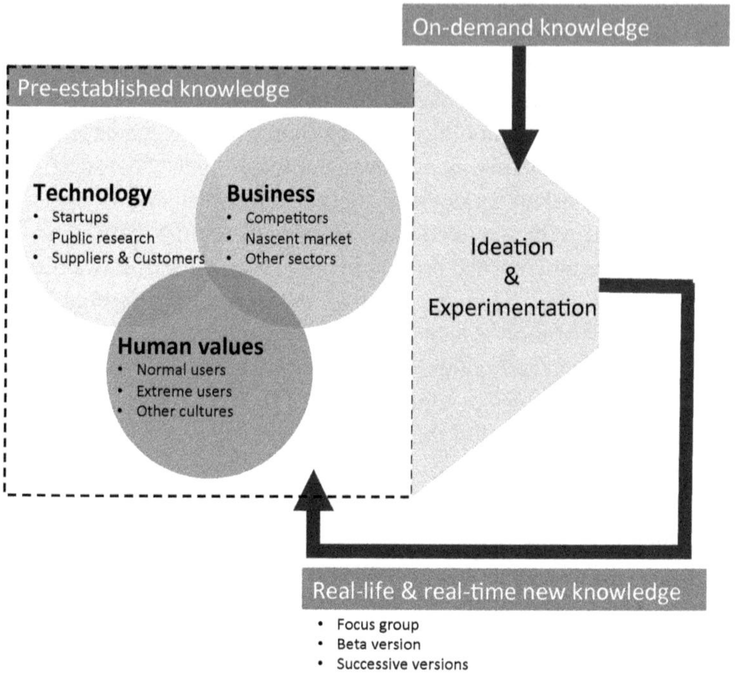

Figure 6.8: Knowledge for innovation intelligence. Intelligence, in order to be relevant to innovation, requires a combination of sources from the three domains domains: technology, business, and human value. Following ideation, the final and most valuable piece of knowledge comes from the results of experimentation, which often then feed into another loop through the innovation intelligence process.

6.5.4 A tool for integrating knowledge in real time

As explained in chapter 4, innovation has become the art of assembling knowledge that can come from disparate areas. Innovation intelligence must integrate an increasingly broad range of knowledge. As shown in figure 6.8, to keep the model simple we propose to look at the knowledge mines as three drivers, three sources, and three types.

> Don't find customers for your products; find products for your customers.
> **Seth Godin**

The three drivers are human, business, and technology. These are the three essential components of successful innovation.

Human. Innovations should improve people's lives. To deeply understand what people want (though they don't necessarily express it), tools such as psychology, sociology, anthropology, and ethnography can be used. As shown in figure 6.8, knowledge mines can be what design-thinking specialists call extreme users, users who are either lead users or not users at all. How do these extreme users behave? What are their preoccupations? For example, in luxury clothes, customers would like clothes with quality performance (that do not need to be ironed, that do not stain, that are more durable), but they still want them to look like other high-end products. The human driver may seem less relevant for B2B business, but innovation is everywhere in companies, not only in the products they sell. Innovation can improve significantly the way collaborators in the company perform their tasks. Nathalie Brunelle, Senior VP of Strategy, Development & Research of TOTAL's Refining & Chemistry branch told us that "operators in our plants will be very different in twenty years. They will be connected. We need to take that into account today." Human is the starting point. Innovation must

---

[iv]The phase *expert of the organization* is used here to indicate a person who has a sufficient understanding of the company and its environment to know what really matters for the company. Such people are called analysts in governmental agencies.

improve people's lives, both at home and at work.

Technology. What is going on in technology? What are the trends? What are the new emerging technologies? Who are the major players? What are the possible applications of these technologies? Is there an innovative use of this device in adjacent sectors? For example, if we look at new materials, what new materials that have appeared in the last four years could bring new functionality to luxury clothing? What is going on with bio-sourced materials? What is going on with self-healing materials? What is going on with faux leather? How could these technologies represent an opportunity – or, if the company doesn't react, a threat – for the company? Possible sources of technology include start-ups, public research organizations, adjacent industries, suppliers, and clients. The challenge, given the vast range of available and emerging technologies, is how to map those technologies that have potential for the company's applications? This is where third-party companies may be able to help.

Business. Is the proposed innovation viable? Is there an estimate of the potential profitability of such a business? What would be the best business model? What are competitors doing? What is going on in nascent markets? What activities in other sectors could inspire me? Is such activity compatible with my company's image?

For all three drivers (human, technology, and business), the net of innovation intelligence must be adaptive. The net's size begins at a relatively macroscopic level, and then, when fields of interest have been identified, the mesh of the net becomes finer in order to zoom into the details.

Innovation Intelligence 231

> We do no market research. We don't hire consultants. The only consultants I've ever hired in my 10 years is one firm to analyze Gateway's retail strategy so I would not make some of the same mistakes they made [when launching Apple's retail stores]. But we never hire consultants, per se. We just want to make great products.
> **Steve Jobs, Fortune, March 2008**

Knowledge mines can also be examined from another perspective: how to collect this knowledge? This brings us to the three sources: desk research, investigation, and experimentation.

Desk Research. Desk research is self-explanatory: a member of the innovation intelligence team is sitting at a desk and collects information related to the three drivers (human, technology, and business). This work can be outsourced, as long as the person performing it has a solid understanding of what really matters for the company. The tool of choice is the Internet, although it has limitations, such as the risk of overemphasis on buzz and hype and the fact that truly new information is not yet available there.

Investigation. Point of view from experts is collected through interviews. The network of receivers is oriented in a specific direction and invited to proactively gather data.

Experimentation. As soon as an initial prototype has been made, it is tested in real life or in a simulation. Such tests generate new knowledge along the three drivers. This new knowledge is incorporated into the integrated knowledge.

The final perspective from which knowledge mines can be viewed is shown in figure 6.8: knowledge can be pre-established, on-demand, or real-time, real-world.

Pre-established knowledge. Pre-established knowledge is already available. It is published in scientific papers, patents, and blogs. It can

232   Chapter 6. Toward Innovation Intelligence

also be in the head of experts. It is "just" a matter of finding the right sources and applying the right filters. Pre-established knowledge is gathered, processed, and analyzed before being used to feed ideation and experimentation.

On-demand knowledge. On-demand knowledge is very similar to pre-established knowledge in that it may already be available (but it is not always). On-demand knowledge will often be required during the ideation and experimentation phase. For example, combining the human driver (high-performance clothes), with the technology driver (self-healing materials), we may decide to make a prototype of a self-repairing T-shirt. What would be the consequences for health? This is a question that may arise during the ideation and experimentation process that was not (and could not be) anticipated during the initial innovation intelligence phase. To answer the question, on-demand knowledge is required.

Real-world, real-time knowledge. Real-world, real-time knowledge is really the hot, new stuff in innovation intelligence. Because the pace of the marketplace is so fast, rapid iteration must be made to adapt to the market. The focus group is no longer sufficient. A first version of the product (a prototype or a pre-series) must be rapidly released, and the market's reaction observed. How are people using the product? Do they use it as expected? What works? What doesn't work? How many are they buying? How much are they willing to pay? When Parrot launched the first version of the drone, they thought people would use it as a video game. But they did not. Instead, they used it to film stuff from above. This new knowledge is essential, and it is the most proprietary. It is today's cutting edge. Innovation intelligence must be structured and activated to capture this real-world, real-time knowledge. Building and strengthening the relationship between the final customer and the company is critical for two main reasons: first, because being in direct contact with the customer is the only way to capture a significant part of the profit margin, and second, because close interaction is increasingly necessary in order to understand the true needs of the customer. Companies such as Apple, Tesla, and

Innovation Intelligence 233

Proctor & Gamble have developed means to acquire superior insights about customers in order to guide ideation and the subsequent filtering of ideas. These companies gain strong insights from their customers thanks to the direct engagement they have with them. They respect and care about their customers' opinions.

To summarize, innovation intelligence is the process that aims at collecting, filtering, and analyzing data to transform it into actionable levers driven by innovation and feeding innovation. Innovation intelligence integrates knowledge about three drivers (human, technology, and business), from three sources (desk research, investigation, and experimentation) and of three types (pre-established, on-demand, and real-time, real-world). Innovation intelligence can be represented as a logical workflow, although in reality it is not sequential but rather an intricate series of iterations. Finally, innovation intelligence is time-dependent, with all the pieces constantly evolving.

6.6 Conclusion

We have seen traditional companies adjusting to the drastic changes in their environment by revisiting the way in which they operate. The process of disruptive innovation is moving out of technology silos, becoming increasingly multidisciplinary, and is supported by top management. In the key aspect of the innovation process, innovation intelligence, knowledge is being gathering from every possible source, and its sound analysis is defining competitiveness on the innovation battlefield.

By observing companies, we see clearly three key levers they are using to redesign their innovation processes.

The first lever is a new figure among executives, the Chief Innovation Officer (CINO). This is still a new function, not yet formalized and stabilized, but the key functions are already clear:

- Direct and motivate innovation intelligence activities
- Encourage and coordinate all functions in this endeavor
- Coordinate creative synthesis of the outcome
- Drive disruptive innovation and align it with strategy

234   Chapter 6. Toward Innovation Intelligence

- Shape the future of disruptive innovation projects

The second lever is symbolized by the innovation lab. Although practical examples do exist, here again its structure is neither rigid nor formalized. It is a multidisciplinary (cross-functional) team that must be agile, lean, and located in a space that fosters creativity. This team pushes disruptive innovation. It analyzes, interprets, and identifies ideas out of knowledge. It is one of the receiving nodes of the intelligence network. It integrates the three key drivers, technology, business, and human value. It also conducts rapid experimentation, evaluating ideas and generating business propositions for the company.

The third lever is innovation intelligence. Traditionally, intelligence was driven separately by individual silos for each of the functions in a company (such as R&D and marketing); today, intelligence should be conducted cooperatively, combining technology, business (including strategy and marketing), and human value, a sector that closely follows customers, their practices, and their values. As knowledge is flooding, innovation intelligence should be processed and interpreted in real time. New ideas or approaches must be projected on markets and checked for viability.

Although the three levers described above are already at work, the tools they need in order to be effective in their jobs are not yet fully developed. The required tools, currently works in progress, will be discussed in the next chapter of this book.

Chapter 7
Tools for Innovation Intelligence and rapid experimentation

We have to adapt and overcome, that's all we can do.

FRANK KNIGHT

In Short. . . Innovation intelligence in a company is performed by a network. Most nodes are not permanent staff of the company's innovation team but rather they are trained as innovation intelligence (II) nodes. In this way, the network is like a tree with branches along which quality knowledge flows quickly to the CINO. Intelligence covers three domains: business, technology, and human. The various parts of the network that explore these three domains should be interconnected and coordinated. The concept of a scout network is a good option for part of the intelligence network. Innovation intelligence is proactive and searching for information very early, before it becomes buzz in the Internet. Desk research and data mining are necessary complements. We discuss the following approaches for speeding up the innovation cycle: automation (high-throughput screening), a challenging idea of limited applicability; functional bricks and platforms, very effective solutions for high-

236 Chapter 7. Tools for Innovation Intelligence

volume systems; and parallel processing in lean teams. We classify
and review the present commercial offerings in terms of tool for to
aid in innovation intelligence efforts. The toolbox is still a work in
progress. But all indications are that progress is being made so that
one day we will have tools such as the Uber of skills or the eBay of
knowledge.

We admit that much of the content of the previous chapters was conceptual. Now we will face the reality, the messy and incomplete toolbox
that can be used to implement what we have described conceptually.
We will focus on tools for assisting large companies in establishing
and operating an effective innovation intelligence process. We will
also introduce some tools for accelerating the innovation process, a key
requirement for innovation in today's environment. Some of these tools
are already quite well known, some are new and effective, some are
new and still experimental, and we hope that additional tools will be
developed in the future. This section should, therefore, be considered
an overview of a rapidly changing situation.

7.1 Intelligence channels

> One of the more paradoxical aspects of the Apple
> Store experience is when this close listening leads
> to a store employee asking if a different item – even
> a less expensive one – might actually fit you better
> than the one you originally had in mind. But this
> doesn't harm Apple's bottom line.
> **Micah Solomon, Forbes, November 28, 2014**

It is impossible to compile an exhaustive list of intelligence channels, or tools. No matter how much effort we make, we will miss some.
For example, informal discussion is a common vehicle for easily un-

Innovation Intelligence 237

derstood intelligence. A casual discussion can lead to a well-balanced exchange in which both parties benefit. Every salesperson does this. It is difficult – if not impossible – to include all such benign interactions in a list of intelligence tools. (We should note, however, that even small interactions such as these may carry important messages, which is one of the many reasons an intelligence network should be created, trained, and motivated to collect and process and all relevant innovation-related knowledge.) We are going to classify intelligence channels first as our three domains: human, technology, and business. Before we dive into the individual channels, however, let's discuss the collective behavior of the network.

7.1.1 Self-adapting network

Although we have described the three separate domains for convenience, we must keep in mind that human, business, and technology form an intricate mix, and that an intense coordination and correlation should be maintained among the three domains of information gathering. In fact, even the best information that a company receives from one of these channels does not have much value on its own. It is their contrast and their matching that gives value to the ensemble.

Note that the completeness of information regarding a potential innovation does not require that the three domains be covered by a balanced effort. Rather, the intelligence network should be sufficiently interconnected for it to immediately adapt to a need for information balancing. For example, if a given piece of technology is discovered in an adjacent field somewhere in China, instead on only reporting the technical data about the technology, the intelligence network should self-activate a complementary search in the other two domains (human and business): Does the technology sell well? How profitable is it? What is its market trend? Has there been any recorded attempt to import it into other businesses? How do customers in this adjacent field use the technology? Do they like it? What are the drawbacks of it? If the technology is found in China, complementary searches should probably

238 Chapter 7. Tools for Innovation Intelligence

focus mainly on China and possibly Japan if the technology is also being sold to Japanese OEMs.

One important reason for having a network with distributed intelligence is related to the screening of the information. The members and affiliates of a large group receive an incredible volume of information each day, therefore a system that would bring back everything and pile it on the CINO's (virtual) desk would be a nightmare for him or her. There should be rules for determining the relevance of each piece of information and delegation of decision making to several levels of sub-nodes. Screening is a difficult task that cannot be done entirely by the book. We think it that the best way to treat an intelligence network is by self learning: nodes should interact and decide among themselves how to treat a particular case. A good example is redundancy. Here comes a piece of information already seen. Should it be rejected? Not necessarily. Indeed, the very fact that this information is showing up again may be a message, a confirmation. A handshake between the two nodes that found the redundant information should solve the case. Remember the excellent motto from 3M: "Never kill an idea, just deflect it!" For an intelligence network, the motto could be modified: "Never bury an idea, improve it and reorient it to another node."

In any case, a good intelligence network never works in only one way; information flows mostly upstream, but some should flow downstream to make the network more intelligent. For example, a node might contact the source of the information, saying the following: "We found your last information relevant for these reasons. Our colleague in India detected something similar – can you explain it? By the way, we are interested in testing umami taste in a new food product – do you have anything along this line?"

7.1.2 Human domain

A large number of companies have created specific labs where representative samples of the customer population test the company's innovative products. This is a quite natural endeavor for a B2C company. We have

Innovation Intelligence   239

seen already mentioned the Carasso Research Center of Danone (see chapter 6), a typical example of such a lab. For a B2B company, getting to know the customer is both simpler, because the customer is well identified, and more difficult, because the customer's purchasing department creates a de facto a communication barrier between the B2B supplier and the end users either at the customer or at the customer's customer. Let's consider the example of Saint-Gobain, a leading provider of building materials. Saint-Gobain has several interfaces between itself and the end user, the homeowner. Architects and building contractors, if not the building subcontractors and workers, all have their say in the value chain. Saint-Gobain has established the DomoLab, where it innovative products can be displayed, discussed, and evaluated by architects, building contractors, and homeowners. Insights are gathered by interviewing homeowners, architects and building-industry workers, in order to gain an appreciation of cultural variations among countries. Another example of a real-world test of new product is Organce, a luxury showroom in Paris where new fashionable clothes are displayed and submitted to the evaluation of connoisseurs.

Offering such test labs at which customers and end users can experience innovative products and provide their opinions is a natural customer-contact tool, but the digital revolution provides opposite to take the tool even further. All new applications on smartphones are prime examples of such extensions. Any new application gathers and automatically records data whenever a user downloads or uses it. The company offering the application then has access to real-time user feedback and statistics about usage. Because a digital product like an application can be improved, with updated versions provided to users in almost real time, this data can be used in a fast, tight loop to improve the product.

Conventional companies that offer physical products dream of being able to achieve such real-time connection with their customers. It is not yet possible today, but it is coming. Connecting objects is a new trend, and soon advanced companies will have the technical ability to follow the products they have sold. Achieving a close connection with the

240 Chapter 7. Tools for Innovation Intelligence

customer via the Internet should be an objective of the most creative people in every company.

There are less ambitious, but still effective, ways to connect with a large number of users of a product or service. One obvious tool is an online forum. We already mentioned (see chapter 4) that Bel, the cheese manufacturer and distributor, is using customer feedback and initiatives to guide the development of its Apericubes, mini-packs that Bel offers in a wide variety of flavors. Car companies are also closely following debates that take place on user forums and their products' buzz in order to both identify problems and to gauge the global interest of consumers.

7.1.3 Technology domain

> If you know the enemy and know yourself you need not fear the results of a hundred battles.
> **Sun Tzu (around 500 BC)**

We will not list again all of the traditional homework that companies must do in order to keep afloat in the knowledge. However, the following shortcomings of many companies do bear repeating:

- Information is rarely processed to a sufficient extent to provide strategic value
- Technology is rarely combined with consumer and business values
- Information processing is so slow that any action based on it is too late

Altogether, this list summarizes the shortcomings of most company cultures with regard to innovation intelligence. The chaotic inflow of information is not valued highly enough. Were the information properly regarded, the company would process it faster and the resulting insight would naturally find its way to the highest levels of the organization.

Let's review some tools that are, in our opinion, of great use in the

Innovation Intelligence   241

technology field.

Scouting is an approach worth considering. The military has always been ahead in terms of organizing intelligence, using it as a key competitive tool. The scouting concept was formalized in the mid-nineteenth century, but the concept had previously been used by Alexander the Great and Julius Caesar.

Armies and new territories

Scouts were recruited by armies to assist in difficult and unknown territories. They were selected for their knowledge of the terrain and ability to detect faint signs of activity (tracks), to help in navigation, and to assess the behavior of hostile parties. Scouts were actively used by the British Army in India and during the Boer Wars in South Africa and by the U.S. Cavalry during the American Indian Wars. The attached photograph shows a party of Apache scouts attached to the U.S. Cavalry in 1870. Most U.S. Cavalry scouts were Native Americans, but some were pioneer Americans who had long lived in the wild. There was always risk that a scout would not remain faithful, but the potential benefit more than compensated for the risk.

Scouts are also used by companies for technological and business intelligence, but the concept is not formalized and varies widely in its application. One of us was well acquainted with the scout system in Japan in the 1990s. Recall that Japan managed to become a major economic player by first being a copycat and then achieving high degree of productivity optimization (a common growth model). Since that time, Japanese companies have maintained a high regard for intelligence and

242   Chapter 7. Tools for Innovation Intelligence

have directed their knowledge-gathering skills toward innovation. Most Japanese scouts of the 1990s were employees of their companies, but external scouts probably existed and were simply difficult to identify as such. Although scouts carried rather modest titles on their business cards[i], they were quite well respected in their companies because they had easy access to high-level executives. A scout was always on duty. They traveled a lot, far more than their colleagues, and spoke English well. Most important, their interest was almost universal. Although each scout had a core technical specialty, he or she took note of many findings well outside that specialty. No doubt they reported to an intelligence organization that could process and refine the information they gathered. Japanese scouts were very active with their networks and very fair in the give-and-take ritual we mentioned in Chapter 5. They were not only technical; they could trigger important business actions such as mergers, acquisitions, or a friendly visit of the company vice president to another company that was doing something particularly interesting.

Scouts also exist, sometimes by another name, in companies other than Japan. For example, the higher ranks of technical employees in the dual ladder system in the United States are implicitly in charge of scouting for their companies.

Every company has some activity that could be the embryo of a scout network. The main challenge is that the activity is often attached to a silo, such as technology or marketing. Such embryos can be purposed to build a scout network, but care must be taken to break the silo barrier. A skilled gatherer of technological information is not a skilled intelligence scout if he or she is lacking in the business comprehension aspect. From the little experience we have on scout networks, it is clear that the network's effectiveness is driven by the importance and status assigned to it, as communicated by the company's highest-level executives.

---

[i]On a humorous note, when Jacques visited a fabrication plant in Japan, he never wore a tie. Because people who wear ties were assumed to be of a higher level, they were not allowed to enter clean rooms at such plants!

Innovation Intelligence 243

In-house scouts are not usually sufficient for facing the knowledge flood. Scouts should behave like nodes and should incorporate their personal networks such that they become extensions of the scout network. Outsiders may also be formally or informally recruited to the intelligence network. For example, many companies form longstanding relationships with public research organizations and universities, establish joint research centers, or sign long-term collaborative contracts. Many of the companies we interviewed – including TOTAL, Faurecia, Air Liquide, and Saint-Gobain – have followed such approaches. Such relationships always include information gathering and alert flagging.

Scouting cannot be subcontracted on a short-term basis. In the longer term, subcontracting is possible if a high degree of mutual trust can be established between the company and the scout.

> I find that a great part of the information I have was acquired by looking something up and finding something else on the way.
> **Franklin Pierce Adams (1881-1960)**

Another source of active intelligence is what we call the *local antenna*. Let's consider the example of BMW, which recognized that electronics and programming were becoming a significant fraction of a car's value. Although Stuttgart, Germany is not a bad place, it is more suited to mechanical engineers and motorists than to creative software developers. BMW decided to set up an antenna called the BMW Group Technology Office in the very heart of Silicon Valley. The key idea of an antenna is to benefit from the ambient boiling knowledge and obtain fresh, firsthand information about innovations. This antenna is not only technical – it covers all three domains of intelligence.

Due to the density and flow of information about new technologies, one of the key elements of an effective intelligence system regarding technology is the screening. Screening can only be performed by a tree-like network, where information is screened and dispatched before

244 Chapter 7. Tools for Innovation Intelligence

it flows toward the decision center.

7.1.4 Business domain

Collecting innovation intelligence in the business domain often overlaps with competitive intelligence, a discipline taught in many business schools and which can offer a multiplicity of excellent textbooks from knowledgeable authors.[87,88,89] For us, the most relevant aspect of competitive intelligence is the analysis and resultant understanding of how competitors are innovating. Observation of the industry to become familiar with all of the players and their successes and failures is a good start for becoming an effective contributor to innovation intelligence. We would recommend extending the analysis to adjacent industries and sometimes even businesses that are completely out of the scope if they share some key characteristics. For example, if you are focused on a giant warehouse building, examine a capital-intensive industry like electricity generation or semiconductor manufacturing. Stepping outside the obvious can be inspiring and provide relevant information from more sources.

Start-up firms serve an important function in innovation intelligence. We have seen their emergence, which has been quite impressive in the field of digital innovation. We decided to put start-ups in this business domain section for two reasons. First, most start-ups, especially those funded by venture capital, are potential targets for acquisition. As a result, when a company finds a start-up that has interesting and relevant knowledge, acquisition is always an option. Second, start-ups are, as described by Henri Chesbrough, small laboratories for testing business models. Therefore, it is key to follow not only the technical content of start-ups but also the results of their business-model experimentation. Nevertheless, start-ups could also be part of the technology section; most of them are really battling at the frontier of knowledge. In fact, when your intelligence network detects an interesting start-up, most likely it will also be found by the technical people. Start-ups' activities make them visible mainly on the technical scene.

Innovation Intelligence 245

Nearly all of our interviewees said that start-ups are among the most interesting elements of the innovation landscape. They all want to keep a close eye on start-ups. As we have said, we live in a rapidly changing and mobile world. Although start-ups communicate extensively in an effort to attract attention whenever they have something to sell (whether a product, service, or the company itself.), the content of their technical communications is often vague and elusive if not wishful.

Many of our interviewees are proactively monitoring the landscape of start-ups. Several techniques are commonly used for this monitoring, and we will review some of them.

Some companies establish or invest in dedicated venture capital funds. The idea is to attract start-ups that would fit into the company's strategy by funding them with venture capital. The main purpose of such investment is not financial but rather to have a front seat to observe how the technology or business model develops. One of the first companies to follow this approach was Intel. Several of our interviewees also do so, including the following: Airbus (Airbus Venture), Orange (Orange Fab), Saint-Gobain (NOVA), Schneider Electric (Schneider Electric Ventures), the Nordic bank SEB Group (SEB Venture Capital), GDF SUEZ (GDF SUEZ New Ventures), TOTAL (Total Energy Ventures). Danone is a partner in a rather large venture capital fund and describes its interest as driven by three axes:

- Intelligence: knowledge from inside about what is going on
- Identification of start-ups to partner with or invest in
- Fostering the ecosystems of companies working on relevant topics

Today it is also possible to enter partnership with large incubators. For a fee, your company, like Faurecia, can have a front seat for watching the start-ups in the pool. This is an appropriate technique if the company's technology of interest is not dispersed across too many start-up breeding places.

Whatever technique is used, there is considerable risk that an interesting fish will be missed. Indeed, today there are start-ups in many places around the world, in Wyoming and in the suburbs of Brisbane.

246 Chapter 7. Tools for Innovation Intelligence

Well-operated scout networks can find start-ups relevant to a company's strategy. Conducting an exhaustive search for start-ups would, however, require a great amount of effort. Start-ups have a fluctuating level of communication, large and loud after an achievement, they can be quiet when struggling with the inevitable obstacles along the way. Still, monitoring relevant start-ups makes sense; start-ups run daring experiments and, if a larger company is paying attention, the larger company can learn from those experiments. We should emphasize again the value of failure. Start-ups do fail most of the time, and a lot can be learned by understanding the reasons for their failure.

Let's take a moment to consider a special event, a symbolic materialization of the collective aspect of innovation intelligence. It is the *learning expedition* or learning trip. If a theme is particularly relevant, if a convergence is detected in a sector of interest, an efficient way to involve many of a company's C-level executives in the intelligence process is to invite them all on a learning expedition to visit many companies (start-ups) and together examine the situation. After an event like this, the company's leaders may view innovation in the sector of interest very differently than they did previously. A successful learning expedition will result in a shared vision of what the company should do in the sector.

7.2 Tools for speeding up the innovation process

7.2.1 Importance of timing and direction

In our opinion, one of the most important ways to speed up the innovation process is based on high-quality innovation intelligence. It is all about asking the right question and then hurrying to implement the solution. We have encountered so many projects that were lost or stuck because the initial momentum was not headed in the right direction. Even more devastating are the projects that are begun too early, when either the market or the underlying technology was not yet ready. Timing is one of the keys to success in innovation: if you start too early, you will suffer and the project's supporters will throw

Innovation Intelligence

in the towel. Moreover, after such a bad experience, the company has been so traumatized that is not likely to restart the project when it would make sense. Too early is a catastrophe, too late gives away the pole position, first-mover advantage, to a competitor. The key is to be on time and point the project in the right direction. Innovation intelligence enables the company to fine-tune the why and the when of an innovation project.

7.2.2 Squeezing the innovation funnel flat: parallel processes

In classic innovation stage gating, as explained in chapter 3, there is a tendency, while running through the funnel, to address one question after the other in sequence. Such an approach necessitates handing off the responsibility from one business function to another, as the project progresses from each question to the next. For example, when the prototype is ready (technical function), the business plan must be developed (business functions), then the project must undergo market evaluation (marketing and sales departments). These hand offs, as well as any associated responsibility reassessments, delay the project.

In-house parallel process. A rapid innovation process necessitates a small, commando-style team, as recommended in chapter 6. Commando-style teamwork has the advantage of being lean and fast. When answering a given key question is not costly, it is worth the risk of answering multiple such questions simultaneously. This parallel approach is particularly easy to do when the team is multidisciplinary. Questions about technology, human values, and business value can all be researched and answered simultaneously. The commando-style structure enables the project's various tasks to follow parallel, collaborative paths, with different team members assigned to each task, which speeds up the process. In addition, each team member has the opportunity to find shortcuts. Squeezing flat the innovation funnel, performing tasks in parallel rather than sequentially, is rather easy for innovation such as a digital application or a service offering.

This parallel approach is more difficult to apply to complex systems,

248   Chapter 7. Tools for Innovation Intelligence

especially those sensitive to product liability. However one can find a lot of information on *parallel engineering*, more frequently called *concurrent engineering*; the approach was initiated primarily by NASA and then formalized in several publications and textbooks.[90] However, such techniques are rather technical and complex; while they may be appropriate for the process of designing a helicopter, they do not help much in a commando-style project.

Regardless, some type of parallel approach is recommended for projects that need to move quickly. Bypassing the sequential approach does not increase the overall financial risk of the project, as long as the innovation lab conducting the project does so in a lean way.

Co-innovation is an additional way to force in the process to include some tasks performed in parallel. Co-innovation will speed up a project only if the collaboration adds capacity and knowledge but not managerial complexity or bureaucracy.

Co-innovation with clients. A joint project with a client can create value rapidly. For example, Airbus currently has two projects with airlines, one about turnaround-time optimization and one about predictive maintenance. The goal of each project is to demonstrate the value within a one year. Working with a partner actually speeds up the process, because having access to the partner's capacity and knowledge enables something similar to parallel processing.

Co-innovation with suppliers. Joint projects with suppliers are similar to joint projects with clients; the main difference is part of the value chain involved. Some industries are already highly structured with integrated value chains – the automobile industry is a prime example. Others are less so. The innovation lab can help to address inefficiencies. The first step is to identify and understand the efficiencies by benchmarking best practices for working with suppliers, in order to reduce the cycle time. The goal here is to generate and test ideas to improve the general performance of innovation.

Innovation management software. Software applications such as HYPE or Inova Software are designed to support a process from idea generation to concept development to project implementation. By using such software, employees of a company can propose ideas and managers can evaluate, rank, and select ideas.

7.2.3 High-throughput screening: an inspiring innovation tool?

High-throughput screening

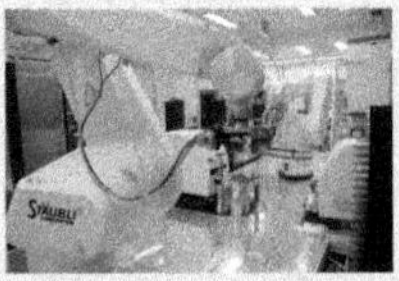

A high-throughput screening (HTS) lab in a biopharmaceutical company looks like a robotized nanotechnology factory. Robots handle plates with more than 1,000 miniature reaction zones and fill them with a series of chemical mixtures or biological samples. The reaction results are measured in parallel by sophisticated imaging. Today, such an operation can simultaneously scan the properties of say, 100,000 different molecules. Many types of reactions, such as reaction catalysis or inhibition, antigen activation, and even living cell growth, can be tested.

In this book, we keep recommending that adjacent fields be explored in search of inspiring bits of knowledge. Because we are discussing how to speed up the innovation process, let's examine an extreme case in terms of processing speed. High-throughput screening (HTS) is a technique widely used in the biopharmaceutical community, but it has so far had little effect in other sectors. This highly sophisticated research technique was developed for new drug discovery. It combines robotics, miniaturization, parallel sensing, and massive data acquisition and handling.[91] The basic tool is a tray called a microplate, which is covered with a matrix array of small recesses called wells. Each well is a mini-reactor, the equivalent of the glass test tube that we all played with during our chemistry classes, but containing less than a drop of liquid. Chemical and biological substances are put into the wells by fast-moving robots. A huge volume of data is generated and analyzed by simultaneously conducting so many tests. Typically, for targeting a given disease, perhaps 10,000 candidate molecules are

250   Chapter 7. Tools for Innovation Intelligence

selected and imported from a compound library, a bank of more than one million substances. A set of initial tests is conducted, using HTS to test all 10,000 candidate molecules simultaneously, reducing the candidate list from 10,000 to approximately 1,000 molecules. The batch then goes for more sophisticated HTS, finally narrowing the list to 10 promising candidates. This small batch will then go to in-vivo tests, and eventually one or two candidates will go on to the most difficult clinical tests. HTS relies on incredibly powerful machinery that was developed by the pharma industry with strong support from public research (mainly the U.S. National Institutes of Health, or NIH). Researchers from Harvard[ii] are going even further;[92] they are dispersing tiny droplets in oil and processing them in microfluidic machinery. Such a method would reduce reagent consumption by one million and speed up the test rate by one thousand.

In the midst of such enormous processing capacity, an innovation practitioner can feel small and helpless – the skills of researchers are not needed any longer, they have been replaced by robots! This is not quite true. Brains are needed now more than ever, but for designing the test sequence rather than performing the tests themselves.

There is something we can all learn from this HTS knowledge of creating fast, automatic processes for the repetitive tasks in innovation, focusing on those that can make the best use of robotics. There have been some attempts to export this knowledge from the biopharmaceutical industry to adjacent industries. As one would expect, the agro-food industry and forensic sciences are prime candidates. The information industry is also following a similar route, which they call Big Data projects. We should keep an eye on that.

7.2.4   Bricks and platforms: magic wands of complex innovation

Although HTS can speed up innovation for simple products (molecules) projected into an extremely complex use (curing a disease), it is not

---

[ii]We noticed that the first words of the abstract for the paper authored by the Harvard researchers are, coincidentally, "The explosive growth in our knowledge..."

Innovation Intelligence   251

easy to apply it to industries that create complex systems such as cars,
airplanes, or automated warehouses.

Dealing with complexity, in particular the assembly of a very large
number of elements from a wide base in order to create a new system,
leads to mind-jamming pain. Coping with such complexity can be done
by regrouping parts of the inherent complexity into subsystems that
can be treated as simple, conceptual objects we call functional bricks.
The following is an old story.

It all started with mathematics, by enclosing in a simple symbol
an underlying set of complex calculus. Examples include operators:
∇ is the gradient vector of a function, $\triangle$ the Laplacian, and $\square$ the
d'Alembertian. All of these simple symbols hide many operations. A
full set of complex calculations can be simplified by manipulating just
symbols. Such a symbol is a sort of functional brick for symbolic calculus; you do not need to repeat the detail of the brick's content, you just
need to pay attention to its rules of use. The first to apply such a conceptual simplification to hardware was Charles Babbage[93] (1791-1871).
Polymath, mathematician, philosopher, astronomer, and mechanical engineer, he is known as the father of programmable computing. He made
this conceptual simplification long before the existence of electronics.
He designed very complex mechanical systems, with gears, levers, and
transmissions, and in designing those systems he used a language of
his own, sets of graphical signs that were conceptual simplifications,
condensing in one sign an ensemble of mechanical parts providing a
given function. In other words, Babbage simplified his design effort
by assembling functional bricks. He designed two machines. His *difference engine*, the simpler machine but which contained 25,000 parts,
was intended to calculate the value of a polynomial. It never worked,
because it was built at a time when mechanical tolerances were insufficient (modern copies of Babbage's design do work). His *analytical
engine* was, in fact, a full-blown computer that could be programmed
by punched cards made of perforated cardboard in the same way as
the Jacquard weaving machine was controlled. Babbage was short on
funding, so his mechanical computer was never built, but his legacy is

252 Chapter 7. Tools for Innovation Intelligence

highly respected by modern computer science experts.

The concept of a functional brick is today one of the most important success factors for a technology to enter into multiple innovative applications. Let's take the example of system on chip (SoC), the typical, modern, all-purpose integrated circuit. It has billions of CMOS transistors, more or less alike but not all performing the same task. Some of the CMOS transistors are parts of the central processor, some buffer data in and out, others deal with embedded logic, others help with video processing, and so on. In fact, SoCs are patchworks of interconnected functional bricks, each subcircuit brick performing a specific task. The semiconductor industry calls such bricks an IP *core*. The underlying message behind this name is the following: "do not copy this circuit, it is intellectual property (IP)." A chip-design company keeps in a huge digital library plenty of IP cores, ready-made circuit designs that serve most of the functions commonly used in integrated circuits. If the company wants to develop a chip for a new application, say, decoding encrypted television services with a new security algorithm, it can design the circuit mostly by assembling functional bricks. Using bricks is much faster than designing the circuit from scratch, because most of the bricks have already been debugged, the bricks' development cost is shared with many users, and the innovative part of the product is concentrated in the assembly of the bricks and on the potential satisfaction of the customer. The software industry follows a similar approach when developing new software programs: large, complex software programs are built by assembling subprogram bricks. Not only it is faster and cheaper that programming the entire software from scratch, but it is also more flexible. If you want to inject innovation into one of your systems, perhaps by adding another feature, you just need to introduce into the assembly a few more functional bricks, make sure the ensemble is coherent and appealing, and the innovation task is done.

Innovation Intelligence

Lego MindStorm and functional bricks

Some creative games are made of functional bricks. This image shows a robot elephant made from the game set MindStorm by Lego. A large combination of creative objects can be easily built by assembling the functional bricks provided by Lego: gears, axles, motors, belts, sensors, driving processor, and so forth. MindStorm is also famous in open innovation circles. The game was first released with a hidden source code for its robot command. Hackers managed to decipher it very fast. Lego found that geeks were exchanging tips on how to improve the code. In response, Lego shifted gears, transitioned to open source, and fostered a fan club which actively contributed to the progress of MindStorm software.

We intentionally selected a game (see inset above) to illustrate the use of functional bricks for designing and building machinery. Designing an object for a specified purpose without having to rework all the inner details is a pleasing intellectual game. The creativity is in the assembly, and the beauty of the result is in its simplicity and the quality of the provided service. Our main point here, however, is that innovation can happen much faster when functional bricks are available. The potential speed of the process is defined by the design quality of the brick interfaces; in order to work cooperatively, the bricks must be easily attached, linked, and connected.

When the set of bricks is wide and rich, innovation can be not only faster but wider, richer, and perhaps even more creative. As a case in point, remember what happened when the miniature camera was made available at an affordable price. Shortly thereafter, camera phones were launched, and a full set of applications and social practices[iii] developed.

[iii] Albert, don't forget to take your daily selfie! (private joke between the authors)

254   Chapter 7. Tools for Innovation Intelligence

In the gradual development of system industries, the condensation of design into functional bricks is a key stage in the maturity of the industry. It is often associated with an innovative period during which new applications are developed and products are differentiated at a limited cost. Thanks to a growing number of applications, more functional bricks are needed, the cost of the bricks decreases, and the virtuous loop of the experience curve can run. In parallel, bricks become a commodity, and only production-efficient companies can compete in brick making. At the same time as the industry is undergoing this transformation with regard to the bricks, the value of the end product is shifting so that it focused increasingly in the design and assembly rather than in the individual bricks. We could have mentioned this phenomenon in chapter 4, but we have placed it here because it is a key factor in innovation speed.

Knowing that a new brick in your business is going to be available, being able to forecast when its price will make it economically viable as a component, and lobbying for this brick to be an easy plug-and-play are key aspects of the innovation intelligence job and also increase the chances of winning the innovation race.

The brick concept was recently significantly improved upon by the concept of a platform. A platform is a meta-brick, a concept developed in the automobile industry and which is now gaining popularity in sectors such as aeronautics, portable computers, and even construction and agricultural machinery. A platform is a predesigned and prequalified package constituting the core, or skeleton, of a complex system. An assembly of interlocking bricks, it will become the seed for a series of different systems based on it. For cost reasons, automobile manufacturers team up to create a common platform. We have provided below an example of a quite broad platform, the Golf platform. Modern platforms can be elastic; for example, some dimensions of the Golf platform can be stretched or shrunk to create a large SUV or a small city car.

The outer layers of the product are left open to modification by car designers, and this is where innovation and differentiation are done by

Innovation Intelligence

Figure 7.4: Car companies are now very agile is designing a common platform with enough flexibility to generate a variety of models ranging from a small city car to a large SUV or a luxury station wagon. Shown above is the Golf platform developed by a consortium led by Volkswagen. The Golf platform is the basis for eight families of cars marketed under four brand names.

the partners sharing the platform. Platforms allow companies to offer the market, at a reasonable cost, plenty of customization. This is a solution to the inherent conflict between two equally urgent demands from customers: on one hand, the customer wants a low price (which necessitates mass production of a standard product), but on the other hand, the customer wants his or her car to be different than others. We are today far from 1909, when Henry Ford declared, "Any customer can have a car painted any color that he wants so long as it is black." Today's models target population segments such as sport, outdoor, cocoon, senior, and so forth. Platform design, which limits customization and innovation to the outer, most visible part of the vehicle, is intended to enable automobile manufacturers to both control production cost and provide innovative new models more quickly.

7.3 Digital tools for innovation intelligence?

7.3.1 A proposed classification

We have researched the companies and interviewed the founders, CEO, or stakeholders of Gerson Lehrman Group (GLG), NineSigma, Expernova, Yegii, ReadCube, MyScienceWork, YourEncore, Viadeo, Maven, ResearchGate, and Mendeley, among others? and, of course, Presans! Although we have decided not to publish it in detail in this book, we have conducted an extensive review of third-party tools that may, today and in the future, play a role in innovation intelligence. In this book, we have decided to instead present a summary of our proposed simplified

256 Chapter 7. Tools for Innovation Intelligence

classification of these tools, present a few patterns and trends that we have identified, and share our vision of where all of this may be going. The range of tools is extremely broad and varied. Nevertheless, we have decided to place tools in the following categories:

- Open innovation and crowdsourcing
- Expert networks and micro-consulting
- Professional social networks
- Innovation software
- Data archives and data mining

For nearly all of these broad classes, extensive studies have already been carried out by other authors. For example, for the category open innovation and crowdsourcing, in 2013 Kathleen Diener and Frank Piller published a report in titled *The Market for Open Innovation*,[94] which is probably the most up-to-date and comprehensive review of open innovation intermediaries. Letizia Mortara?also published a quite complete report in 2010 titled *Getting Help with Open Innovation*.[95]

Figure 7.5 is a visual representation of the first three items in our proposed simplified classification of tools for innovation intelligence. It is not intended to provide a complete picture of our classification, which also includes innovation software, data archives, and data mining, or to capture the entire reality, which is slightly more complex.

Open-innovation intermediaries are companies such as Innocentive, NineSigma (see inset below) in the United States, ideaken in India, and Presans in France. These intermediaries focus on innovation. They promise to find *non-obvious* experts who are off the beaten track or working on different applications. These companies are all quite small (a few tens of employees and less than EUR 10 million in revenues). In section 7.3.2 we will explore in detail the way these companies operate.

NineSigma: will they catch the digital wave?

We have interviewed a few people who work at NineSigma, including Andy Zynga, the current CEO, as well as clients who

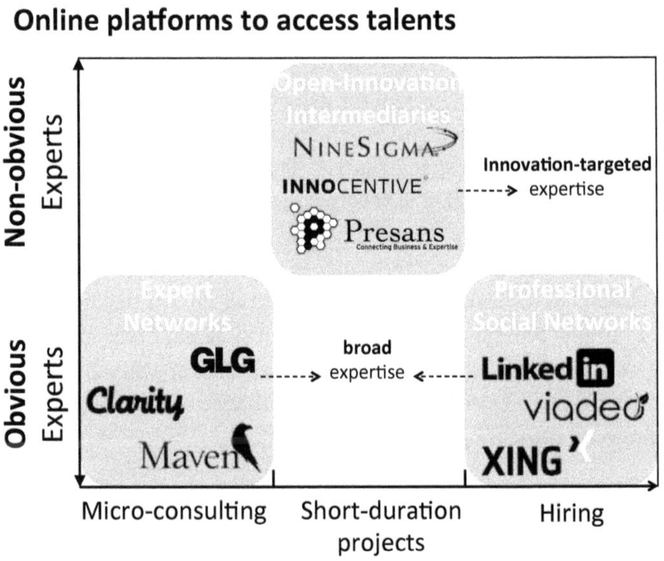

Innovation Intelligence 257

Online platforms to access talents

Figure 7.5: Innovation-intelligence tool classification. This diagram shows a classification of selected commercial tools that aid in some aspect of innovation intelligence.

have used NineSigma's services. Since its founding in the year 2000, NineSigma has undergone two main evolutions. First, although the company originally focusing on technology search, NineSigma extended its presence in the value chain on both the front-end (helping to select the problems that have a higher chance of being solved via its platform) as well as on the back-end (helping to select among the experts who answer a request for proposal). Second, NineSigma is beginning a digital transformation. Created almost fifteen years ago, NineSigma does not have a culture in advanced information technologies such as data mining. The company's information system for managing experts and requests for proposals was developed by an external IT service company based on NineSigma's specifications. That was probably the right strategy back in the early 2000s, when the company's key need was to build the expert network and the client portfolio. But this shortcoming has become an issue. In recent years, NineSigma has attempted to begin its digital transformation, for example by launching its NineSights online community. Like many companies facing the digital wave, NineSigma will find it challenging to catch the wave. The solution may be an alliance with one or more digital pure players.

Expert networks are companies such as Gerson Lehrman Group (GLG), Clarity, and Maven. They promise instant access to experts around the world. Their focus is not necessarily innovation. GLG has existed for over fifteen years and grown to a relatively large size. The most recent figures are already a few years old, but our estimation is that it represents over eight hundred collaborators around the world and revenues probably greater than EUR 500 million. GLG is not playing in the same league as open-innovation intermediaries. The more recently established payers, such as Clarity and Maven, are also gaining momentum. They both focus on providing instant access to *obvious* experts. In the case of open-innovation intermediaries, I don't know what kind of experts can bring me insights, so the intermediary

Innovation Intelligence 259

company will need to conduct a search for non-obvious experts; in the case of expert networks, I know what kind of expert I need, so I can simply perform a keyword search on the expert network's platform, find the right expert, and engage him or her for a micro-consultancy.

Professional social networks are companies such as LinkedIn, the largest and most well known, and its little brothers and sisters Viadeo in France and XING in Germany. Their focus is on employment. The value proposition of these companies is two-pronged: the B2B offering and the B2C offering. The value proposition is evolving due to commoditization (again!). There are two aspects to the B2B side of employment, helping companies to hire talented people: sourcing and selecting. When professional social networks first appeared, they promised to enable potential employers to find passive job seekers, in other words to recruit people who already had positions (90% of the talented people). On the B2C side of employment, the side that most people know, they promised to people to track their networks. As time has passed, both the B2B (sourcing) and B2C (networking) offerings have become commoditized. They have become the basics. Social networks need to provide additional services. On the B2B side, the trend is to move toward selection, the second key activity of employment. For example, Viadeo is now proposing a service called Face to Face. Even if the employer is not currently hiring, what talented people might it be interested in? With such a service, Viadeo aims at gaining an understanding of latent demand and to become more efficient in helping headhunting companies with selection. On the B2C side, the offering has also evolved. For example, members of the famous Generation Y are heavy users of social networks. They expect digital tools to help them with their careers. Their careers are very different from those of their parents. Young professionals – *slashers*, as they are also called – don't remain with companies for very long, don't trust companies, and don't rely on companies to train them. They change companies to gain new experience, to add lines to their CVs. Social networks are preparing offerings to help them in slashing. For example, the social network might notify a slasher that people who have

260   Chapter 7. Tools for Innovation Intelligence

occupied his or her current position have moved on to XYZ afterward. Or the social network might give the slasher access to information about how to achieve his or her career goals, for example, if today you do this and in the future you want to do that, then you should consider doing XYZ next. Of note, a new company, Kudoz, launched in September 2014 and promises to be the Tinder[iv] of Talents. Although professional social networks currently focus on employment, we can easily imagine that tomorrow they might develop services related to micro-consulting, thus stepping on the toes of expert networks.

Innovation software applications are provided by companies such as HYPE Innovation, Inova Software, Mindjet, and Motivation Factory. These companies propose a range of software to help client companies support their innovation process. Innovation software focuses mainly on the ideation and experimentation aspect of innovation rather than on the innovation intelligence. However, the leaders in this field are sufficiently established that they could diversify in a credible manner toward innovation intelligence.

Data archives and data mining providers are companies such as Expernova (see inset below), Intellixir, Questel, Collexis (owned by Elsevier), and Presans for data mining, and companies such as MyScienceWork (see inset below) and Mendeley for data archives. These companies focus on archiving various sources of information (scientific publications, patents, reports, and so forth), developing slick interfaces to search for and rank relevant data, and facilitating access to knowledge. They also focus on cross-referencing, consolidating, and structuring various sources of information in order to transform data into information and knowledge... and maybe one day reach complete intelligence.

[iv]You don't know what Tinder is? What century are you living in? Google it! Admittedly, I didn't know either.

Innovation Intelligence 261

MyScienceWork: toward the iTunes of knowledge?

MyScienceWork was created in 2010 by Virginie Simon and Tristan Davaille. The impetus was the time wasted when accessing relevant scientific publications. In just a few years, they have opened offices in France, Luxembourg, and San Francisco, California. The young company has collected several tens of millions of scientific publications in order to build enhanced scientific archive services. CEO Virginie Simon, not worried by other older players such as Academia, ResearchGate, or Mendeley, is dreaming of nothing less than building the "iTunes of knowledge, a mix of Google Scholar and LinkedIn." An ambitious challenge!

Expernova: a robust piece of software

Expernova was founded by Pascal Magnier. In 2004, the young Magnier completed his thesis on the evolution of R&D in large corporations. In 2007, while working at Pernod Ricard, he faced a concrete issue: he needed to find solutions to recirculate specific types of waste. An expert was found in a completely empirical way: by word of the mouth. That time he was lucky. In 2008, Magnier decided to found a start-up that would help companies to find experts around the world. Like similar companies, such as hypios and Presans, at around the same time (2008-2010), realizing that convincing experts around the world to register on its online platform would take too much time and too much money, Expernova decided to develop tools to find the digital traces that experts leave on the web. Since its creation, Expernova has undergone several major evolutions. Client companies are not interested in obtaining just a list of names, a list of potential experts. That can be done with a simple Internet search. Therefore, the main evolutions of Expernova have been to provide more value – additional

262 Chapter 7. Tools for Innovation Intelligence

analytics and statistics – via the company's platforms. Perhaps most importantly, the recent evolution is orienting Expernova's platforms toward use cases that process and package raw data into usable, targeted information. Many exciting challenges lie ahead for this company. It has a good set of bricks toward robust innovation intelligence.

7.3.2 The myth of the so-called open-innovation platform

This section is based on our field experience and regular conversations with companies that use some of the tools we have just described, experts who market their expertise via these tools, and with the main players in the tools marketplace during the past five years.

The term open innovation is currently fashionable. Moreover, like any buzzword, it is overused. However, as we have already discussed, open innovation is the natural response to the knowledge flood: it is more efficient to fetch certain pieces of knowledge outside of the organization than to build the knowledge in-house. That said, the term open innovation is neither a panacea nor a magic potion, despite some claims to the contrary.

One of the tools used for open innovation that has piqued the interest of both academics and companies over the past decade is the so-called *open-innovation platform*, or *open-innovation intermediary*. The buzz around this concept is even worse than that around open innovation itself. Thanks to, or because of certain enthusiastic promoters, people have begun to believe that an open-innovation online platform (especially if it came with a semantic search engine, another buzz word!) would enable companies to post their problems online and random people to respond with solutions, the best one receiving payment from the company. Thanks to the Internet, everything has become possible, and furthermore, at low cost! Such is the birth of a myth!

We will detail two key messages:

- **Data mining is a requirement.** State-of-the-art data-mining

Innovation Intelligence   263

technologies are required for the identification and management of potential experts likely to deliver relevant, high-quality answers for the company. We are speaking about millions of experts!

- **Innovation without human interaction does not exist.** Senior personnel trained in robust methodologies are needed to extract the essence of the expert's knowledge and transform it into actionable recommendations for the company.

> The best experts will not spontaneously register on an online platform.
>
> **what we at Presans have learned from our experts**

There are tens of millions of experts in the world. Imagine that a company wants to access external knowledge and expertise away from its core business to solve a technological problem or make a strategic decision related to innovation. How can the company engage and motivate the best experts, the most unexpected ones, yet the most relevant? How should the company extract the essence of the expert's knowledge to transform it into actionable levers?

To access global expertise, the company may decide to use a dedicated online platform. The company can choose from the following three types:

- **The old-school platform.** This platform has fifteen years of experience, so it has many client references (not always satisfied). This platform generally explains that the solution to a posted problem can be provided by anybody who has registered on its website. This platform can have up to several hundred thousand registered users, or solvers as they typically call them, but it will fail to tell customers that less than 5% – or even less than 1% – of those registered users are active on the website. Therefore, such a platform is very far from the tens of millions of experts around

264 Chapter 7. Tools for Innovation Intelligence

the world. In addition, the best experts do not spontaneously register on such a platform. They don't register on any online platforms. The best experts are busy; they don't have time to waste. Their expertise is rare and it is expensive; they don't want to sell it on a platform that may pay them if the client uses their answer. On this platform, typically a posted problem generally will be poorly formulated, and the answer necessarily will be unsatisfactory.

- **The on-demand hunting platform** (automated, targeted broadcast search). This is what we have learned from our global network of experts: to mobilize the best experts, you must give them a guarantee that if they work they will be paid (not just "may be paid"). Since there are millions of experts in the world and they have published hundreds of millions of documents on the Internet (scientific publications, patents, conferences, social networks, and so forth), finding and engaging the best expert is like finding a needle in a haystack. We live in a world in which information is a commodity. To analyze this information, we need data-mining tools to facilitate the work (and prepare the information for human analysis). This is why the most recent platforms, such as Presans and hypios, have tried to leverage data mining to develop Google-like expertise in order to build and maintain up-to-date database of a few million experts, and most importantly, to engage the experts in a selection process on-demand. The point is to filter millions of experts around the world down to a few hundred of the most relevant experts, who are then automatically contacted, down to a few dozen experts who submit a proposal. Finally, based on the proposals, the best and often most surprising experts will be selected and paid for a micro-consulting project.
- **Home-grown platforms.** Many companies – including several of our interviewees for this book – have tried to create their own platform, incorporating a portal for the company's innovation activity. Such home-grown platforms range from mere showrooms

Innovation Intelligence

265

for ongoing innovation to open calls for contact and expertise. Some companies have gone as far as opening contests for ideas. To quote Jean Philippe Paré from Danone, "To leverage external competence, we tried to set up our own Internet platform... but we realized that it does not work." The case is not yet closed, however. Companies can use their own platform to connect with activist communities and learn a lot from the interaction. We think that company innovation drivers should indeed experiment with a company platform, but the best objectives are consumer contact, opinions from application activists, the company acting an insider in the buzz machine, and possibly guiding preselected contacts to a more selective portal. Fishing the idea of the century via such a platform may well be an urban myth[v].

> Companies want more than a list of experts, more than being put in contact with an expert. They want insights.
> **what we at Presans have learned from our clients**

When the company that has made the choice to use a platform has realized that it should use one that is technology-enabled, that can map global expertise, it still has another choice to make:

- **The fully automatic platform with semantics search magic sauce.** These platforms have contributed to the buzz that culminated around 2010. Younger than the old-school platforms, these platforms are approximately five to seven years old. They have done a lot of communication. In fact, that is almost the only thing they have done. They are champions of the concept. They have developed a semantic search engine in which companies can ask questions and, a bit by magic, the platform automatically

---

[v]We are speaking here about platforms to source technologies or talents. Such platforms may be well-suited to collect insights from users. An example could be *Imagine with Orange*, the crowdsourcing platform of Orange.

266 Chapter 7. Tools for Innovation Intelligence

finds relevant experts who will (maybe) provide answers. It just works! There is no need for the company to be specific with its question. These platforms claim that it is even better to be as vague as possible to unleash the experts' crazy imaginations.

- **On-demand expert-hunting platforms that do not forget that customers and experts are humans.** Platform customers have told us that they want more than a search-engine expert, more than a list of experts, more than being connected to experts, more than a 100%-online platform. They want insights. They want actionable levers. They want help to reformulate, open, and break down their problems and their questions. In this case, the platform must seek the ideal experts for the company in the same fashion as a headhunter would search for the best executives to fill a C-level position. Then, when thirty targeted proposals from leading experts around the globe show up, client companies want help to select the most appropriate one. They then want help to coach and manage the expert while he or she works on the micro-consulting project. Finally, the client company wants help to synthesize and translate the expert's knowledge into actionable levers. None of this work can be automated. It can only be performed by who have a combined business and technology culture. The people for this job are the meta-experts we introduced in chapter 5.

- **Innovation contests.** One of us has already contributed to a book[96] on this topic. Innovation contests represent about 80% of the entire intermediary business in the sector of open innovation. Contests have their roots far back in human history, but the Internet has provided the ability to reach large numbers of possible contenders. Innovation contest performance was analyzed by Angelika Bullinger[97,98] and Christian Terwiesch.[99] Bullinger et al found a counterintuitive result: the most innovative answers come from questions which are either very sharp and narrow or very broad and vague; questions that are in between obtain less innovative answers. Terwiesch demonstrated that the best

Innovation Intelligence 267

innovation contest processes are multistep, beginning with an initial selection from among the crowd, and then branching to more focused interrogations of a smaller ensemble of contenders. Based on our years of experience, we would say that contests require far more preparatory design than simply throwing a hook in the middle of the ocean and hoping for the best. Defining very precisely the strategic objective of the contest is a prerequisite. Another issue to weigh carefully is the balance of reward and effort that is proposed to contenders. Contests are difficult to optimize and, despite the volume of browsers, they are not magic tools.

7.3.3 Toward robust tools for innovation intelligence?

What are the trends in tools for innovation intelligence? Companies are demanding tools that will enable them to become more efficient at innovation. They want to achieve better results by being more exhaustive, by being faster, and by being better at filtering information. However, we cannot really say that there is currently an industry of tools dedicated to helping companies improve their innovation intelligence. There is only a heterogeneous ensemble of small companies trying to find the right positioning. No leader has yet emerged with the winning solution. In our opinion, the solution will probably strike a balance between Big Data and expert insights.

Despite the fragmented and heterogeneous offerings of tools, we can tell that the market is boiling. There is stuff in the air. Although the Uber of skills and the eBay of knowledge have not yet emerged, they will. It's just a matter of time. Like in any other industry, the digital barbarians will come, and everything will change. Powerful tools enabling companies to tap into the spare brain capacity of experts or the knowledge reservoir will appear. We already can observe a few trends:

- **Democratization of expertise.** Fifteen years ago, the first platforms, such as GLG, appeared. Suddenly, companies could

268 Chapter 7. Tools for Innovation Intelligence

access expert insights. Experts from among the middle and top management of large companies, for example, would release information. Costs were high, but the insights provided were highly valuable. Over the past couple of years, new players such as Maven and Clarity have appeared. These companies propose to put the long list of needs in contact with the long list of expertise. They say, "You need expertise in carpentry, we'll find you a carpenter." These companies are gaining momentum and democratizing expertise. Expertise is becoming a commodity. Wages are decreasing. Although these new players are probably toward the lower end of micro-consulting, tomorrow, armed with their network and momentum, they can move along the value chain toward higher-end services. We don't exclude the possibility that these companies may tomorrow be in GLG's protected garden, or in that of NineSigma's or Presans'.

> The formulation of a problem is often more essential than its solution, which may be merely a matter of mathematical or experimental skill.
> **Albert Einstein**

- **Embracing more of the value chain.** At the same time as we observe newcomers commoditizing expertise, we also see older players trying to provide more value via their Internet platforms (see section 7.3.2 for our discussion of the myth of the so-called open-innovation platform). Client companies are no longer interested in getting just a list of experts. It is not good enough to receive more or less serious ideas or solutions to problems from zillions of random people. Client companies want more than that. They want insights. They want solid opinions. They want integrated knowledge. They want intelligence. U.S. company YourEncore seems to understand where the value is: YourEncore

Innovation Intelligence 269

focuses on experienced people and on strong interaction between the client companies and the experts reachable through the platform. Value is no longer in the size of the expert network. The size of the expert network is a prerequisite (our friend Noriaki Kano strikes again). But the real value is in formulating the right question, extracting insights from people's heads, and combining the right insights. Many platforms have failed or will fail because they focus on solving the problem. Complex problems are solved not by focusing on the solution or answer but by focusing on the question. Platforms will probably increasingly focus on asking the right question. We predict that, ultimately, there will be more platforms enabling interactions between experts within and outside companies, platforms through which on-demand teams of experts can be leveraged. Creating such platform is an incredibly complex challenge, for various reasons, but it will be done eventually. Among these platform players, we observe a trend towards verticalization to embrace more of the value chain. This may include specialization in an industrial sector.

- **Increasing role of Big Data and data mining.** More and more digital pure players are appearing. In France, three players were founded between 2008 and 2010, all of them trying to automatically create a network of experts based on the traces experts leave on the Internet. Although one of these companies is now undergoing a Chapter 11 reorganization, the two others, Expernova and Presans, have taken very different approaches and are developing well. Since then, copycat companies have appeared and disappeared. Many other start-ups have appeared around the world and tried to give sense to raw data. They have tried to transform hundreds of millions of scientific publications, patents, reports, and so forth into actionable intelligence. At the most recent LeWeb, the largest conference dealing with digital technologies in the world, in Paris an entire session on science and research start-ups was organized..[100] The session was chaired by Victor Henning, cofounder and CEO of Mendeley, which was recently acquired by the academic publishing company Elsevier for several tens of millions of dollars.

- **Double-stage consolidation.** Consolidation is currently happening among these players. In the last few years, major acquisitions were made by larger players such as Elsevier and Mindjet. For example, Elsevier, looking for new growth drivers, over the past ten years has acquired companies such as Collexis and Mendeley, each for healthy valuations. Although it is not clear yet what Elsevier will do with these data mining companies, the acquisitions were clearly attempts to find new growth drivers. Although Elsevier's historical business still generates good revenues, digital barbarians are reshuffling the cards. People want free articles, so it is also a matter of time before Elsevier's historical business is seriously damaged. Consolidations between first-generation platforms, those not technology-enabled, and the more recent second-generation of platforms that have developed powerful data-mining tools. Finally, traditional consulting companies, such as McKinsey, The Boston Consulting Group (BCG), and Arthur D. Little, spend a considerable amount of money on expert networks, and it is very likely that these traditional consulting companies will also be disrupted by digital barbarians. If they want to survive, the consulting companies will need to adapt by embracing the digital revolution.

7.4 Conclusion

It is hard to be draw definitive conclusions after hovering above a complex landscape that is a work in progress. One point seems rather clear, however: tools and processes coming from traditional industries are working fine except that they need to be realigned consistent with the new positioning of innovation in the enterprise, closer to the decision center and encompassing far more functions than solely a technical one. This is true for a scouting network and for rapid innovation processing. The situation is far murkier when considering the introduction of

Innovation Intelligence 271

digital technology potential into the innovation endeavor. Pure digital players, such as Google, Amazon, and LinkedIn, have found their way to innovate, a drastically different innovation practice compared that of traditional players. As a result, they dominate on their own terrain.

We have seen many indications that the digital wave can make a decisive contribution to innovation performance in traditional companies. Apart from the simple impact of Internet searching being used on a daily basis by every employee, the situation is not yet stabilized for more specific digital tools that would assist companies in improving their innovation performance. There is intense activity from many companies with diverse origins and approaches; if a universal solution exists, there is no sign of it yet. We are convinced that significant progress is within sight, particularly with regard to improving and adapting to innovation modern tools in semantic search and Big Data. We can only recommend that innovation drivers in companies monitor activity at the frontier of knowledge in this tools sector. Meanwhile, the best approach is to do reality checks on less ambitious existing tools and define the best use for them in your particular sector.

Chapter 8
Conclusion and Perspectives

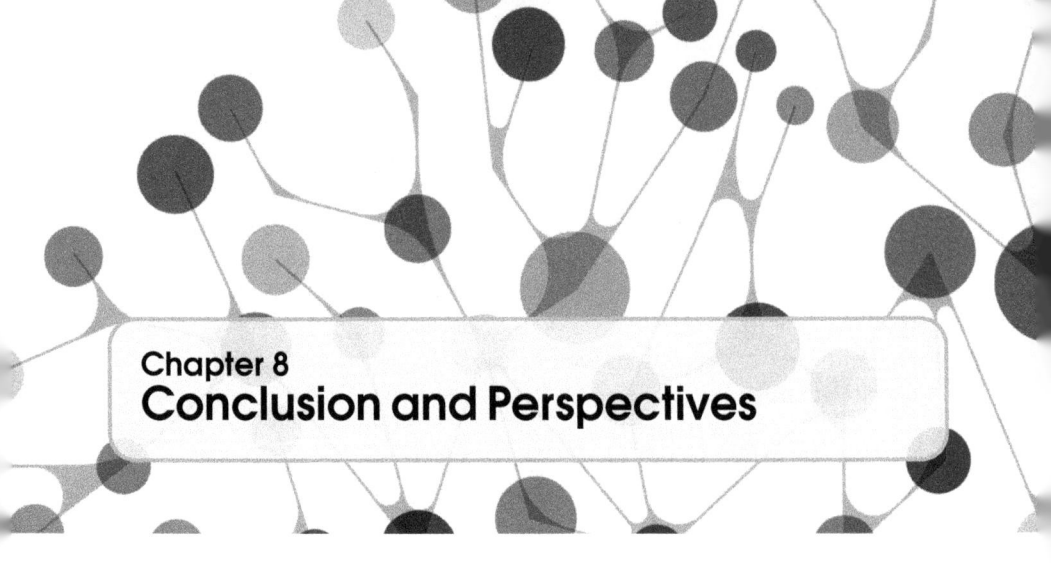

I think and think for months and years. Ninety-nine times, the conclusion is false. The hundredth time I am right.

ALBERT EINSTEIN

"What I am dreaming of is an application on my iPhone or my computer that would produce a one-page synthesis and the analysis of everything that the leading experts know on a given topic, the sum of all the knowledge in one brain." This is how Jean Botti, CTO of Airbus Group, concluded our interview.

We are entering a third Industrial Revolution, this one related to resource optimization and mainly due to digitalization. In this book we have covered an intangible resource, knowledge and its mediators, experts, and its main consequence, innovation. We have demonstrated that the knowledge sector is subject to rapid changes that drastically affect the economy.

The tight link between knowledge and innovation was illustrated by an iconic case, the birth of Parrot's quadricopter drone. Parrot a midsize company and not so long ago a start-up, specialized in wireless peripherals for mobile phones. Then, without having any background in flying objects, the company decided to make a drone. The team

274 Chapter 8. Conclusion and Perspectives

succeeded in this endeavor by acquiring the necessary knowledge and blending all of the technologies to make the device user-friendly. The success of the project was recognized at a live demo in the hallways of the Consumer Electronics Show in Las Vegas, Nevada.

Following evidence from Parrot's case, we have established the deep relationship between innovation and knowledge. Innovators use knowledge from the outside world, not only as inspiration but also as building bricks. While mapping knowledge resources for innovation, we have found the territory vast and rapidly changing. The evolution of knowledge is a dynamic process: new knowledge is generated as innovation waves amplified by new applications. We are currently in the middle of the huge digital wave.

Global knowledge is growing at an accelerating rate; we describe this phenomenon as a knowledge flood. Its origins are many, including the globalization of knowledge creation, but growth has intrinsic roots as knowledge and learning themselves lead to faster knowledge creation. The knowledge flood is spreading across new domains and both its creation and its repositories are fragmented in multiple areas. Particularly relevant to innovation are application-driven research centers and the boiling world of start-ups. Altogether knowledge as such is becoming a commodity; it is more efficient to seek knowledge than is to create it. Open innovation is a natural solution in this environment.

Driven by the acceleration of the innovation cycle, most products face an urgent threat of commoditization. Product designers are reacting by utilizing the ever-increasing content of the technology toolbox, generating even more complete and complex products. A parallel trend is that many products are becoming full-service packages around basic customer demands.

The digital wave is striking an unprepared industrial infrastructure. Digital innovation is incredibly fast and inexpensive, making it possible for almost anyone. Traditional players are having difficulty adapting to the new pace and the new competition. Digital barbarians take advantage of this inertia: they insert themselves between customers and traditional businesses and capture the relationships and the profit

Innovation Intelligence

margins themselves. However, digital technology can also be seen as a fantastic opportunity to improve practically any business that is willing and able to adapt to it.

Experts are key players in the innovation. They provide companies with external knowledge that drive their innovations. Experts in the knowledge flood must adapt by both specializing and exploring adjacent knowledge. To assist in innovation, experts must be able to learn fast, extend their coverage via networks, and intelligently exploit those networks. Industry players will need experts more than ever, an ever-changing variety of them, many from outside the company. Successfully managing expertise requires that a company acquire what we call meta-expertise, expertise about expertise and experts.

Despite often being triggered by a new technological offering, innovation requires that coordinated attention be paid to three domains: technology, business, and human value, which is a subtle perception of customer needs. We have conducted interviews of many executives who drive innovation at their companies. The sum of it can be condensed to explain the shaping of three new items:

A figure: Chief innovation Officer. This not yet a standard C-level position, but the trend has begun and is gaining momentum. This person drives disruptive innovation, sets innovation culture in a multidisciplinary way that cuts across the functional areas of the company, and coordinates and supervises innovation intelligence. Because this role requires coordinating several functions, not only technical but also business development and markets, it is moving closer to the CEO.

A lab: Innovation lab. This lab can be permanent or temporary. Small, lean, and multidisciplinary, it is capable of analyzing all three domains (technology, business, and human). The innovation lab identifies ideas and concepts from the intelligence inflow and quickly determines whether they are viable. It is an agile system for generating business propositions outside the realm of business as usual.

An activity: Innovation intelligence. Innovation comes from outside. It requires cross-correlated information on customer tastes and needs, on competitors'

276　　　　　　　Chapter 8. Conclusion and Perspectives

successes and failures, and on new ideas and technologies. Data should be collected about the field itself and then rapidly processed and transmitted; innovation demands responsiveness. Innovation intelligence should be positioned as a highly valued activity, with that tone set by top management and with proactive contributions from all functions of the company.

We have surveyed the tools available to assist companies in both intelligence and accelerating the pace of innovation. Some tools, such as platforms, functional bricks, and scout networks, work well as long as they are coordinated and managed with a sense of urgency. New tools are coming from the digital and service arenas. Many of these tools are well adapted to a precise task, but a universal tool does not yet exist. Progress can be expected from a combination of tools in the digital arena. The winning tools for innovation intelligence will most likely rely on a combination of Big Data and digitally enhanced human networks.

As Jean Botti pointed out, "The machine has become more intelligent than humans. Do you know Watson?" Botti was referring to the artificially intelligent computer system developed by IBM and which is able to answer questions posed in natural language. Watson won the *Jeopardy!* game show, beating two former winners. Such tools are not yet available for innovation intelligence. But it is just a matter of time.

Bibliography

[1] H. Rosa. *Social Acceleration : A new Theory of Modernity*. Columbia University Press, 2013 (cit. on pp. 3, 79).

[2] J. Rifkin. *The Third Industrial Revolution; How Lateral Power is Transforming Energy, the Economy, and the World*. Palgrave MacMillan, 2011 (cit. on p. 12).

[3] S. Heck and M. Rogers. *Resource Revolution; How To Capture the Biggest Business Opportunity in a Century*. Amazon Publishing, 2014 (cit. on p. 13).

[4] B. Segrestin and A. Hatchuel. *Refonder l'entreprise*. Seuil, 2012 (cit. on p. 15).

[5] E. Störmer et al. *The Future of Work: Jobs and skills in 2030*. Report. UKCES, 2014 (cit. on p. 16).

[6] E. Mouchous et al. *La révolution des métiers. Nouveaux métiers, nouvelles compétences: quels enjeux pour l'entreprise*. Report. EY and Linkedin, 2014 (cit. on p. 16).

[7] M. Beatson. *Megatrends: The trends shaping work and working lives*. Report. CIPD, July 2013 (cit. on p. 16).

[8] S. Enlart and O. Charbonnier. *A quoi ressemblera le travail de demain?* Dunod, 2013 (cit. on p. 16).

[9] W. Isaacson. *Steve Jobs*. Simon & Schuster, 2011 (cit. on pp. 34, 218).

| 278 | Chapter 8. Conclusion and Perspectives |

[10] A. Hatchuel and B. Weil. "C-K design theory: An advanced formulation". In: *Research in Engineering Design* 19.4 (2009), pp. 181–192 (cit. on p. 41).

[11] D. Braha and O. Maimon. *Mathematical Theory of Engineering Design: Foundations, Algorithms and Applications*. Kluwer Academic Publishers, 1999 (cit. on p. 41).

[12] A. D. de Figueiredo and J. Campos. "The serendipity equations". In: *Int. Conf. on case based reasoning*. 2001 (cit. on p. 42).

[13] G. Garel and E. Mock. *La Fabrique de l'Innovation*. Dunod, 2012 (cit. on p. 42).

[14] URL: http : / / www . pinterest . com / pin / 134193263866652808/ (cit. on p. 45).

[15] URL: http://en.wikipedia.org/wiki/Hiriko (cit. on p. 45).

[16] J. T. Duane. "Learning curve approach to reliability monitoring". In: *IEEE Trans. on Aerospace 2* (1964), p. 563 (cit. on p. 46).

[17] P. Ghemawat. "Building strategy on the experience curve". In: *Harvard Business Review* 42 (1985) (cit. on p. 46).

[18] *The long tug of war over RU 436* (). URL: http : / / www . newsweek.com/long-tug-war-over-ru486-191256 (cit. on p. 46).

[19] URL: http : / / www . computerweekly . com / feature / A - history-of-cloud-computing (cit. on p. 48).

[20] G. S. Hornby. "Automated antenna design with evolutionary algorithms". In: *AIAA Space*. 2006 (cit. on p. 49).

[21] R. Subbu, K. Goebel, and D. Frederick. "Evolutionary design and optimization of aircraft engine controllers". In: *IEEE trans. On Systems, Man and Cybernetics ; Part C : Applications and Reviews* 35.3 (2005) (cit. on p. 49).

Innovation Intelligence 279

[22] D. R. Paretkar et al. "Buckling of an Adhesive Polymeric Micropillar". In: *Journal of Adhesion* 89 (2013) (cit. on p. 55).

[23] R. G. Cooper. *Product Leadership: Pathways to Profitable Innovation*. Basic books, 2004 (cit. on p. 58).

[24] URL: http://en.wikipedia.org/wiki/Streetlight_effect (cit. on p. 59).

[25] *History or the Federal Judiciary*. Federal Courts Improvement Act of 1982. US Federal Judicial Center (cit. on p. 61).

[26] J. L. Borges. *Ficciones*. Vol. The Babel Library. 1944 (cit. on p. 71).

[27] A. C. Doyle. "The great Keinplatz experiment". In: *Belgravia Magazine* (1885) (cit. on p. 75).

[28] D. J. de Solla Price. *Little Science, Big Science*. New York, Columbia Univ. Press, 1963 (cit. on p. 76).

[29] J. Tague, J. Beheshti, and L. Rees-Potter. "The law of exponential growth : Evidence, Implications and Forecast". In: *Library Trends* 30.1 (1981), p. 125 (cit. on p. 76).

[30] R. B. Fuller. *Critical Path*. St Martin's Press, 1981 (cit. on p. 77).

[31] G. S. Hawkins. "Mindsteps to the Cosmos". In: *World Scientific* (2002) (cit. on p. 77).

[32] K. Popper. *Conjectures and refutations : the growth of Scientific Knowledge*. Taylor & Francis, 1963 (cit. on p. 78).

[33] B. Henderson. URL: https://www.bcgperspectives.com/content/classics/ (cit. on p. 78).

[34] R. Kurzweil. *The Singularity is near*. Viking, 2005 (cit. on p. 79).

[35] *Industry Tap*. URL: http://www.industrytap.com/ (cit. on p. 80).

Chapter 8. Conclusion and Perspectives

[36] M. Zeleny. "Management support systems toward integrated knowledge management". In: *Human Systems Management* 7 (1987), p. 59 (cit. on p. 80).

[37] J. M. Smart. "The Transcension hypothesis". In: *Acta Astronautica* (2011) (cit. on p. 81).

[38] T. Modis. "the limits of Complexity and Change". In: *The Futurist* (2003) (cit. on p. 81).

[39] J. Huebner. "Declining trend for innovation". In: *Technology forecasting and Social Change* 72 (2005) (cit. on p. 82).

[40] U. Axelson and M. Martinovic. *European Venture Capital: Myths and Facts*. Tech. rep. BVCA, 2013. URL: http://www.bvca.co.uk/Portals/0/library/Files/News/2013/European_MandF_Report_21Jan13.pdf (cit. on p. 86).

[41] URL: http://upstart.bizjournals.com/companies/startups/2013/05/07/mattias-guilotte-immigrates-to-usa.html (cit. on p. 88).

[42] URL: http://eu-research.blogspot.fr/2009/02/number-of-researchers-by-world-region.html (cit. on p. 89).

[43] H. Chesbrough. *Open innovation*. Harvard Business School Press, 2003 (cit. on pp. 89, 96, 98).

[44] S. Johnson. *Where good ideas come from?* Penguin books, 2010 (cit. on p. 90).

[45] L. Hoddeson. "Between Sciences and Technology". In: *Elsevier* (1990). Ed. by P. Kroes and A. Sarlemijn (cit. on p. 91).

[46] G. K. Tea and E. Buehler. In: *Phys. Rev.* 87 (1952), p. 190 (cit. on p. 91).

[47] URL: http://www.wired.co.uk/news/archive/2012-03/07/wayra (cit. on p. 95).

[48] URL: http://en.wikipedia.org/wiki/Bell_Labs (cit. on p. 97).

Innovation Intelligence 281

[49] URL: http://www2.dupont.com/Phoenix_Heritage/en_US/1880_b_detail.html (cit. on p. 96).

[50] URL: http://en.wikipedia.org/wiki/Not_invented_here (cit. on p. 98).

[51] *Physics Entrepreneurship and Innovation*. Tech. rep. American Institute of Physics, 2013 (cit. on p. 98).

[52] M. D. Henry and J. L. Turner. *The Court of Appeal for the Federal Circuit's Impact on Patent Litigation*. Tech. rep. 2005. URL: http://www.immagic.com/eLibrary/ARCHIVES/GENERAL/U_GA_US/G050629H.pdf (cit. on p. 102).

[53] URL: http://en.wikipedia.org/wiki/United_States_Court_of_Appeals_for_the_Federal_Circuit (cit. on p. 102).

[54] S. Kinukawa. *Patent breadth and cumulative innovation: a natural experiment in the mid 80's*. Tech. rep. Keio Universty, 2006. URL: https://www1.gsec.keio.ac.jp/imgdata/working/26_pdf.pdf (cit. on p. 103).

[55] URL: http://en.wikipedia.org/wiki/Kano_model (cit. on p. 108).

[56] MacDuffie and Fujimoto. *Why dinosaurs will keep ruling the auto inductry*. Harvard Business review, 2010 (cit. on p. 111).

[57] URL: http://gramaziokohler.arch.ethz.ch/ (cit. on p. 119).

[58] *Digital Skills for Tomorrow's World*. Tech. rep. UK Digital Taskforce, 2014. URL: http://www.ukdigitalskills.com/ (cit. on p. 132).

[59] URL: http://en.wikipedia.org/wiki/K._Anders_Ericsson (cit. on p. 140).

[60] O. Lelebina. "La gestion des experts en entreprise". PhD thesis. Centre de Gestion Scientifique, Mines-Paritech, 2014 (cit. on p. 141).

282 Chapter 8. Conclusion and Perspectives

[61] B. Wilder. *Some like it hot*. 1959 (cit. on p. 142).

[62] B. Bloom. *Developping talent in young people*. Ballantine Books, 1985 (cit. on p. 143).

[63] URL: http://en.wikipedia.org/wiki/Robert_Stroud (cit. on p. 144).

[64] URL: https://hbr.org/2007/07/the-making-of-an-expert (cit. on p. 144).

[65] K. A. Ericsson. *The Cambridge Handbook of Expertise and Expert Performance*. Cambridge University Press, 2006 (cit. on p. 144).

[66] I. Berlin. *The hedgehog and the fox*. 1953 (cit. on p. 146).

[67] M. Gladwell. *Outliers*. Little, Brown and Company, 2008 (cit. on p. 147).

[68] URL: http://en.wikipedia.org/wiki/House_(TV_series) (cit. on p. 148).

[69] R. J. Sternberg. "Intelligence as developing expertise". In: *Contemporary Educational Psychology* 24 (1999) (cit. on p. 148).

[70] R. R. Bernstein et al. "Arts Foster Scientific Success". In: *Journal of Psychology of Science and Technology* (2008) (cit. on p. 150).

[71] T. A. Stewart. *Intellectual capital: the new wealth of organizations*. Nicolas Brealey Publishing, 1997 (cit. on p. 152).

[72] R. Lamont. *Understanding the dual ladder*. URL: http://www.computersciencesalaryrange.com/understanding-the-dual-ladder/ (cit. on p. 155).

[73] T. Allen and R. Katz. "The dual ladder : Motivational solution or managerial disillusion ?" In: (1985). URL: http://dspace.mit.edu/bitstream/handle/1721.1/2117/SWP-1692-12737256.pdf?sequence=1 (cit. on p. 155).

| Innovation Intelligence | 283 |

[74] URL: http : / / home . kpn . nl / stam7883 / graph _ introduction.html (cit. on p. 165).

[75] URL: http : / / www . computerworld . com / article / 2515874 / computer - hardware / timeline -- parc - milestones.html (cit. on p. 171).

[76] I. Buchem. "Serendipitous learning: Recognizing and fostering the potential of microblogging". In: *Form@re, open journal* (2011) (cit. on p. 175).

[77] URL: http : / / www . bestthinking . com / thinkers / science / social _ sciences / psychology / michael - smithson (cit. on p. 179).

[78] R. B. Duncan. *The ambidextrous organization: Designing dual structures for innovation.* Killman, R. H., L. R. Pondy, and D. Sleven. The Management of Organization, 1976, pp. 167–188 (cit. on p. 188).

[79] J. G. March. "Exploration and exploitation in organizational learning". In: *Organization Science* 2 (1991), pp. 71–87 (cit. on p. 188).

[80] W. Miller and L. Morris. *4th generation R&D: managing knowledge, technology and innovation.* Wiley, 1998 (cit. on p. 197).

[81] A. D. Fiore. "A Chief Innovation Officer's actual responsibilities". In: *Harvard Business Review* (2014). URL: https : //hbr.org/2014/11/a-chief-innovation-officers-actual-responsibilities (cit. on p. 197).

[82] *Bill Poston.* to be published. URL: http : / / thechiefinnovationofficer.com (cit. on p. 197).

[83] B. Jaruzelski, V. Staack, and B. Goehle. *Proven Paths to Innovation Success.* Tech. rep. strategy+business, 2014 (cit. on p. 206).

[84] *Baromètre Act One - HEC 2013 des Directeurs de l'Innovation.* Tech. rep. HEC and Act One, 2013 (cit. on p. 207).

284 Chapter 8. Conclusion and Perspectives

[85] URL: http://dschool.stanford.edu/dgift/ (cit. on p. 216).

[86] E. Ries. *The lean Startup: How today's entrepreneurs use continuous innovation to create radically successful businesses.* Crown Publishing, 2011 (cit. on p. 217).

[87] J. J. McGonagle and C. M. Vella. *The Manager's Guide to Competitive Intelligence.* Westport, CT: Greenwood Publishing Group, 2003 (cit. on p. 244).

[88] B. Gilad and T. Gilad. *The Business Intelligence System.* New York: American Management Association, 1988 (cit. on p. 244).

[89] L. Kahaner. *Competitive Intelligence: How to Gather, Analyze, and Use Information to Move Your Business to the Top.* New York: Touchstone, 1997 (cit. on p. 244).

[90] P. Biren. *Concurrent engineering fundamentals.* Prentice, 1996 (cit. on p. 248).

[91] L. M. Mayr and P. Fuerst. "The Future of High-Throughput Screening". In: *J. of Biomolecular Screening* 13 (2008) (cit. on p. 249).

[92] J. J. Agresti. "Ultrahigh-throughput screening in drop-based microfluidics for directed evolution". In: *Proc. Natl Acad Sci USA* 107 (2010) (cit. on p. 250).

[93] M. Moseley. *Irascible genius : A life of Charles Babbage, inventor.* Hutchinson, 1964 (cit. on p. 251).

[94] K. Diener and F. Piller. *The Market for Open Innovation.* Tech. rep. RWTH Aachen University, 2013 (cit. on p. 256).

[95] L. Mortara. *Getting help with open innovation.* Tech. rep. University of Cambridge, 2010 (cit. on p. 256).

[96] A. Meige. *A guide to Open Innovation and Crowdsourcing.* Paul Sloane. Kogan Page, 2011 (cit. on p. 266).

Innovation Intelligence 285

[97]   Bullinger. "Community-based innovation contests: where competition meets cooperation". In: *CIM* 3 (2010) (cit. on p. 266).

[98]   Bullinger. "Innovation Contests – Where are we?" In: *AMCIS 2010 Proceedings* (2010) (cit. on p. 266).

[99]   Terwiesch. "Innovation Contests, Open Innovation, and Multi-agent Problem Solving". In: *Management Science* 54.9 (2008) (cit. on p. 266).

[100] URL: http : / / blog . leweb . co / 2014 / 11 / future - science-15-science-research-startups-selected-present-leweb/ (cit. on p. 269).

List of Figures

1	Albert Meige, photo by Arthur De Tassigny	xxiii
2	Jacques P.M. Schmitt, photo by Arthur De Tassigny	xxiv
1.1	James Watt, PD	11
2.1	Henri Seydoux, photo courtesy of Parrot	25
2.2	Novadem team, photo courtesy of Novadem	28
2.3	Henri Seydoux, photo courtesy of Parrot	34
3.1	C-K theory, CC	41
3.2	Swatch collection, DR	42
3.3	Origin of knowledge, A	43
3.4	Rudolf Diesel, PD and Fire Piston, DR	51
3.5	George De Mestal, DR and Epizoochory, CC	51
3.6	Schindler rope, DR	53
3.7	Video game players and BMW, DR	54
3.8	Nanopass needle, DR	55
3.9	Geckskin, DR	55
3.10	Innovation cycle, A	56
3.11	Stage gating, A	59
3.12	U.S. patent rate, A	62
3.13	GPS patent rate, A	63
3.14	Steven Sasson, DR	64

LIST OF FIGURES

4.1 Scientific publication rate, A 73
4.2 Geographical distribution of scientific paper authors, A . . 75
4.3 Doubling rate for accumulated knowledge, A 76
4.4 Market penetration time, A 79
4.5 WKID pyramid, A 81
4.6 Speed limit sign, A 82
4.7 Start-up firm creation rate, A 86
4.8 Mattias Guilotte, DR 88
4.9 Celine Lazorthes, DR 89
4.10 Float zone, PD 91
4.11 Chromatron, DR 93
4.12 Bell Labs corridor, DR 97
4.13 Small companies' R&D investment, A 100
4.14 Change in U.S. jurisprudence, A 102
4.15 Cisco Systems headquarters, DR 104
4.16 Philips Research Eindhoven, DR 106
4.17 Kano model, A 108
4.18 Diagram of an automobile transmission, DR 111
4.19 NutriCook, photo courtesy of Groupe SEB 114
4.20 Measuring devices, DR 115
4.21 Nespresso, DR 117
4.22 Air Liquide business model, A 118
4.23 Brick assembly, DR 119
4.24 Philippe Letellier, photo by Céline Fernbach 133

5.1 Benjamin Bloom, DR 143
5.2 Silo digger vs. chipmumk, A 146
5.3 Deep well, DR 147
5.4 Polymaths, A and PD 150
5.5 Experts' contributions viewed as a funnel, A 157
5.6 Serendipity, PD 159
5.7 Moore's law, A and PD 160
5.8 Graph theory, A 164
5.9 Flea market, DR 166

5.10 John Karlin, photo courtesy of Alcatel-Lucent USA 169
5.11 Meeting at Xerox PARC, DR and Xerox PARC, DR 170
5.12 Consumer Electronics Show, DR and Apple Campus 2, DR 172
5.13 Puzzle, photo by Olga Berrios, CC 174
5.14 Conference, DR 176
5.15 Logo presans, courtesy of Presans SAS 178
5.16 John Harrison, PD 180

6.1 Chief Innovation Officer (CINO) role, A 198
6.2 CINO role at Airbus, A 205
6.3 Evolution of the CINO role, A 206
6.4 iLab, courtesy of Air Liquide 211
6.5 Three dimensions of design thinking, A 216
6.6 Sequence structure in design thinking, A, after Guido
    Kovalskys, Stanford d.school 217
6.7 Innovation intelligence cycle, A 226
6.8 Knowledge for innovation intelligence, A 228

7.1 Apache scouts attached to the U.S. Cavalry in 1870, PD . . 241
7.2 Highthroughput screening lab, DR 249
7.3 Robot elephant made from Lego Mindstorm game set, DR 253
7.4 Golf automobile platform, A and DR 255
7.5 Innovation-intelligence tool classification, A 257

DR: Droit Réservé; CC: Creative Commons; PD: Public Domain;
A: created by the authors.

List of Tables

3.1 Knowledge distribution during an innovation wave 66

4.1 A few examples of companies that use external knowledge in their innovation projects 95

4.2 The top ten fastest-growing companies in the United States, 2011 – 2014 129

Lightning Source UK Ltd.
Milton Keynes UK
UKHW022013170619
344563UK00020B/679/P